# The
# Coming
# Race
# War in
# America

# The Coming Race War in America

*A Wake-up Call*

# Carl T. Rowan

LITTLE, BROWN AND COMPANY  Boston New York Toronto London

*To the relatives of those tragic victims whose lives have already
been snuffed out by heinous hatreds*

The author is grateful for permission to include the following previously
copyrighted material:

Excerpts from *Nixon* by Stephen Ambrose. Copyright © by Stephen Ambrose.
Reprinted by permission of the author.

Excerpts from *Science and Politics of Racial Research* by William Tucker. Copyright ©
by William Tucker. Reprinted by permission of the author.

Excerpts from speeches by Jeremi Duru, John Morcos, Dorian Baucum, and Taryn
Richardson reprinted by permission of the authors.

ISBN 0-316-75980-5
Library of Congress Catalog Card Number 96-77914
10   9   8   7   6   5   4   3   2   1

MV-NY

Published simultaneously in Canada by Little, Brown & Company (Canada) Limited

Printed in the United States of America

# Contents

# Preface

Sensational, inflammatory journalism has never been my style. I have never written dire prophecies of human disasters except when there was compelling evidence that calamity was at hand. I do not endanger a reputation for accuracy and responsibility, gained over a career of almost half a century, when I warn you that a terrible race war is coming in the United States. It is coming fast.

Signs of a searing, stupid conflict are almost everywhere: in the cruelly bigoted rhetoric that often befouls the well of the House of Representatives; in the swastikas and Ku Klux Klan symbols that festoon our military barracks; in the "for kicks" murders of two black people near Fort Bragg, North Carolina; in the Harlem death of a man in a fire provoked by black critics of a Jewish merchant; and in the widespread lawlessness of some eight hundred militias and paramilitary groups that have sprouted up in the fields and urban haunts of America.

I see so many violent harbingers of a larger, utterly tragic conflict that I am loath to express my fears to Americans whose hearts and minds are numbed to the reality of what is happening in America. But I am too late in my blessed journalism career to begin hiding unpalatable truths from my readers.

I know that for many who read this, a race war will seem unthinkable. Those Caucasians who profess to believe that white racism is no longer a major problem in this country are likely to declare me a "troublemaker" and argue that white Americans are not paranoid nuts of Third Reich mentality who want to war on black citizens. The Caucasians who say this are part of a rising problem, because they are in denial of both the magnitude and the danger of white violence in America. They are dismissing the purveyors of hatred who have sprung up in America, the leaders of whom are, with few exceptions, vowing to "take back America for the White race."

These are maniacal bigots who directly or indirectly killed 168 innocent people in the Oklahoma City bombing. They stockpile grotesque amounts of weapons and bombs for other terrorist assaults. Incredibly, they get sympathy from conservatives, black and white, who seem to share their contempt for the government.

In July 1996 Walter Williams, an economics professor at George Mason University, wrote a column saying:

"The Freemen aside, it is my impression that most militia members are not common criminals who rob, rape and murder. To the contrary, at least the ones I've seen are working, churchgoing, patriotic family men and women. They, like most other Americans, are becoming increasingly fearful of their government. What distinguishes them, misguided or not, is a willingness to prepare to resist a government seemingly hell-bent on making a mockery of our constitutional guarantees."

I don't know which militia members this black man, Williams, has met. They surely can't be the ones who take as their bible an utterly racist book, *The Turner Diaries*, in which the script for the Oklahoma City bombing was set forth in grim detail. Williams can't have met the militiamen who rail that Jews are the products of an illicit liaison between Eve and the Devil, and that blacks are subhuman.

These cults of white supremacy are determined to provoke black Americans into fighting a race war. Unfortunately, the rage within millions of black people who are hopelessly trapped as the American underclass is so great that many are spoiling for a fight. A race war can come easily and spread rapidly.

Many privileged blacks do not yet see how easily armed bands of white supremacists can attack black institutions and assassinate black leaders and thus goad blacks into responses of unprecedented fury. These "comfortable" blacks are saying that even alienated blacks know that they cannot win a race war, because white politicians and law enforcement officials would side with the militiamen at first and put the black rebels in concentration camps and graves before moving to suppress the white supremacists. Well, not if the white provocateurs have been attacking white judges and law enforcement officers, as is already the case in the northwestern states.

In many ways, the early salvos have been fired in a race war that will worsen. Each day brings stories of killings of racial passion. We have seen Louis Farrakhan raise the specter of possible black collaboration with foreign terrorists, and white American politicians talk about building "stockades" in which to warehouse black malcontents.

As surely as though they were Third Reich propagandists paving the way for a blitzkrieg, we see the right-wing hatemongers all over the American media, spewing forth the venom that energizes the white supremacists. A spirit of violent paranoia pervades this society because of a drumbeat of *Bell Curve* claims that white men are being cheated — deprived by black people who were inferior at birth and are not qualified today for the jobs and other "goodies" that they get.

I am sure that some critics, white and black, will express shock that I, the recipient of so many honors and accolades over a long and marvelous career, would unload so much anger and outrage onto these pages. I *am* indignant, precisely because I know how far this country has come since I was a terribly impoverished boy in Jim Crow Tennessee. I know how much greater we could be as a nation but for the fact that over the last generation many craven politicians have given aid, comfort, and encouragement to violent racists. I am absolutely certain that the still-suffering survivors of that Oklahoma City atrocity will not be the last Americans to know the anguish of seeing loved ones killed by domestic madmen.

Have I no confidence in the ability and determination of law enforcement agencies to protect Americans, me included, from those who threaten openly to murder and maim in a quest for white supremacy? I have no such faith because, as I document in the chapter on O. J. Simpson and elsewhere in this book, the law enforcement people are too often collaborating with the most brutal of the racists.

I find no consolation in the fact that those vowing to overthrow the U.S. government — "the System" — in order to guarantee the primacy of "the White race" will kill whites who get in their way as cavalierly as they slaughter blacks. And I make no apologies for the force of my criticism of those who have helped to create a genuine American crisis.

I will remind readers of this book that nowhere, on any page, do I say that a ghastly race war is *unavoidable*. We can help to avert what the bigots call "Armageddon," but only if we stop denying that a grave threat exists and move with resolve against the most dangerous of the self-styled revolutionaries. In the final chapter I have spelled out the steps of wisdom and justice that are necessary to keep us safe and free.

But in one more moment of candor, let me say that I am not optimistic that this society is up to the challenge before it.

Carl T. Rowan
*Washington, D.C.*
*July 4, 1996*

# The
# Coming
# Race
# War in
# America

**Chapter 1**

# America's Violent Decline

H ow do you tell when a great civilization is in decline? When a great nation is on the rocks spiritually, morally, racially, and economically?

I look closely at my country, and everywhere I see signs of decadence, decay, and self-destruction.

Respect for law and order has declined drastically, except in the phony speeches of politicians.

The nation's capital is awash with special counsel and special prosecutors, taking testimony from the President, the First Lady, key members of the cabinet and the Congress — all accused or suspected of criminal wrongdoing. The FBI is far short of being trustworthy, its agents and former agents deep in partisan politics. Local police departments reek with corruption, including condoned lawlessness by some policemen. Our prisons bulge with record numbers of young Americans, mostly the fruit flies of the drug trade, while the big bumblebees of the crime and drug syndicates peddle their wares with impunity.

Every day our newscasts begin with stories of grisly murders, sexual assaults, grotesque abuses of children, mass killings on job sites, and worse.

America is sinking in greed. Our workers fear tomorrow and

their bosses grab what they can today. A corporate fatcat can get a $10 million reward for "downsizing" his firm — that is, putting thousands of employees out of work.

Public morality has probably never been lower. Lawmakers writhe and wrangle over how to deal with television programming that spews out sexual rot and gratuitous violence morning, afternoon, and night — prime time sewers. Congress makes believe that a meaningless "rating system" and a V-chip will solve the problem.

Racism has not been as virulent throughout America since the Civil War, with short fuses burning on a thousand powder kegs. We have seen our greatest law enforcement agency, the FBI, sit for weeks in a stalemate with a small Montana cult, the Freemen, whose leaders preach that the descendants of northern Europeans are "God's chosen people," that Jews are "the children of Satan," and that African Americans and other people of color are by nature dumb and immoral.

We see the Freemen and other hate groups like the Aryan Nation, the skinheads, the Ku Klux Klan, and assorted militias piling up arms for what they say is a coming race war in America that will precede the return of Christ.

These are the adherents of a "Christian Identity" movement whose followers refuse to pay governmental levies, but collect taxes themselves. They rake in millions through extortion, the widespread use of bogus checks and phony credit cards, and simple extortion.

But local law enforcers and even the FBI are afraid to tangle with them, wary since their disastrous confrontations with the David Koresh cult in Waco, Texas, and the Randy Weaver group at Ruby Ridge in Idaho.

Official, open coddling of these groups pretty much ensures that the race war these white supremacists predict will really come.

I know that these harsh judgments about America as it nears the turn of the century are not what most Americans want to hear. In the wake of the fall of the "Evil Empire" that was the old Soviet Union, with the still-limited development of China and the Third World, and the starkly limited hegemony of European and other "first world" nations, Americans prefer to boast that the United States is the last of the great powers. As proof we cite our nuclear arsenals and the fact that we have the only quick-strike forces capable of moving into Bosnia, Africa, and the Middle East, to wage war or peace, within hours of a White House go-ahead to strike. We like to boast of our economic might, even though we've seen a frightful decline in good, high-paying jobs. We like to think that we are the world's cultural giant because our movies and music, our top television shows, are coveted the world over, this much to the dismay of foreign leaders who think the cultural fare that we export carries the seeds of national destruction.

So much of what Americans boast about nowadays is superficial, even delusionary. Look below the surface. I have done so and concluded that this country, for which I have fought in war and peace, is in precipitous decline. The leaders of Rome, Greece, the Third Reich, the British Empire, never saw the onset of decadence and internal rot in time; we can, and we must, if the United States is not to succumb to its internal hatreds and moral excesses, to be consumed by its own self-destruction.

Who can overlook the decline of marriage as an American institution, with Hollywood and television stars, and so many social and political leaders, abusing drugs and having sex and babies out of wedlock? Our teenagers see no stigma in this lifestyle. Licentiousness and depravity have made the United States a hollow remake of Sodom and Gomorrah, with even preachers and priests, nuns and schoolteachers, unveiled as the practitioners of child abuse, as marriage killers, and as outright murderers.

Take a look at this society's decline in terms of organized religion. Preachers preach and rabbis teach, but fewer and fewer people listen, and those who visit churches and synagogues rarely heed what they hear. Look at what the Greeks and Romans have written that they saw too late — and what we see now, everywhere in this nation: racial and religious bigotries, blind nationalisms, and myriad other injustices tolerated and even glorified by our philosophers, politicians, Presidents, the "wise men" allowing this, the greatest of societies, to be consumed in hatred.

Look at the piling up of economic injustice and ask how long we can live in peace and prosperity.

The January 22, 1996, issue of *U.S. News & World Report* carried an article about how WORKERS TAKE IT ON THE CHIN which noted:

- that in 1982 dollars, U.S. workers had suffered a decline in earnings, from an average of $298 weekly in 1970 to $256 in 1994
- that during the last five years "the upper class" has gained economically by 76 percent, while the middle class has risen by 6 percent, the working class by 2 percent, and the poorest class by 6 percent
- that in 1945 the top 1 percent of U.S. families held 32.4 percent of the nation's wealth, but in 1992 that top 1 percent held *42 percent* of the wealth. Here was indisputable evidence that while the privileged were assailing attempts of the New Deal and the Great Society to redistribute wealth from the rich to the poor, the rich have been getting richer while the poor have lapsed into deeper poverty

A less conservative publication would have been accused of spreading "inflammatory class warfare verbiage" or "an anticapitalist, pinko diatribe."

What we have to recognize is that we are a society stumbling into a vast darkness, because we do not really seek answers to the issues that I have raised; issues that are of concern to all of us. Instead we look for scapegoats!

The result: in just the last decade we have seen some gruesome manifestations of racial and ethnic hatred in America — literally, murder in the streets, blood spilling everywhere. We have seen political fights in Congress over who should get the most of America's goodies — fights that have caused shutdowns of the federal government and mind-boggling gridlock in Washington. One senses that our nation is split irrevocably and that there is no one to bring us together again.

The blame game seems to be played with every American failure.

Some U.S. auto dealers blame Japan's supremacy in selling certain products on "unfair trading practices." From time to time the U.S. industrialists who feel cheated, and the politicians who deplore the trade imbalance with Japan, create almost enough hysteria to foment a trade war between Washington and Tokyo.

Some American industrialists find scapegoats in the men and women of organized labor, claiming that the "exorbitant" demands of U.S. workers drive them to move plants to Taiwan, Singapore, and, yes, Mexico, where they can enjoy cheap labor. So these employers have engaged in economy-crippling wars with the organized-labor movement, which itself is struggling to emerge from a long, tragic decline.

Still, it is clear that organized laborers and their pay, health care, and other demands are not the cause of the rot in industrial America. If greedy union leaders are not responsible for the disappearance of "good jobs" — of high-paying posts as computer chip makers and camera makers and even shirtmakers and shoemakers in the United States, then who is?

The political flamethrowers, such as Governor Pete Wilson of California, think they see advantage in blaming our economic decline on the great influx into the United States of "illegal aliens." They are bent on making immigration the issue on which many politicians in California, Texas, Colorado, Florida, and other states will rise or fall in the 1996 elections and the remaining years of this century.

The one explosive issue that may trigger the actual burning of America, and certainly exacerbates the ever-widening divisions between and among its citizens, is "affirmative action." Almost every presidential and congressional candidate now strives to convince voters that black, Hispanic, Asian, and female recipients of undeserved economic preferences are really to blame for the economic malaise that has produced so many millions of "angry white men."

These simplistic blame games have already created a disrespect, even hatred, not only for the poor, but for government officials at all levels. They are seen as the ones who proposed, enacted, and protected the laws that supposedly have lowered the levels of life of white men. Others who think their plight is far worse than that of white men have also made the government their worst villain. The government is seen as the invader, controller, and circumscriber of the lives of everyone — the middle class that has lost ground, the underclass that never had sufficient chance.

So citizen militias, operating publicly and secretly, have sprung up across America — a fact that exploded into our consciousness with the dreadful bombing of the federal Alfred P. Murrah office building in Oklahoma City in 1995.

Some Americans prefer to think that some grotesque mental illness affecting only a handful of individuals would provoke the bombing of a huge building and the murder of 168 people — but only the next bombing will show us the level to which "the government" has become the enemy of "the people."

Yes, I can virtually guarantee you that there will be other bombings of the magnitude of the one that occurred in Oklahoma City. That is because the forces that prompted the Oklahoma City crime have influenced hundreds of thousands of other Americans who nurse precisely the same hatreds that were unleashed in Oklahoma.

Note, for example, that the crazy defiance and the spirit of violence of the Montana Freemen did not end with their "surrender" to the FBI. They still defied the authority of the federal courts. In late June, in a Billings, Montana, courtroom, one of the Freemen, Steven Charles Hance, said to U.S. magistrate Richard Anderson, "You're going down, son." The Freemen had already been charged with threatening the life of another federal judge, and yet they were handled with kid gloves.

We cannot afford to ignore the fact that the Freemen are just a tiny part of a nationwide horror — the sprouting up of highly armed militias and paramilitary groups across America, all of them expressing some degree of racial paranoia and hatred. The most watched of these "patriot" right-wing groups are the Militia of Montana, the Unorganized Militia of the United States, the Michigan Militia, Police Against the New World Order, the Idaho Sovereignty Association, United Sovereigns of America, the North American Freedom Council, and the Texas Constitutional Militia. But those pressing to create a constitutional crisis by promoting a ghastly race war are going underground.

The nation was stunned late in June 1996 when federal officials announced that they had arrested ten men and two women in Phoenix on charges that they had plotted to blow up buildings that housed the Bureau of Alcohol, Tobacco and Firearms, the Internal Revenue Service, the Secret Service, and other federal agencies. These twelve members of a group called the Viper Militia, which almost no one had heard of, had gone so far as to videotape the columns in these buildings where explosives should be put so as to most effectively cause the buildings to collapse. Their plan had been foiled through a marvelous piece of police work. An Arizona law officer infiltrated the group and in meeting after meeting listened to the militiamen boast of how they would quickly kill any infiltrator.

Police learned quickly that these twelve alienated Americans had the explosives and weapons with which to carry out what would have been a devastating act of domestic terrorism. In the home of one Viper alone, that of Gary C. Bauer, the group's ordnance expert, federal agents found almost one-half ton of ammonium nitrate. This little Viper Militia group had stashed away in one Phoenix house half a ton of ammonium nitrate; fifty-five gallons of nitromethane; a highly toxic yellow powder explosive called picric acid; many blasting caps; and more than seventy automatic rifles. This tiny band of self-styled revolutionaries had, right in residential Phoenix, the ingredients for a bomb at least half as large as the one used to blow up the Alfred P. Murrah federal building in Oklahoma City, killing 168 people.

The evidence mounts that many of the eight hundred or so militia groups that have sprung up in this country are amassing even greater caches of explosives and firearms, and that the serious terrorists are operating in units of fewer than a handful of people, so as to prevent infiltration by lawmen.

Yet, FBI and other officials in Washington tell me that Americans as a whole are not yet sufficiently aware of the gravity of the situation. These "patriot" criminals are now regularly robbing banks with automatic weapons. They are planning assassinations and attacks on police and military units. They are suspected of the sabotage derailment of an Amtrak train outside Phoenix in October 1995.

Incredibly, within weeks, for most Americans it was as though the events in Phoenix never occurred. The Viper Militia had produced no bodies to bury, no loved ones to mourn, so the threat didn't seem as real as was the Oklahoma City bombing.

It may be years before we learn how many paramilitary groups like the Vipers were driven underground by the arrests and seizures of weapons in Arizona.

But overt or covert, all these groups profess to believe that dangerous conspirators, including Jewish bankers and publishers and animal-like blacks, have usurped the U.S. Constitution, corrupted the courts and the banks, and moved to take arms away from loyal citizens. Their solution is to fight what the fringe leaders call "the System" by setting up common-law courts, robbing banks, and engaging in terrorism.

You cannot dismiss all these whites as mere "angry men" who shout a lot about their grievance but aren't likely to become violent. They have done violence almost beyond comprehension in Oklahoma City. And "they" were clearly influenced by a weird novel, *The Turner Diaries*, published in 1978 under the pseudonym of Andrew Macdonald by a former physics professor named William Pierce. This uncompromising racist, Pierce, has become the prophet of a Caucasian war, and his book has become the bible of the "save the White race" movement.

In May 1996, I wrote to the National Alliance in Hillsboro, West Virginia, to purchase a copy of William Pierce's *The Turner Diaries*. Along with the book I got a sheet stating:

> For far too long, we of European descent have allowed clever aliens to rob us of our identity and our history and to impose on us an alien morality in which the highest virtue is to hate our own race.
>
> The time has come for a courageous rethinking of all our values — for a new morality for White people, based firmly on Nature's laws and on the highest ideals of our Race-soul; a morality in which the first principle is the survival and advancement of our race — a principle to which all other things are subordinate.

Clearly, the lives of all those people who died in Oklahoma City were subordinate to the mad-dog, white-supremacist goals of those who are waging war to gain the power to say who can live in America. I have read the most racist of all the literature of slavery days, and of the bitter conflicts of the 1950s and 1960s, and I recall nothing as bigoted as *The Turner Diaries*. Almost every page reeks with talk of "depraved blacks raping white women," "the corruption of our people by the Jewish-liberal-democratic-egalitarian plague," details of the assassination of white editors who side with blacks; with the conclusion that "it is frighteningly clear now that there is no way to win the struggle in which we [whites] are engaged without shedding torrents — veritable rivers — of blood."

I am aware that white people who have just begun to read this book are probably fixated on the question of when and why angry blacks will begin the race war. There is no question in my mind that the disciples of William Pierce will start the fires of what some of them refer to as "Armageddon." Pierce wrote the "fictional" details of how to blow up the FBI headquarters in Washington, D.C. His scheme, right down to the use of ammonium nitrate fertilizer, was copied in the Oklahoma City tragedy. It is known that right-wing militiaman Timothy McVeigh, who was indicted on charges of carrying out that bombing, regarded *The Turner Diaries* as his gospel.

When Mike Wallace of CBS's "60 Minutes" confronted Pierce in the mountains of West Virginia, he found a man who would express no sorrow about the Oklahoma City bombing, just regret about the timing of it.

"[The bombing] does not make sense under the present conditions that we have when there's no group capable of actually taking on the federal government and defeating it," Pierce said. "I do not believe that we are in a revolutionary phase yet. I believe that the people have a lot of waking up and understanding to do first."

By way of "educating" the people, Pierce told Wallace that he had sympathy for the Montana Freemen and the Unabomber, favored shipping American blacks to Africa, and admired more than any man Adolf Hitler — an admiration he expressed by keeping two original copies of *Mein Kampf* right over his shoulder in his office.

Pierce has sold some two hundred thousand copies of *The Turner Diaries* since 1978. He has made a deal with publisher Lyle Stuart, a Jew, to republish the book and give it wider circulation. Stuart told Mike Wallace that he wants the world to know what Pierce stands for.

The Clinton administration's timid handling of the Freemen emboldened not just the Freemen, but lawless militiamen everywhere. Some of the most reactionary politicians in America went to that Jordan, Montana, farmhouse to try to negotiate a peaceful end to the standoff, but came away saying that the Freemen did not want a peaceful end to the dispute. That event made it clear that if the FBI and state law enforcement units continue to be intimidated, these groups that declare themselves to be beyond the jurisdictions of the law agencies of "the System" will strike out violently, making a race war inevitable.

Are you worried yet?

Just note that amidst all the concern about *The Turner Diaries,* the FBI's National Security Division was issuing a bulletin to police agencies that some militia leaders had issued directives for their "Project Worst Nightmare," in which militia units were told to prepare to "shut federal operations down" in the event that federal forces were used to assault the Montana Freemen farmhouse. The private militias were given "targets of opportunity," including communications facilities, senior federal law enforcement officials, and "selected news media."

In May, the FBI made more headlines by confirming that it had learned of anonymous threats to alcoholic beverage producers and broadcasters who air alcohol commercials, federal government officials, members of the news media, and Jewish executives and physicians.

The threat to kill government officials was based on cries that the Freemen standoff was a plot to attack all militias and seize their weapons. The threat to Jews involved an alleged plan to murder twelve hundred Jewish executives and physicians if Israel did not withdraw its military from Lebanon immediately.

In Georgia, just before the Olympic Games in Atlanta, federal treasury agents arrested two members of the Georgia Republic Militia on charges that they were plotting to make dozens of pipe bombs for use in a "war" against the United Nations and the "new world order." Fears were expressed that Robert Starr, the militia commander, and William James McCranie, Jr., planned to explode devices during the Olympics. A pipe bomb was exploded, with no evidence of involvement by the Georgia Republic Militia. The FBI poured hundreds of agents into efforts to identify the perpetrator of a crime that killed one woman and injured more than a hundred people.

How far can the madness go? The incidents and developments cited above represent mostly the homegrown threats. Add in the likelihood of foreign terrorists intervening in alliance with whatever groups stand up against Pierce and his Hitlerite punks and you have the makings of a terrible conflagration — one worse than the Civil War. Worse because the 200 million handguns on America's streets will come into play, along with the automatic guns and other weapons held by militias, weapons stolen from U.S. armories and gun stores, and sophisticated weapons provided by some foreign countries.

In April 1996, the FBI declared that Islamic radicals represent "the greatest threat coming to us domestically in the United States."

John P. O'Neill, chief of the FBI's counterterrorism section, said investigations of international terrorists had increased by 600 percent since the bombing of New York's World Trade Center in February 1993. "No longer is it just the fear of being attacked by international terrorist organizations — attacks against Americans and American interests overseas," O'Neill added. "A lot of these groups now have the capability and the support infrastructure in the United States to attack us here if they choose to. . . . Our largest growth area is in the anti-government movement, particularly in the area of militias. . . . We are seeing a threat from the international groups and the domestic groups at the same time."

Although international Islamic terrorists and local militias all profess to hate the U.S. government, they surely will not be on the same side in an American race war. They will be killing each other, turning the United States into a killing field, with blacks, Jews, Hispanics — well, everybody — forced to become combatants or to be slaughtered.

Clearly, no one in America can gain from such a war. But how to stop it? Tragically, the hated "System," as Pierce has labeled our federal government, must do some of what Pierce and the militiamen say they fear. Federal authorities must rein in to some degree the militia leaders who talk openly about killing federal judges and assassinating other elected officials, and who espouse murdering newspaper editors and destroying banks by writing billions of dollars worth of phony checks.

In April 1996, O'Neill warned against walking into what he called "a crescendo" of anti-government feeling fueled mostly by the Waco siege of the Branch Davidian compound and the shoot-out with the Weavers at Ruby Ridge. He said the image of a U.S. Army tank, with a white star painted on the side, moving against a civilian target, contributed to the anti-government movement "more than anything else." That thinking virtually paralyzed the FBI, leading to a long standoff during which

most of the militia leaders decided they could do almost anything they wanted to do.

The American dilemma now? If we can restrain the crazy, violent, paranoid white men, conceding the existence of millions
of white people who secretly sympathize with William Pierce,
we will have a chance to pacify the millions of nonwhites who
are more than ready to rumble.

We have gone too long without taking "the race problem" seriously enough to put it on a war footing. But we have a little
time in which to try to avert the spilling of what Pierce calls
"torrents — veritable rivers — of blood."

Before the big rumble, we are going to have a propaganda
war, the guts of which are discernible in this "60 Minutes" exchange between Wallace and Pierce:

WALLACE: (Voiceover) The central message of his novel *The
Turner Diaries*, indeed, his own abiding conviction, is that
the United States is being ruined by blacks, Hispanics,
Jews — just about everyone but those he calls his people,
Aryan whites.

The breakdown of our society, you blame, basically, mainly
on blacks and Jews.

DR. PIERCE: No, not — not primarily. I — I blame it on the fact
that we have . . .

WALLACE: Dr. Pierce . . .

DR. PIERCE: . . . allowed this society to become excessively cos-
mopolitan; that we have not had real white leadership in this
country.

WALLACE: That's the buzzword; that's the code word, "cos-
mopolitan."

DR. PIERCE: Mm-hmm.

WALLACE: That's Jews and blacks, and you know it is.

DR. PIERCE: Well, if you want to put it that way, but it involves
a lot of other people, too. It involves the mestizos coming
across the — our southern border. And . . .

WALLACE: Race mixing?

DR. PIERCE: Race mixing is — is one of the things which is
causing the breakdown of American society, and the alien-
ation of the people generally.

The people who sold me the copy of *The Turner Diaries*, the price hiked from $5.95 to $12.95, sent me gratis a copy of a National Vanguard Books catalog that listed dozens of racially inflammatory titles, plus many U.S. Army manuals such as *Boobytraps, Incendiaries, Explosives and Demolitions, Improved Munitions Handbook,* and an assortment of fiction about "Race and Revolution."

The centerpiece of this catalog is a long article headlined WHO RULES AMERICA?, with a subhead declaring that *The Alien Grip on Our News and Entertainment Media Must Be Broken.* Who are the "aliens" in this tirade of hatred? Michael Eisner of Walt Disney Company and Capital Cities / ABC; Gerald M. Levin of Time Warner Inc; Sumner Redstone of Viacom; David Geffen, Jeffrey Katzenberg, and Steven Spielberg of DreamWorks; the heads of the Newhouse newspapers-books-magazines-and-cable empire, Samuel and Donald Newhouse; the publisher of the *New York Times,* Arthur Ochs Sulzberger, Jr.; and the publisher of the *Washington Post,* Donald Graham. You've guessed it. All of the people being assailed and threatened in this screed are Jews.

"The Jewish control of the American mass media is the single most important fact of life, not just in America, but in the whole world today," this article screams. "There is nothing — plague, famine, economic collapse, even nuclear war — more dangerous to the future of our people."

What are Jews doing to justify such extreme condemnation? The catalog says:

> The Jew-controlled entertainment media have taken the lead in persuading a whole generation that homosexuality is a normal and acceptable way of life; that there is nothing at all wrong with White women dating or marrying Black men, or with White men marrying Asiatic women; that all races are inherently equal in ability and character — except that the character of the White race is suspect because of a history of oppressing other races; and that any effort by Whites at racial self-preservation is reprehensible.

I am sure that many Jews hate being tied to African Americans whenever the advocates of a race revolution spread their bigotry. It must be especially irritating when some African Americans like Louis Farrakhan make attacks on Jews a major thrust of their efforts to gain followers and make money. But neither Jews nor blacks can escape the fact that the white-supremacist killers wish both groups a common destiny of either expulsion from these shores or genocide.

I am one black man who wants Pierce and the militiamen to know that there will be no expulsion and no timid voluntary return to Africa.

If decent Americans become afraid to stand up to the threats and violence of the white supremacists, things will become worse very fast. Pierce and his followers will believe that they are in what he calls "a revolutionary phase" in which the federal government "can be defeated."

The conflict that I foresee will be as crazily complex as it will be violent, cruel, and heinous. We now see the skinheads and Ku Klux Klansmen emboldened in their campaigns against blacks, Jews, Catholics. We see the Muslims at war not only against Jews, but against the Italian mayor of New York, Rudolph Giuliani, and against America as a whole, as reflected in terrorist bombings. We hear black students talk about "the basis of truth" in a speech full of anti-Semitic invective by Nation of Islam minister Khalid Muhammad at Kean College in New Jersey. We see blacks in political struggle with Hispanics. And from Los Angeles to Detroit to New York, we see a growing underclass at war against "the establishment."

This dreadful upsurge in hurting and hatred in America, the increase in murders that are both random and born of rage, flows in part from the denied but obvious racism and contempt for the poor that were so venomous during the Reagan years, and before that from the spineless neglect and indifference of the Nixon and Ford years. But that is history. A race war of destructive proportions that will shock the world is probable because of these facts:

While President Clinton is no closet bigot, he is not as committed to racial and social equality as were Harry Truman, John F. Kennedy, and Lyndon B. Johnson. Clinton has fed the fever over welfare reform, even after discovering that "the poor must work" rhetoric was hollow, because for millions of impoverished men and women our society has no jobs, offers no training, and will not pay for day care for their children. He has gone along with the pretense that building more and more prisons at obscene costs is a solution to the crime problem. In an effort to prove that he is not "soft on crime" he has not only voiced the "lock 'em up" mentality, but led the way to designate more federal crimes as reasons to execute offenders.

During the heat of the presidential primaries, Clinton looked like a leader only because the warring Republicans looked so atrociously unpresidential. Pat Buchanan revealed himself to be shamelessly anti-Semitic, anti-black, and anti-Hispanic, thus destroying what little chance he had of winning the GOP nomination. The winner, Bob Dole, began immediately to play the race card, as have all the winning Republican candidates since Eisenhower. They bring the race war closer, but either don't know it or don't care.

Sophisticated hatemongers are in their heyday in the American media. The Rush Limbaughs, Howard Sterns, Pat Buchanans, and other socially and morally blind electronic pamphleteers write the nation's bestselling books because they moderate and dominate the nation's most-listened-to or most-watched radio and television shows.

Limbaugh and others of his ilk have manipulated public opinion in dangerous ways.

The idea is to make Limbaugh look great while making poor people look like bums, environmentalists appear to be "wackos," and decent-minded people look like enemies of democracy.

The politicians who love Limbaugh have virtually destroyed the social safety net in America, but they still rant about "reverse discrimination" and the so-called "special privileges" given to minorities. White male paranoia has become epidemic. This despite the fact that the median net worth of black households in this country is $4,604, or just one tenth the median net worth of white families — $44,408. The comparable figure for Hispanics is $5,345.

On talk shows and elsewhere I am frequently asked why "blacks get all the college scholarships." The General Accounting Office report that 96 percent of all the scholarship money in America goes to whites has done little to wipe out the white cries of persecution, many inspired by the likes of Limbaugh but reverberating in political campaigns across America.

Black judges and generals, cabinet officers and columnists, and talk-show hosts and television anchors are prominent symbols of the racial progress that has taken place in this society over the last two generations. But these symbols create a veneer that hides the truth that for the overwhelming mass of black people, Hispanics, and other nonwhites, precious little has changed during the thirty years that gave us the so-called civil rights revolution.

This harsh truth was never clearer to me than on August 27, 1993, when some seventy-five thousand people marched on Washington, D.C., to commemorate the celebrated March on Washington of 1963 when the Reverend Dr. Martin Luther King, Jr., gave his great "I Have a Dream" speech.

Only the most embittered flamethrowers could argue that no racial progress had been made over those thirty years. Sane people of sufficient age remembered that in 1963 petty apartheid was still a deeply ingrained way of life in the old slave states, and Jim Crow held sway over more of the North than most Yankees would admit. Black children were getting their heads battered and bloodied simply because they tried to buy a hamburger or drink a cola in Jim Crow restaurants, or even fancy department stores. Black travelers were being humiliated on buses and trains, or when they sought shelter in "white" hotels and motels. Jim Crow was king from Indianapolis, Indiana, to Indianola, Mississippi.

That 1963 March on Washington provoked the Congress to pass the Public Accommodations Act of 1964, which erased most of the ugly racism manifested in segregated movie theaters, recreation facilities, and other public places. That law gave a measure of dignity to black people. Few Americans have tried to force blacks into the backs of buses, or deny them the right to sit among whites at theaters, in restaurants, and now even in beauty parlors and dance classes. We have had problems with Denny's and other fast-food operations, but for the most part a black man's dollar has come to look as green and good as that of anyone else. Stores that once refused to let black women try on dresses or other garments now spend billions of dollars a year pitching their merchandise to black women.

But those who perceive a dramatic decline in racism in the

United States, or who embrace Ronald Reagan's line that it no longer exists, will point out, accurately, that black political power was relatively inconsequential in 1963.

That 1963 march struck the consciences of millions of white Americans and enabled President Johnson to secure passage of the Voting Rights Act of 1965. As a result, by the time of the 1993 march, blacks from Georgia, North Carolina, Louisiana, Mississippi, had been elected to Congress, and some eight thousand other black elected officials were holding office.

It was notable in 1963 that no black person had ever been a member of a President's cabinet. In 1963 there were no black syndicated newspaper columnists, no black presidents of major white universities, no black military men who even dreamed of becoming chairman of the Joint Chiefs of Staff. And no one listening to King's dream would have stretched it to a belief that by 1993 blacks would have served as mayors of Atlanta, Washington, D.C., Baltimore, Philadelphia, New York, Cleveland, Detroit, Los Angeles, New Orleans, and other cities.

But therein lies a damning story of the indelible curse of racism. It was only when the cities were watching their tax bases erode as affluent whites and some privileged blacks fled to suburbs, urban crime rates began to soar, and the public schools were falling into disrepair that the white power structure said: "OK, let's turn this mess over to a black mayor. And let him have a black police chief and a black superintendent of schools. Let them wrestle with this fucking problem!"

Political leaders moved deliberately to create "black majority" districts — in some cases creating district boundaries that looked absurd. Now politicians who benefited from gerrymandering for decades are screaming that gerrymandering to benefit blacks is unconstitutional. These efforts to rip away the political power blacks have obtained also carry the seeds of violent upheaval.

Then the businessmen who called the shots moved their businesses out of the cities. And Republican Presidents, seeing that our cities were populated more and more by blacks, Hispanics, immigrants legal and mostly illegal, who tended to vote for Democrats, said the big cities could "DROP DEAD!"

The Fair Housing Act of 1968 has never been much more than

a joke. Big cities such as Chicago, New York, Detroit, may be more segregated in terms of housing now than was the case twenty-eight years ago.

Jim Crow is maintained as much by bankers and mortgage companies as by hood-wearing white hoodlums. In city after city investigative reporters and others have established the fact that even a black person of exceptional prestige and large financial resources has a more difficult time getting a housing loan than a white applicant with lesser qualifications. The difficulty is magnified if the black applicant is trying to integrate public housing projects in formerly white neighborhoods! In January 1996 we saw the spectacle of FBI agents and U.S. marshals accompanying four black families, including eight children, into the Vidor Village federal housing project in Vidor, Texas, an all-white suburb of Beaumont. The Department of Housing and Urban Development had taken over the project after nine previous black residents were driven out by harassment and threats of violence.

The result is that there is no sense of community that reaches across racial lines. So walls of fear, suspicion, and hatred are maintained. And that makes the unthinkable, a race war in America, possible.

The long-heralded 1954 Supreme Court decision *Brown v. Board of Education* has failed in many important respects to wipe out Jim Crow in public education and to give blacks the most basic opportunities they were guaranteed forty years ago. The University of Alabama, which once was violently opposed to the admission of any black citizen, can now field a predominantly black football team, or even an all-black basketball team. Cheering fans may think for a moment that racism has vanished. But a visitor to the public schools of Birmingham, Atlanta, Washington, D.C., or Summerton, South Carolina, sees only token integration.

Now, the most pernicious discrimination in public schooling takes place in the North — in the cities such as Boston, Chicago, Detroit. White flight to suburbs, gerrymandering of school district lines, unfair distributions of everything from books, computers, and discretionary funds for teachers have poisoned such relationships as exist between black and white children.

Blacks gained dignity from the Public Accommodations Act

and political power from the Voting Rights Act. But the whole truth is that there can be only limited dignity and self-respect for those who live in poverty; and there is only limited political power for Americans who have no money and can afford no lobbyists or political action committees.

The curse of racism was never more evident than in the fact that while some blacks found dignity and political clout and economic opportunity over the last thirty years, the great mass of black Americans have not. And that fact lies at the heart of the breakdown of so many American families, the rise in rage and violent criminal behavior, and the worries about personal safety that we all feel.

In July 1963 unemployment was 5.1 percent for white Americans and 10.2 percent for nonwhites; in July 1993 joblessness was 6.0 for whites and 12.9 for blacks. In 1963 unemployment for white teenagers was 16.5 percent, but 31.2 percent for nonwhites; in 1993 it was 15.6 for white teenagers, but 32.7 percent for blacks. Over all these years you could bet your life that black unemployment would at any time be at least double that for whites. That is how and why black people have become the heart of America's permanent underclass.

In 1963, people marched on Washington in part to protest the fact that the median income of black families was only 53 percent of the median income of white families. That march provoked social legislation during LBJ's presidency that lifted black families to the point where they had $64 for every $100 available to the white family. But then came the racist "white blacklash" that wiped out the heart of Johnson's bid for a "Great Society." Black family income fell, so today the normal black family has $57 for every $100 available to the normal white family. That is pitiful, tragic "progress."

No law has provided for blacks and other minorities what ought to be the most basic of civil rights: the opportunity to work and earn a decent living. I have lived through all the promises of urban renewal, the War on Poverty, Community Action programs, Community Development corporations, Model Cities, Community Development block grants, Urban Development action grants, Enterprise Zones, and now "Empowerment Zones." But no life-changing money went into urban ghettos or the pockets of rural poverty, because slicksters already eating at the federal gravy train found ways to siphon off, or just plain steal, the monies intended to revitalize the most depressed neighborhoods. Ronald Reagan has been out of office for years now, but prosecutors are still trying to convict and imprison all the HUD officials and their co-conspirators who looted that department of billions of dollars on Reagan's watch.

You ask why, even with all the new evidence of bigotry, greed, exploitation of the underclass, anyone would be upset enough to start a race-class war. White Americans who have not endured the roller-coaster nightmare of political promises and burgeoning hopes, followed by dashed dreams and more of the traditional neglect, deliberate abuse, and institutionalized racism will never understand why some people stop hoping and start fighting.

From the time I was in elementary school in then Jim Crow Tennessee I have heard optimists, the self-styled keepers of "the American dream," say: "We can never change this generation of adults, but the kids will solve the problem. They haven't been fed racism in mother's milk."

We are sliding headlong into terrible racial conflict that will dwarf the Los Angeles riots precisely because the baby boomers have not grown up devoted to racial equality the way we thought or hoped they would. In fact, white youngsters — the children of the baby boomers — have swallowed more of the stereotypes that engender fear and hatred in recent years than at any time I have known. Thus, when they see that white girls are fornicating promiscuously, with larger and larger percentages getting pregnant out of wedlock, a "social scientist," Charles Murray, and his mouthpieces can alarm the nation with warnings that white girls have begun to act like black girls.

In his State of the Union address in January 1994, President Clinton exhorted the nation to "remember that even as we say no to crime, we must give people, especially our young people, something to say yes to." He said, "We must take the guns out of their hands and give them books."

But white denial makes good steps difficult to achieve. There are only a few white people — the skinheads, assorted Klansmen — who will openly say they are racists. But corporate boardrooms, local governments, education districts, are full of powerful men and women who are virulent bigots but will become stridently indignant and threaten to sue if someone calls them a racist. So racism thrives, safe behind a curtain of politically correct language. What constructive things have we actually given to the millions of underclass youth that they can say yes to? Not even books. Most readers of this book will have seen on TV numerous times the wretched public schools for blacks in which there are no encyclopedias, only a few termite-ridden books, not even a magnifying glass, let alone a modern piece of scientific equipment.

For almost seven years I have run a scholarship program for black high school seniors, and I have seen needed and deserved grants go to many hundreds of youngsters who display the learning, achievement, and personal integrity manifested by children who have been given a decent chance. But I see, with growing alarm, that millions of the children who can't get nominated for a Project Excellence scholarship have never been given a fair shake, never been offered even a tiny stake in this society.

White Americans expect blacks to say yes when they get only the backs of white people's hands.

Do they expect black youth who are desperate for ways to make an honest dollar to say yes to 40 percent or higher unemployment?

Do they expect proud and angry young black men to say yes to a Congress that allocates billions for new prisons but refuses to fund "dead-end" public service jobs? A "dead-end" job is a blessing for all of us compared with the dead people we keep counting in our pockets of unemployment.

We are at the brink of tragic racial strife because young black men have, in shameful numbers, been given prison cells to bolster the pretense that the bureaucrats are making progress in "the war against drugs." Bureaucrats fired the first salvos in the race war when they let the white kingpins of the drug trade, corrupt cops and sheriffs, and rich drug-buying actors, publishers, athletes, lawyers, and stockbrokers skate free.

For a generation we have seen a law enforcement version of genocide: our failed drug war has incarcerated, or destroyed the reputations of, a fourth of the young black men in this country.

And now we hear a Democratic President, Bill Clinton, endorse "boot camps" for first-time violators of the law. And Newt

Gingrich urging a "wartime" stance in which the federal government builds detention camps.

Welcome to the old South Africa and Nazi Germany!

There is a limit to how much oppression black Americans will take, no matter how much comfortable African Americans such as Carl Rowan tell them that they can never match the firepower of national guardsmen, or the troops that would surely be deployed to put down a black rebellion. Surely the Mayan Indians in Mexico's southern state of Chiapas knew that their Zapatista National Liberation Army was no match for the military power that Mexico's corrupt then-president Carlos Salinas de Gortari could throw against them. But rage and desperation provoked the Indians to seize San Cristóbal de las Casas and other towns and villages, to take over a radio station, bust open a prison, take many hostages, and make it clear that life in Mexico could never be the same. They wouldn't take it anymore.

If Gingrich and others think 33 million black people will accept his "stockades" in dumb docility, they had better ponder these facts:

- In every war, in every crisis, no group of Americans has been more loyal than African Americans. But the African American potential for destruction is incalculable should even a thousand desperately angry blacks become allies of the foreign terrorists who wish to do great harm to this country. The gates to the new concentration camps will swing shut much too late to stop those who think it is time for rebellion.

- There are now five million or more Muslims living in the United States, a million in deeply troubled California alone, and close to a million in New York. Some 42 percent of the Muslim residents are United States–born African Americans. We would be fools to assume that they will listen only to moderate black pacifists. Louis Farrakhan was surely referring to them when he said in Iran that "God will give the Muslims the honor of destroying America."

Let me reiterate that black involvement in a race war will largely be reactive — a response to deliberate provocations by the soul brothers of William Pierce and the other white supremacists, but also to those "law and order" Americans whose abuses of the criminal justice system drive blacks to say, "We've had enough!" It will be for the most part a black-versus-white war, because the rapidly growing Latin American population has not yet quite learned that the paranoiacs who spew forth rhetoric about killing to save the white race have no more respect for brown people than they do for black people. But Hispanics are sure to learn a lot faster than most Americans think. That is why from the White House to Capitol Hill to the largest and smallest city halls in America, there should be no priority greater than making the moves of justice that will prevent a race war.

You are saying, perhaps, that there can't possibly be provocations that are serious enough to provoke a race war. Then you have no idea of what goes on in America every day. Consider, for example:

## Two Days in December

It was December 6, 1995, a routine night at Fort Bragg, near the Fayetteville, North Carolina, home of the fabled 82nd Airborne Division of the U.S. Army. Many of the fifteen thousand members of this elite unit just sat around drinking beer — not yet sobered by the prospect of having to do duty in Bosnia or any other trouble spot.

One small gathering of drinkers included Private James N. Burmeister II, twenty, of Thompson, Pennsylvania, Private Malcolm Wright, twenty-one, of Lexington, Kentucky, and Specialist Randy Lee Meadows, Jr., twenty-one, of Mulkeytown, Illinois — all Caucasians. With each beer, Burmeister spoke with more agitation about wanting to earn his "spider web tattoo" — a symbol that he had committed a murder "for the cause." The "cause," later testimony showed, was white supremacy and the right-wing political agenda.

According to police and court records, Burmeister and Wright set out that December night, with Meadows driving, to find some black people to harass. They came upon a black man, Michael James, thirty-six, and a black woman, Jackie Burden, twenty-seven. After racial insults were hurled, one of the military men shot the two blacks to death.

Police arrested Burmeister and Wright on charges of first-degree murder. They charged Meadows with two counts of conspiracy to commit murder.

When police searched Burmeister's rented room, they realized that these were not random, drunken killings. They found a Nazi flag, white-supremacist literature, pamphlets on Adolf Hitler and Nazi Germany, and a videotape of the movie *Natural Born Killers*. Among the hate literature was a clandestine newsletter published at Fort Bragg called *The Resister*. A group called "Special Forces Underground" was publishing this newsletter, which in recent issues had railed against the United Nations, opposed United States policy in Haiti, and declared support for "individual rights, strict constitutionalism, limited government, isolationism, laissez-faire capitalism and republicanism." Police also found a 9mm Ruger that they said was used to execute Mr. James and Ms. Burden.

When Burmeister, Wright, and Meadows admitted that they were skinheads — a neo-Nazi white-supremacy group that in recent years has become increasingly violent across most of the nation — military authorities at Fort Bragg and in Washington were aghast. Could a brutal, racist, revolutionary group have invaded the army and its celebrated "special forces" in such a frightening way? They must have remembered the two army men who had become buddies at Fort Riley, Kansas, and had been accused of bombing a federal building in Oklahoma City on April 19, 1995. And just two months earlier, at Fort Bragg, a sergeant had been charged with a predawn sniper attack on soldiers who were warming up for a morning run. He had killed one member of the 82nd Airborne and wounded eighteen others.

Here were killings far more disturbing than any number of hate-inspired assaults by whites on blacks, Jews, Asians, and homosexuals. Here was a possible cancer within America's most vital military forces, an affliction of right-wing hatred that would leave everyone, including the President, vulnerable to wanton murder.

Naturally, neither Pentagon nor White House officials wanted to portray the problem as a national security threat. On December 12, Secretary of the Army Togo D. West, Jr., announced a worldwide investigation of the presence of political extremists in army ranks, and a determination to oust from the military the hate groups that seemed to be gaining influence in American life. But West's announcement was shrouded in a maze of military mumbo jumbo and political caveats about what the country could do or should do about, or to, haters in military uniforms.

The Pentagon said army regulations prohibit soldiers from active participation in groups that espouse supremacist causes, attempt to create illegal discrimination based on race, creed, religion, or sex, or that advocate the use of violence. The Pentagon said soldiers are discouraged, but not prohibited, from merely being members of hate groups, receiving mail from them, or attending their meetings while off duty.

Lieutenant Colonel Kenneth McGraw, spokesman for the Special Operations Command at Fort Bragg, told the media that the extremists who published *The Resister* and opposed U.S. policies were not in violation of any regulations.

Was anything being said, or planned, that would deter those ready to kill to earn a tattoo? Or even those military men who printed in *The Resister* things that went to the heart of the army's ability to fulfill a mission? Such as:

"The U.S. military has become a slave service for the wealth redistribution schemes of internationalists and gangs of weeping do-gooder mystics. One need simply note the circling of media carrion eaters to predict in which third world toilet these altruists will flush hundreds of millions of U.S. tax dollars and the lives of U.S. servicemen. Peacekeeping is a monumental fraud."

Secretary West said that he believes the extremists of Christian militia mentality or other haters "are not a sizable proportion of our Army." But the question arises, "How large, how well-organized, do these groups have to be if they have access to army training, army weapons, army secrets?"

Burmeister was not the only unheeded symptom of racial troubles in the military. Race riots had occurred in Korea years before. The navy had had hate-based eruptions on some ships. White members of hate groups on army bases in Germany wrote racial slurs on the cars of black soldiers. Skinhead groups in Colorado armed themselves with guns stolen by sympathizers on military bases.

Sad to say, the upsurge of violent racism in armed groups in America involves more than the United States Army, Navy, and

Marine Corps. It now includes every police force in any city and county in America, the National Guard, federal agencies, and even some private "protective" groups.

On that December day in 1995 when Secretary West declared his intention to "ferret out" the haters in the army, I reacted with pessimism. I explained why with these words:

> Do you remember that half a year ago we were shocked by revelations about an orgy of racism by law enforcement officers at a "Good Ol' Boys Roundup" in Tennessee? White officials and ordinary agents of the FBI, the Secret Service, the Customs Service, the Drug Enforcement Administration, the U.S. Marshals Service, the Internal Revenue Service, the Immigration and Naturalization Service, the Bureau of Prisons, and even the District of Columbia Metropolitan Police would gather in Ocoee, Tenn., hiding behind a "Nigger Check Point," to get drunk and vent their racism. Employees of the Bureau of Alcohol, Tobacco and Firearms had begun this event, called "sickening" by President Clinton, in 1985.
>
> ATF Director John W. Magaw and the heads of the other law enforcement agencies promised investigations in July. Even though there are videotapes of some of their employees attending those "roundups of hatred," we haven't seen a single report of any punishment being meted out to anyone.
>
> It's time we faced the fact that some people — white, black, brown, or whatever — have violent, authoritarian personalities. The only places where they can legally get a gun, bayonet, or baton and occasionally use them to maim or kill is in a law enforcement agency or the military. We know about the crisis they have brought to the policing of America's cities. We are learning, much too late, of the frightening problems these authoritarians, especially those driven by hate, are bringing to our legitimate military — and to the "militias" that are springing up.

Human history is replete with lessons that hatred begets hatred; that one despicable act guarantees a reprisal; that the corrosive juices of racial rage corrode everything beyond all the laws of physics. On December 8, 1995, just one of two mad-dog days in December, we got another lesson on the ways in which racial and ethnic hatred poisons weak minds, provoking incredible cruelties, rending the fabric of an entire society.

Do not leap to any conclusion that I am saying that whites alone are doing the evil and saying the ugly things that provoke violence in America. Just as I have always held that racism is a destructive disease that respects no race or class, so blacks and others are guilty of the kind of demagoguery that makes a race war possible in America. Consider for example:

Hostility in Harlem

On December 8, in the business heart of Harlem, surely the best-known black community in the world — yes, better known than Soweto in Johannesburg — an itinerant black laborer and former street vendor, Roland Smith, walked into Freddy's Fashion Mart, a store on 125th Street owned by a Jew, with a gun and a container of gasoline.

In what would become known across America as "the Harlem Massacre," fifty-one-year-old Smith shot four people to death, spread his gasoline wide, then killed himself as he burned down the store, taking the lives of three more people.

The massacre of eight people, including five Latinos and a black security man, Kareem Brunner, tells us how the incendiary language of racism, in even the simplest dispute, produces raging infernos — in actuality and in the minds of millions of people far away.

I didn't learn this just reading about "the Harlem Massacre." I cut my reportorial teeth in Mississippi, where Emmett Till and Medgar Evers were murdered by racists. I was in Birmingham at the time of the racist bombing of the Baptist church in which four black girls were murdered while attending Sunday school. So I cannot forget how race hatred overrides all pretenses of logic, no matter what the race of the haters.

People who lived near the charred store refused to believe that a race war had erupted so near them. John Perkins, twenty-seven, told the *New York Times:* "This guy had to be crazy. This isn't about race. This is the act of a crazy man."

Roland Smith may have been deranged — out of his mind at

losing his right to make a living as a street vendor. But no sane person could doubt that Smith was driven to his act of multiple murder by violent street cries of racism, telling him that he had to wreak retribution on white "crackers" and Jewish "blood-suckers." Smith died foolishly, thinking that he was protecting Harlem from Jews, Indians, Koreans, all those people whom he had heard the Reverend Al Sharpton describe derisively as "interlopers."

Just as whites in Bensonhurst had killed and maimed to keep black New Yorkers out of "their part of town," Smith had been driven to kill to keep nonblack businessmen out of the "African American part of town."

At issue was what seemed a simple dispute over a lease and sublease. Freddy's Fashion Mart was owned by a Jew who, according to the *New York Times*, "lives in the insular neighborhood of Brooklyn's Sephardic Jews, where children attend yeshivas and even the hardest-charging businessmen shut off their cell phones and beepers for the Sabbath."

Fred A. Harari had been so hard-charging that his Harlem store was a great success. So much so that he wanted to expand, using space that he had subleased to a black man, Sikhulu Shange, who had for fifteen years used the space for the Record Shack. Harari's notice that he would not renew the sublease quickly became the basis for war. What might have been a simple landlord-tenant dispute quickly became a deadly symbol of the murderous level of racial conflict in America.

The black newspaper the *Amsterdam News* asked: "Could this be the beginning of a systematic attempt to drive viable black-owned businesses out of Harlem? Prior to the 1950s, blacks could not shop on 125th Street, let alone run their own business operations in the area."

The irony, which the *Amsterdam News* should have known, was that the actual owner of the property in dispute was a black church, the United House of Prayer for All People, a Pentecostal church founded in Charlotte, North Carolina, in 1926, by Bishop C. M. (Sweet Daddy) Grace, a man who became a superhuman figure in Harlem. He supposedly "healed" people, then sold them cold cream, toothpaste, eggs, coffee, and other products with such success that soon he could buy a twenty-room mansion in Montclair, New Jersey.

The late Sweet Daddy's church not only owned the property at 272 West 125th Street, where Freddy's and the Record Shack coexisted; it was one of the biggest landlords on the street. So this was no case of white predators trying to force blacks out of that part of Harlem. It was quite simply a case of a black landlord squeezing a Jewish tenant for more money, with the Jew in turn squeezing a black subtenant to give back his space or pay about double what he had been paying.

Shange knew that this black church lay behind his problems, but he never told protesters how angry he was at the United House of Prayer. And the church lay low, even as the protesters became more violent in their language and threats. It was so much easier to let the public believe that a Jew was abusing a black subtenant.

Every black demagogue played the "evil Jew" theme. Morris Powell, a black street vendor of pies and oils on 125th Street had been exhorting African Americans to "buy black," to keep their money away from the Jews, Koreans, and others he saw as driving him out of business as they exploited unsophisticated black consumers.

Powell's message was not unlike that of the Reverend Louis Farrakhan, leader of the Nation of Islam, who had great appeal in arguing that black survival depended on African Americans emulating their Jewish "oppressors." Blacks had to "carve out a place in the world to get respect and have a homeland — that's what we need to do," Powell had said.

Powell fashioned himself after Marcus Garvey, the black man who led a failed "back to Africa" movement. He saw himself as the essence of black pride as he wore his African "kofi" and festooned his Vendors Association Shoppers Mart with African cloth and clothing and numerous portraits of Malcolm X. His marquee shouted Buy Black.

Morris Powell was for years a fierce — and eventually unsuccessful — defender of the black street vendors on 125th Street. The city, including black mayor David Dinkins, believed that some six hundred black vendors had become a nuisance, clogging the street, irritating pedestrians, paying no taxes — all the while stealing business from tax-paying merchants in the area. But the city's attempt to shut down the vendors failed, making Powell a more formidable force than ever before.

But that emboldened Powell to the tragic point where he could decide not only who could do business on 125th Street, and in Harlem, but who could not. His street harangues against Freddy's and other businesses owned by nonblacks led to angry accusations that he had fomented Roland Smith's gun murders and the torching of Fred A. Harari's place of business.

Powell had poisoned the mind of Roland Smith as surely as if he had given him an injection of some mind-bending drug when Powell stood outside Freddy's ranting against its Jewish owner. His pickets screamed about "Jew bastards." Blacks who dared enter Freddy's were taunted as "cracker-lovers" and "black traitors." Brunner, twenty-two, the store security man, was warned, "You'll get yours."

Court records, tapes, and eyewitness reports indicate that in late November pickets were screaming:

"Kill the Jew bastards."

"Burn down the Jew store and its employees and customers."

"This block is for niggers only; no whites and Jews allowed."

Conrad Muhammad, head of the Nation of Islam in New York and a supporter of the boycott of Freddy's, said Sikhulu Shange "symbolized the plight of black people in Harlem and their inability to find safety nets and support. . . . And so he [Shange] is a cause célèbre."

He became a bigger cause célèbre when the Reverend Al Sharpton showed up to characterize nonblack business people as "interlopers." If Sharpton wasn't a racist, no one was. I remembered that in the old days, when he was trying to make a name for himself in Brooklyn and nationally, he would call white people "faggots," and any black who opposed him was denounced as "a yellow nigger." No opponent was as "black" as Sharpton. And he preached class conflict, calling any African American opponent "a cocktail-sip Negro." The staple insults "Oreo" and "Uncle Tom" were too tame for Sharpton.

So this was the "black leader" who joined the pickets outside Freddy's to declare:

"We will not stand by and allow them to move this brother so that some white interloper can expand his business on 125th Street. . . . We are not turning 125th Street back over to the outsiders [as was] done in the early part of this century. This is a sin and a shame and a disgrace. . . ." The passions of black protesters were inflamed beyond rationality.

Fred Harari was frightened. So he went to the state supreme court in Manhattan to ask Judge Harold Tompkins to sign a restraining order requiring the pickets to stay at least fifty feet from his store.

But the wheels of justice turned exceedingly slowly in Tompkin's courtroom that morning of December 8. First, Anna Hong, Harari's lawyer, arrived in the courtroom ninety minutes late with the papers requesting the restraining order.

Then the courtroom was consumed in a series of legalistic technicalities and human failures. The judge asked if Hong had, as required by law, notified city authorities of the hearing. She had not, pleading that she had only three and a half weeks experience. Judge Tompkins ordered her to call the corporation counsel's office at once. Ten minutes later Ms. Hong said she was having trouble reaching the right city officials and asked the judge to adjourn the hearing until Monday, three days later.

"I'm not going to adjourn it with this affidavit of emergency staring me in the face," Judge Tompkins said, "because if someone gets killed over the weekend, I am not going to have it on my conscience, do you understand that?" He gave the young lawyer three City Hall numbers to call.

Minutes later Ms. Hong said, "Your Honor, I just called my office, and my office has informed me that some people came in the plaintiff's store, shot people with a gun, and burned the store down."

It was some two hours earlier, just after 10 A.M., that Roland J. Smith, a former street vendor who had been arrested for resisting police efforts to clear the streets of vendors, and who had gone to prison for refusing to submit to the military draft, had decided that he alone would save Sikhulu Shange from Fred Harari and the rest of the Jews. He had, in a burst of gunshots and an inferno of his making, killed seven people and himself.

All tragedies such as "the Harlem Massacre" become fodder for politicians, including the politicians who have created the climate of rampant racism that threatens not just Harlem, but every city, every neighborhood, in America.

On December 9, New York mayor Rudolph W. Giuliani, and

the then police commissioner, William J. Bratton, held a press conference to declare that the gunman-arsonist had been provoked by the racist, anti-Semitic remarks made by picketers outside the store. Fingers were pointed immediately at Sharpton, who pleaded only a minor role in the protests.

"We never said we were going after whites or Jews," Sharpton said. "We were trying to help a property owner."

With his rhetoric, Sharpton helped to turn a real estate squabble between a black church landlord, a Jewish leaser of space, and a black subleaser into a cataclysmic war between blacks and Jews, blacks and interlopers, and blacks against a mayor trying "to change the color of New York."

Sharpton's was an incredibly irresponsible performance in the eyes of anyone of any race, except for those African Americans already alienated from this society to the point where no reason could sway them.

Sharpton began taking the offensive: "If anyone even infers I called for violence, they're going to have to prove it. Nobody except an outright imbecile would say I would use violence."

The New York media suggested a lot of "outright imbeciles" were among Sharpton's followers. I could only think how much Sharpton's words sounded like those of former Alabama governor George Wallace, when, in a sickbed interview with me, he denied that his racist outbursts had encouraged whites to kill four black girls in the bombing of the Baptist church in Birmingham. Wallace had told me, "I love everybody," and said, in effect, that only imbeciles would think he had provoked any of the white-supremacist crimes that were committed while he was high on the political stage.

Wallace had a way with words. Sharpton had survived his many excesses by cleverly turning phrases. And, sure enough, there would be a few Jewish wordsmiths who would intensify black-Jewish warfare by blaming the tragedy of 125th Street on blacks in general. Richard Cohen of the *Washington Post*, the self-declared identifier of "cowardly" black leaders, wrote that "the Harlem massacre had many accomplices — and they were all, leaders and followers alike, in Washington with Louis Farrakhan." Here was an absurd assertion that showed that Cohen had no idea that hundreds of thousands of black men came to the Million Man March out of their personal grievances, frustrations, and anger, and not because of the anti-Jewish rhetoric of Farrakhan. Cohen was thus stigmatizing black people in his far-reaching column as surely as Morris Powell was denigrating all Jews in his radio broadcasts.

Here was the rhetorical fodder of war.

Who will learn what from those two days in December, those days of racism manifested in such deadly ways?

We all must first learn the lesson that there is nothing special about Fayetteville, North Carolina, or Fort Bragg or Harlem that makes them harbingers of our race wars. Give me two days in any month of any year now and I can show you events of comparable insanity.

There hasn't been a year in my lifetime that the United States has been free of racist eruptions in Detroit, Harlem, Little Rock, Springfield, Illinois, Atlanta — well, most of our cities, north or south, east or west. But even in the years when one hundred lynchings of black people were commonplace, there was a general feeling that things had to get better. Since 1993, civility has almost disappeared from America's political discourse. Exploiting racial fears and hatreds has become the great American political pastime. And hate crimes flowing from naked racism have become so numerous that we must fear that hatred will consume the next generations, not that they will vanquish bigotry. Consider this limited recital of race-inspired violence since early 1993:

- In Tampa, Florida, two white men chose a black tourist from New York at random, doused him with gasoline, and almost burned him to death.
- In Jackson, Mississippi, three white teenagers who shouted racial epithets as they set fire to two black churches were sentenced to prison terms of three to four years.
- In the unlikely community of Morocco, Indiana, a 99 percent white farming town about eighty miles south of Chicago, thirteen-year-old Angela Scheerings found a death threat in her locker at the North Newton Junior-Senior high school after she and five other white girls emulated the black

"hip hop" culture by wearing baggy pants and braiding
their hair. A sixteen-year-old white male, Brandon Belt,
later told the Associated Press: "This is a white community.
If they [the "wiggers," or "white niggers"] don't want to be
white, they should leave."

- On January 8, 1996, in Knoxville, Tennessee, the Inner
  City Community Church was burned down. It was an event
  that would have gone without national notice but for
  the fact that its associate pastor was a beloved graduate
  of the University of Tennessee, a six-foot five-inch, three-
  hundred-pound black man, Reggie White, who had been an
  All-American collegiate football player and had been for
  eleven years one of the greatest defensive linemen in the National Football League. The church was burned just before
  White would play in the most important game of his life —
  against the Dallas Cowboys for the championship of the
  National Football Conference and the right to play in Super
  Bowl XXX.

Within weeks, the nation was in an uproar over a series of
torchings of black churches, mostly in the South. It seemed that
burning down black churches had become a greater sport than
football. White Americans, again in inexplicable denial, argued
over whether there was a conspiracy, and seemed infinitely
pleased when no one could produce evidence that x number of
white people had sat down in place y and declared it a policy to
burn down black places of worship. They seemed happy enough
to declare that the torchings of these churches were just manifestations of many individual acts of racism. Deval Patrick, the
assistant attorney general for civil rights, pointed out that if
lawmen were dealing only with individual acts of bigotry, the
situation was infinitely worse than if there had been a conspiracy.

Who needed a certain meeting of certain people at a certain
time and place to declare a "conspiracy"? If all of these people
read *The Turner Diaries* and the other publications put out by
Pierce and the other haters, they had reason enough to make
common cause in the burning of black churches.

- I have not forgotten January 14, 1995, when four young
  black men from Guthrie, Kentucky, were angered by a Confederate flag flying from the rear of a truck driven by a nine-

teen-year-old white man, Michael Westerman, with his twenty-one-year-old wife, Hannah, as passenger.

The black men, Freddie Morrow, Damilen Darden, Marcus Merriweather, and Tony Andrews expressed anger when Westerman's flag-festooned truck pulled into a Guthrie convenience store. Racial insults began to fly. The four blacks drove off to get some "backup" buddies. Two carloads of black teenagers followed Westerman and his wife, who hurried across the state line toward Springfield, Tennessee. The intention, Morrow said, was to stop Westerman's car and fight him — one lone white male prey to become the victim of eight or more blacks. But as is so often the case, merely stupid intentions turn into deadly tragedies over race.

As the car in which Morrow was riding drew even with Westerman's vehicle, Morrow said, someone yelled "Shoot! Shoot! Shoot!" And he did, mortally wounding Westerman.

Hannah Westerman testified that she squeezed into the driver's seat and drove the four-wheel-drive pickup truck through ditches into a parking lot, only to see three black men approaching her vehicle. She raced back onto the highway trying to get to the Springfield hospital. But there were black men, at least one with a weapon, blocking her way. So she sped off to a hospital in Clarksville, Tennessee, where her husband soon died.

Andrews agreed to testify against the other black men and was allowed to plead guilty to charges that brought him only two years of probation. Almost a year to the day after this grisly murder scene, on January 12, 1996, Morrow and Darden were convicted of murder and civil rights intimidation in a non-jury trial presided over by Judge Robert Wedemeyer.

So many lives wrecked by race hatreds symbolized by the banner of one side of a war over slavery that supposedly ended 130 years earlier! Could anything be worse? Yes, it has been, and it will be.

• There was the incident of December 7, 1993, when an ill-fated twelve-car commuter train, the Long Island Express, left New York's Pennsylvania Station at 5:33 P.M. At the Jamaica stop, a thirty-five-year-old black man, a native of Kingston, Jamaica, boarded the train carrying a concealed 9mm Ruger semiautomatic pistol. As the train approached the Merillon station, at about 6:10 P.M., the black man,

Colin Ferguson, pulled out his gun and began to shoot people. In a few moments he emptied the fifteen-shot magazine, reloaded it, and continued to shoot. In those moments of rage, Ferguson killed six people and injured seventeen — all his victims white or Asian.

After three passengers subdued Ferguson, police found his pockets full of notes expressing his hatred of Caucasians, Asians, and "Uncle Tom Negroes."

Andre Antrobus, a friend of Ferguson's from Brooklyn, said, "He hated white people because he thought white people controlled the system. . . . He'd say no matter how much he tried to do good, the system would take him back down."

I do not make dire predictions lightly. I have never been an alarmist. In fact, I may have been a youthful Pollyanna in 1952 when I wrote in my first book, *South of Freedom*, "After more than three centuries, America's race problem still is a creeping miasma that overshadows our economic lives, frustrates our social lives and enshrouds our sexual lives in curiosity and untold fear. [Yet], I do not believe that man was born to hate and be hated; I cannot believe that the race problem is an inevitable concomitant of democratic life."

By 1964, when I was Director of the United States Information Agency in the Johnson administration, I had grown a little wiser. I had seen enough bigotry in the fast-food joints of Maryland, in the State Department, in the Memphis airport, and in the private clubs of the nation's capital to take seriously the 1880 declaration by Benjamin Disraeli that "no man will treat with indifference the principle of race. It is the key of history."

I had learned enough about racism to tell a Howard University audience in 1961:

If you ask me what I would like most to see happen in world affairs today, I would not give top priority to a disarmament agreement or a settlement of the Berlin dispute or any such thing. I would give top priority to having it demonstrated that, beyond any doubt, a bi-racial or multi-racial society can exist in harmony and mutual respect.

I feel that long after conflict between the West and Soviet Communism has faded we shall still be plagued by this issue of race. . . . Racial bitterness and bigotry, that racial arrogance ingrained over generations, is the ugly and ominous time bomb that spells danger to mankind.

But I was still part Pollyanna, a man with hope for America, when I heard President Johnson say to a joint session of Congress:

In our time we have come to live with the moments of great crisis. Our lives have been marked with debate about great issues — issues of war and peace, prosperity and depression. But rarely in any time does an issue lay bare the secret heart of America itself. Rarely are we met with a challenge, not to our growth or abundance, or our welfare and our security, but rather to the values and the purposes and the meaning of our beloved nation.

The issue of equal rights for American Negroes is such an issue. And should we defeat every enemy, and should we double our wealth and conquer the stars and still be unequal to this issue, then we will have failed as a people and as a nation.

Well, the terrible headlines of this generation, the current demagogic rhetoric in Congress, the proposed draconian "solutions" to every American social problem, make it clear that we are not equal to "the issue of equal rights for American Negroes."

How did we get here? How did the American dream become such a hellish nightmare? For answers we must look honestly and fearlessly at the people the late Justice Thurgood Marshall called "the gatekeepers." That means that we look at the occupants of the White House during the recent years when racism became tolerable again, if not fashionable. We must look at the routes and means that presidential candidates and the leaders of Congress have taken in their quests for power. We must look at our opinion leaders, the media and academia, to determine whether they have breathed new life into the concept of superior and inferior races, laying down wittingly or unwittingly justification for a new orgy of bigotry in America. Can the likes of Louis Farrakhan, Rush Limbaugh, and other church and media purveyors of divisiveness lead us to anything but a race war? And how much are the gatekeepers to education and employment in America responsible for putting us at each other's throats over such issues as who deserves a scholarship — or over the broader issue of "affirmative action" in the workplace?

Or must we find blameless the gatekeepers, the politicians, the opinion-makers, finding that we are hating and killing because we are afraid and feeling helpless in the face of a terribly high crime rate, a sexual revolution that ensnares and kills our teenagers and makes some of us feel dirty, and an economic revolution that renders us insecure?

# Chapter 2

# The Politics of Racial Strife

In 1995 we saw on several fronts the opening salvos of the race war that some refuse to believe possible. The O. J. Simpson trial unleashed racial passions deeper than any in America since the Civil War over slavery. It pitted not only blacks against whites, but husbands against wives, sons against fathers. Here was a murder that couldn't possibly merit a national orgy of hatred and anger, compared with thousands of other murders that took place in the U.S. in 1994. But the sole issue of race — of a black celebrity allegedly killing his long-abused white wife and her white friend — grabbed Americans by their throats, their gonads, what was left of their brains, and immersed them in spasms of anger and hatred. The jury verdict provoked Americans to abandon the "presumption of innocence," to attack the jury system, to acquiesce in barring the larger "public" — via TV cameras — from courtrooms, and to declare in effect that Simpson was a convict who could not get rich from selling his story the way almost everyone else associated with the case was doing.

Another race missile was lobbed into this growing war in what seemed to some to be nation-praising "Powellmania." The country, especially the Republican party, crawled out to the precipice and looked retired black general Colin Powell in his eyes. What Powell saw in return convinced him that this America is not yet ready for an African American president. That Powell said he would not run gives us more reasons to fear the future than reasons to believe we have lifted or ever can lift politics above racism.

"Powellmania" turned out to be a remarkable case of national schizophrenia. By 1995, it was obvious that millions of white people, including a lot of Republicans whom I know, were convinced that something profoundly wrong had America in its grip. They sensed the spirit of violence in the air. Most of them looked at a black military hero, Colin Powell, and saw him as a force for drawing together the American people. Yet many of those white Americans who said this publicly had to say to themselves privately, "I don't think this nation is ready yet for a black President. Am I really ready for a black President?" As these Americans thought, it became obvious to them that certainly the people who blew up the federal building in Oklahoma City, the people fighting the FBI and other authorities in Montana, at Ruby Ridge, Idaho, in Waco, Texas, were not going to see the granting of political power to a black general as the solution for anything. It was clear that Clinton was going to run for reelection, and there was not a ghost of a chance that Powell could win the Democratic nomination, even if he wanted it, which was not the case. When it became clear that Powell was leaning toward the Republican party, the average political observer could see that most of the bedrock supporters of the GOP would not tolerate a presidential nominee who supported abortion rights and affirmative action and other programs against which the Christian right had set its face years ago.

When Colin Powell announced that he would not run for any elective office in 1996, and when he later told me in an exclusive interview that he absolutely would not accept the vice-presidential spot on a ticket headed by Senator Bob Dole, a great puff of air rushed out of the new American political dream. Whites and blacks alike sensed that there would be no great symbol to draw Americans together. And that in itself made a race war infinitely more likely.

I do not predict that little bands of Americans — white,

brown, black — will sit in coffee klatches and plan a race war. Not any more than you would have predicted that Bill Clinton, Newt Gingrich, and Bob Dole would sit in their personal war rooms and plan a course of conflict that would lead to nation-wounding shutdowns of the federal government. With "race" underlying most of the issues that were at the heart of the "balanced budget" impasse — that is, welfare, Medicaid, Medicare, federal support for education, and whether to give tax cuts to whom — no planning of a crisis was possible.

A foreboding sense that the future will be dark is feeding the spirit of divisiveness, the assumptions of inevitable fratricide, among Americans.

I have said in speeches for more than thirty years that "nothing much changes in America except as it is run through the political system." I know now that we face an almost unbelievable conflict because our politicians have failed. Repeat, our politicians, not our political system, have victimized us.

For generations, some of our politicians looking for an almost certain way to win found that an appeal to racism was the last, even the first, resort. Theodore Bilbo, Eugene Talmadge, "Cotton Ed" Smith, Strom Thurmond, and James Eastland were among the many southerners who found that naked exploitation of white racism brought not only victory, but political longevity and seemingly endless control of the most powerful committees of Congress. They reigned, however, in an era when few other than white men could vote in the South, so their brazen bigotry posed no threat to their fiefdoms.

While Truman and Eisenhower angered these men, and constituted marginal threats to "the System," Kennedy and Johnson were the first Presidents to make the southern bigots question their loyalty to the Democratic party.

On the day in 1965 when LBJ dramatically begged a joint session of Congress to pass the Voting Rights Act, he made a remark to me that I did not fully comprehend until recent years.

"You want me to give this fuckin' speech and say the things you've written for me. Like 'we shall overcome.' And I'm going to do it, because I know it is right. But I ain't so goddamn sure as you are that 'we shall overcome.' You ever thought that we might be liberating some blacks and at the same time sounding the death knell of the Democratic party?"

"No President, no black official of honor, has any choice but to support the voting rights bill," I said, at the time not giving a good goddamn about the impact on the Democratic party or on American politics either then or half a century later.

Johnson was ruthlessly faithful to his commitment to open up voting to all Americans, in all states. Cynics of the time said he was just guaranteeing himself longtime power by "locking up the Negro vote." But Johnson couldn't "lock up" any bloc of votes in a time of widespread uprisings against the Vietnam War. The course of politics would prove him prescient about the fate of the Democratic party.

Even as Johnson and I talked, the conventional wisdom everywhere was that the great racist ogre of the 1950s and 1960s was George Wallace, the governor of Alabama who proclaimed the survival of racial segregation "today, tomorrow, and forever." Wallace won great notoriety because he didn't just block Negroes at the doors of Alabama's schools; he carried a convincing message of white domination to voters in the North and West in 1968, winning the support of 20 percent of them.

At the executive level, the privately corrupt, power-grabbing old director of the FBI, J. Edgar Hoover, was viewed as the most dangerous and obdurate foe of the people's right to assemble in peaceful protest, to give angering speeches, or even to practice civil disobedience. Others, such as Birmingham police commissioner Bull Conner, vied for the dubious title of greatest foe of civil rights for blacks. But historical records make it clear that no single American did more to stunt the movement toward racial and ethnic equality in America than Richard Milhous Nixon.

Nixon was brilliant in his anti-black tactics because he was a slick demagogue, and he was especially deceitful during 1961 and 1969, the years when he was "on probation," and lacked the power to dominate American social policy. He was not out front in any white-supremacist way when he was groping for the political support he needed for a "comeback" in which he would become President.

Nixon was the shrewdest of anti-black propagandists in his double-talk, particularly in his undermining of court-ordered busing to wipe out Jim Crow. He added "forced" to the word "busing" and tacked on "to achieve racial balance." Thus, Nixon made "busing" so inflammatory a word that most whites and many blacks cried out against it.

At the height of the "civil rights revolution," Nixon knew when to be silent, to hide his hostility to the legislation that would deliver a measure of dignity to black people. He gained unjustified credit with a few civil rights leaders by saying that "the most common and justifiable complaint of Negroes and members of other minority groups is not that their constitutional rights have been denied, but that their personal dignity is repeatedly insulted."

How devious of Nixon to classify the issue as "personal" rather than constitutional. This cloaked his secret hatred of civil rights laws, feelings he revealed to the discerning in a *U.S. News & World Report* article of August 15, 1966, in which he said of the Public Accommodations Act: "Not all the police in the nation could enforce the public-accommodations section of the 1964 Civil Rights Act if there were not a commitment on the part of the people to accept the law. If Negroes must repeatedly haul restaurateurs in court before they can be served a meal, then the guarantee of equal accommodations is illusory."

Nixon was the most prominent mouthpiece for those who argued that "you can't legislate morality," and that "civil rights laws will do more harm than good." Stephen Ambrose wrote in his book *Nixon* that "Johnson's position was 'now.' Nixon's position was 'later.' This put him squarely in the middle, as a supporter of civil rights, but not quite yet."

Ambrose offered this additional evidence of Nixon's two-faced civil rights position:

That Nixon tried to play both sides of the fence on the explosive race issue was as obvious as it was inevitable. He firmly upheld the Supreme Court's school-desegregation decisions, and stated unequivocally that segregation should not be perpetuated. But he went on to describe as "dangerous" the Johnson Administration policy of withholding federal funds from school districts that refused to integrate public schools, despite the fact that the power to withhold funds was the only effective weapon available to the federal government. . . .

That Nixon actually detested the civil rights movement would help bring on his downfall. He did not believe in civil protest, especially acts of civil disobedience. However, the politically shrewd side of him knew that most law-abiding Americans joined him in hating black marchers and demonstrators.

So in hundreds of speeches he talked about respect for the law as follows:

> The recent riots in Chicago, Cleveland, New York and Omaha have produced in the public dialogue too much heat and very little light. The extremists have held the floor for too long. One extreme sees a simple remedy for rioting in a ruthless application of the truncheon and an earlier call to the National Guard. The other extremists are more articulate, but their position is equally simplistic. To them, riots are to be excused upon the grounds that the participants have legitimate social grievances or seek justifiable social goals. I believe it would be a grave mistake to charge off the recent riots to unredressed Negro grievances alone. To do so is to ignore a prime reason and a major national problem: the deterioration of respect for the rule of law all across America. — *U.S. News & World Report*, August 15, 1966

"Law and order" was the central piece of Nixon's political being in the 1960s. Ambrose wrote:

> First, Nixon insisted, the black community had to reject lawlessness and the society as a whole had to re-establish law and order. His constituents, generally, were far more receptive to hearing him talk about law and order than listening to him discuss uplifting the ghetto, so it was law and order that he talked about the most.
>
> In so doing, he indulged his penchant for hyperbole. America had become, according to Nixon, "the most lawless and violent [nation] in the history of free peoples." And "far from being a great society, ours is becoming a lawless society." He denounced the "growing tolerance of lawlessness" among civil rights groups, and "the increasing public acceptance of civil disobedience." He got in a shot at the universities, which had helped blur the distinction between "where civil disobedience may begin and where it must end."

Ambrose concluded that "Nixon advocated bringing blacks into the body politic after they had learned how to behave."

The real Nixon need not say that he opposed the Voting Rights Act of 1965. He could simply signal whites that blacks were "not ready" for the ballot, or election to public office. He would consider black Americans "not ready" until he saw evidence that "they had learned how to behave."

This racial stereotyping by Nixon was lost on millions of Americans, except for the right-wing Caucasian soulless brothers who shared Nixon's fear of blacks voting freely.

Of course, Nixon was far more outspoken about race in private than in public. Pulitzer Prize–winning reporter Seymour Hersh, drawing from previously unreleased tapes, wrote in the *New Yorker* in 1992 that "Nixon made a 'stupendous' gaffe during a ceremonial photo session with senior officials of 'a major professional organization' when he asked them about scholarships for blacks. Told that such a program existed, Nixon remarked: 'Well, it's a good thing. They're just down out of the trees.'"

Hersh also asserted in that article that Nixon's private conversations were filled with racial slurs. In his biography of Henry Kissinger, titled *The Price of Power*, Hersh wrote of Nixon:

"'There seems to have been an unrelenting stream of antiblack remarks from the president during his first year in office. In his telephone conversations with Kissinger, he repeatedly referred to blacks as 'niggers,' 'jigs,' and 'jigaboos.' Some of the slurs were obviously results of Nixon drinking bouts, but [National Security Council] aides who monitored Kissinger-Nixon telephone calls came to believe that Richard Nixon, drunk or sober, was a racist."

Nixon survived the early 1960s by being a stealth bigot. He was simply smarter than George Wallace, who was crudely direct in imploring the nation to return to "states' rights," which meant long-embedded racism. Wallace was far from subtle in his efforts to demonize the federal government, which represented security for most Americans whatever their race. Wallace was too up-front as a demagogue, as an inspiration for church bombers and vicious cops, to win the presidency. Nixon knew this, but he also knew that he needed millions of the anti-black voters who would go to Wallace by default if he did not establish himself as the potential "President of the white man."

So Nixon chose Maryland governor Spiro Agnew as his running mate in 1968 with the cynical expectation that he and Agnew, who could do piano duets, would make ugly music together. Nixon would pretend to take the high road while Agnew would shamelessly do the dirty stuff.

On the issue of academic freedom, Nixon told a University of Rochester commencement audience on June 5, 1966:

> Academic freedom is no "academic question"; it is one of the most powerful forces in human history. Princes, presidents, even generals tremble in its presence. Academic freedom is a free society's greatest single advantage in its competition with totalitarian societies.

During the 1968 campaign he would send Agnew out to insult educators and assail college officials for opening their campuses to "the riff-raff" of America, meaning blacks, Hispanics, the groping poor.

A political revolution was in its infancy, and the drifting toward a race war had begun.

Nixon and Agnew employed "the southern strategy" as shamelessly as any nominees ever — more so than Wallace, who was clearly a racist, but who directed his populist appeal to voters in Maryland, Michigan, and other non-Dixie states.

The southern strategy was quite simply a brazen attempt to drive a wedge between the white people of the South and the Democratic party to which they had given their loyalty for generations. The strategy was to convince whites that the people who really controlled the Democratic party now supported blacks exclusively, having abandoned white people in the most unjust ways. Nixon, Agnew, and others made Hubert Humphrey a pariah in the South, repeating over and over their claims that at the 1948 Democratic National Convention Humphrey drove a stake in the hearts of white southern politicians. They talked about how, in the Congress, there was no greater enemy of the South than Teddy Kennedy. They talked about how John F. Kennedy and Lyndon Johnson had run

roughshod over white people in the South by forcing school desegregation down their throats in Little Rock public schools, at
the University of Mississippi, and elsewhere. Nixon, Agnew, and
others launched a massive campaign to lure Democratic defec-
tors into the Republican party, succeeding with longtime Democrats such as Strom Thurmond. The southern strategy was
designed to accomplish exactly what Lyndon Johnson had
warned me might occur to the national Democratic party.

Nixon was a superb strategist in his rhetoric about the South.
He expressed sympathy for the Americans he professed to see as
victims of bigoted Yankees like Humphrey. In May 1966 he told
the North American Newspaper Alliance that "the Democratic
Party in the South has ridden to power for a century on an annual tide of racial oratory. The Democratic Party is the party
which runs with the hounds in the North and the hares in the
South." He said, "The Democratic Party in the South is in grave
crisis — and the silence of Johnson and Humphrey and Bobby
Kennedy is deafening."

In 1968, political pundits credited Agnew with winning five
southern states for himself and Nixon. Nixon was grateful, and
in 1970 told his aide John Ehrlichman that he had great
sympathy for southerners. He said, "The people are going
through an agony down there and we shouldn't make it worse
for them."

It mattered little to Nixon that in May 1970, after six black
people had been shot dead at a civil rights rally in Augusta,
Georgia, and two black women were killed and twelve wounded
when Mississippi state police opened fire on a dormitory at Jackson State College, fifteen presidents of universities came to the
Oval Office to protest. Stephen Ambrose relates in *Nixon* what
happened:

> A spokesman read an opening statement to Nixon. It accused the
> President of adopting policies that had led to "anger, outrage
> and frustration" among blacks. The statement said specifically
> that "the 'Southern strategy' leads to the conclusion that blacks
> are dispensable." It went on to cite "the neglect of urban prob-
> lems; insufficient support of education; your nomination of jus-
> tices to the Supreme Court; your hesitancy to support strong

measures to assure the voting rights of black citizens; your failure to use your great moral influence to bring the people of this great nation together."

It was a damning and bitter indictment, and it hurt. Back in the fifties, Nixon had had a better record on civil rights than any other national politician; at that time he was the only one who would go into the south and tell southerners that segregation was morally wrong. In the sixties, he had been off the firing line, more or less a bystander during the so-called Second Reconstruction. Now, in 1970, he was the chief executive officer of the government, charged with the responsibility for implementing the laws and rulings laid down in the sixties.

It made him uncomfortable, philosophically as well as politically. He later described his position in a memo to Ehrlichman: "I am convinced that while legal segregation is totally wrong, forced integration of housing or education is just as wrong." In practical political terms, he saw himself as a loser whatever he did. He felt he would never get credit from blacks, no matter how vigorously he enforced the law (he told Ehrlichman, "The NAACP would say my rhetoric was poor even if I gave the Sermon on the Mount").

The Republican southern strategy worked in the 1968 election as never before, signaling an end to a "solid South" wed to the Democratic party. But even the most astute political pundits were slow to see that the Nixon-Agnew appeals to racism were in fact a "national strategy." The high levels of support for Wallace outside the South did not impress upon politicians and political scholars the reality that when Nixon railed against "forced busing to achieve racial balance," he was heard as loudly in Boston as in Birmingham; with as much passion in Detroit and Denver as in Dallas, or Danville, Virginia.

Nixon was in fact a segregationist, on both class and racial grounds. As President, he opposed vehemently government plans to put low- and middle-class housing in affluent neighborhoods. He was adamant in opposing government efforts to desegregate racial patterns in housing. Ironically, it was his desire to pacify blacks to the point that they would stay in ghettos that led Nixon to support tax breaks for companies that would invest in center-city "enterprise zones." He talked often about giving blacks "a piece of the action," "a piece of the pie," so they could be content in their own neighborhoods.

Like Minister Louis Farrakhan of the Nation of Islam, though for different reasons, Nixon came to support a version of black economic separatism.

In public, Nixon could sound statesmanlike in urging racial justice in economic matters, as when he said at the 1956 Alfred E. Smith Dinner:

> America cannot afford the moral, the economic and the international cost of prejudice and discrimination. We know the moral cost — the quiet suffering of millions of our fellow men whose only crime was that they were different in race or religion or color from others in their communities. We know the economic cost — the loss of thousands of skilled craftsmen, engineers, teachers, lawyers and doctors, whom we need if we are to develop our resources to the full, but who are not trained because they are denied the equality of opportunity for education which is their right. I can testify from experience as to the international cost. Every instance of prejudice in America is blown up a thousand fold by the enemies of freedom and does irreparable harm to our cause abroad. I have often expressed the idea that the world struggle today is a contest for men's minds. It is mainly in the realm of the spirit, and only secondarily in the military, diplomatic and economic fields.

In private, he argued that blacks pursuing "open housing" were seeking an unattainable goal. He justified a federal commitment to "enterprise zones" on grounds that "there is a lot of suffering" in the slums. To "keep the natives happy," Nixon proposed the "negative income tax," which we now know as the earned income tax credit, recently assailed by Republicans. He was strongly for setting aside a percentage of government contracts for minority firms, a concept that is now being attacked viciously by Republican governors who are leading efforts to wipe out "affirmative action" programs.

Millions of white men have concluded that the "piece of the action" that Nixon had allocated for blacks was coming from their pie. Nixon's cynical gesture of throwing crumbs to the ghettos has boomeranged, and now fuels the race war.

Nixon and Agnew succeeded in convincing a lot of voters in every region that Humphrey, his running mate, Ed Muskie, and all Democrats of their ilk, were hostile not only to the South, but to all white people — that most Democrats had become monsters who gave unfair advantages to blacks and other social misfits, were soft on crime, and were dangerous appeasers of America's enemies abroad.

Voters who knew that the "soft on crime" and "appeasers of communism" charges were hogwash were perfectly prepared to believe that those controlling the Democratic party were hostile to white people, despite the fact that Humphrey and Muskie were Caucasians.

Nixon and Agnew had played "the race card" as shrewdly and unconscionably as any politicians could, and they had won in the face of deep public doubts about Nixon's stance on the war in Southeast Asia, about both his and Agnew's personal integrity, and their devotion to "law and order."

Passions over the Vietnam War and suspicions as to who was "a crook" would vanish with time, but "the race card" would endure. There was hardly an issue in American politics that did not offer Republicans a chance to play the race card, undermining the Democratic party in the South and elsewhere, as Johnson had warned me might occur. In fact, beginning with Nixon and Agnew, appeals to racism became a staple of Republican politics — a controlling factor that seemed dominant even in the 1996 campaign.

During all the great social and political changes in America, no person has mattered more than the nation's Presidents, with the possible exception of Woodrow Wilson's wife, who almost single-handedly consolidated Jim Crow in the nation's capital. So it seems fitting at this point to discuss the Presidents since Nixon and assess their contributions to the race-war mood that permeates American life today.

Gerald Ford is almost a cipher in this passage of history. He was never much more than a bumbling caretaker who expended most of his brainpower defending his pardon of Richard Nixon. His boldest gambit in the House was to lead a pathetic campaign to impeach Supreme Court justice William Douglas.

As Ford presided over one of the nation's worst recessions, with black families suffering far more than whites, as is always the case, I went to the White House to ask President Ford if he had any special plans to give relief to blacks.

"No," he said, "just my overall efforts to revive the economy. Carl, all ships rise with the tide."

Ford's naïveté was such that he apparently never realized that in America, a lot of black ships still lie on the bottom, no matter how high the tide rises.

I recall leaving Kansas City and the Republican convention in 1976, telling myself that Ford's lifetime achievement had been his fighting off a powerful candidacy challenge by Ronald Reagan and winning the GOP nomination. Then the plodding Ford lost to Democrat Jimmy Carter, the "nice guy" Georgia governor whose impact on the nation's race relations was almost as weak.

Carter was not a bigot in the style of a century of Georgians who had ridden to Washington on the backs of blacks and low-caste white people of the South. He was in fact one of the most decent Presidents ever to move into the White House. But he came to Washington as an outsider and he left as an outsider, because he never really found the levers of power in the Congress.

Carter once told this story about himself: "I tried to treat Congress the way I treated the Georgia legislature. And Congress treated me like a governor of Georgia."

He loaded the Congress with proposed legislation that just went nowhere.

And none of that proposed legislation was a great civil rights initiative, primarily because Carter was not a forceful man given to nation-shaking social initiatives. Carter was too overwhelmed by what his opponents called "the misery index" — the combination of the unemployment and interest rates — plus a crisis of Americans being held hostage in Iran. When I asked the late Justice Thurgood Marshall to rank the Presidents, he put Truman at the top and Reagan at the bottom, and said of Carter: "Generally speaking, I think his heart was in the right place, but that's the best I can do with him."

But all this is misleading about Carter's overall impact. First of all, he made his cabinet look reasonably like America, naming Patricia Roberts Harris, a black woman, as secretary of Housing and Urban Development, and later as secretary of Health and Human Services. He also named the former black mayor of

Atlanta, Andrew Young, ambassador to the United Nations, but then lost all credit among blacks by firing Young after Jews protested that he had held meetings with Palestine Liberation Organization officials.

Carter's greatest contribution to racial sanity came in his appointment of judges. Nixon and Ford had not named a single black to any federal appeals court; Carter named eight blacks to serve with 123 white appellate judges, and also named thirty black persons to serve as federal district judges — jurists who now struggle ideologically in a federal system where 55 percent of the judges were named either by Reagan or by Bush.

But the economic situation was so bad during the presidential campaign of 1980 that these appointments, the Camp David Accords, the treaties returning the Panama Canal to Panama, won few votes for Carter. He could not combat Reagan's clever debate line that if all the jobless people stood in line, it would stretch from New York to California.

Carter's inner goodness was no match for the inner and outer meannesses of the Republicans who regarded his election as a fluke, and who ended his power tenure as quickly as they could.

So, in 1981 this country got the President who is more responsible than any for the fact that white racism is both tolerated and even fashionable again in America.

No President in my lifetime ever played the race card to such political benefit as Reagan did. His fulminations about welfare, his loud support of states' rights, his publicity stunts — including opening a reelection campaign in Philadelphia, Mississippi, where three civil rights workers (two Jewish, one black) had been murdered — helped to rip most of the South away from Democratic control. His words also carried great force in the North. He could even say in Illinois that no more racism existed in the United States, and the media would simply charge his words to senility. Few people dared accuse Reagan of being a racist. But in his "lovable" way, he was.

I saw before that 1980 campaign that Reagan was a precursor of Pat Buchanan, throwing out glib phrases that hit the racist nerves of white voters. In 1966 Reagan said on his radio show: "Every day the jungle draws a little closer. . . . Our city streets are jungle paths after dark, with more crimes of violence."

Listen to the echoes as New York talk-show host Bob Grant

rails against "black savages," and Pat Buchanan tells a London audience, "Look what they've done to my city [Washington, D.C.]! They're playing bongo drums on street corners."

I knew that black and poor families would suffer dearly if Reagan won when I heard him explain his economic plan: he claimed that he could pump trillions more dollars into the military, cut taxes, and still balance the budget. On October 28, 1980, in a televised debate with Jimmy Carter, he said:

> I believe that there is enough extravagance and fat in government. As a matter of fact, one of the secretaries of HEW under Mr. Carter testified that he thought there was $7 billion worth of fraud and waste in welfare, and in the medical programs associated with it. We've had the General Accounting Office estimate that there are probably tens of billions of dollars lost in fraud alone.

Reagan never found those "tens of billions," so he ran up rivers of red ink with what his running mate George Bush had called "voodoo economics." Reagan's humongous deficits still burden the nation and are at the heart of the current stupid war in Congress.

Yet, Reagan never stopped throwing out his stories, mostly false, which poisoned race relations. One of his most shameful was of a "hardworking taxpayer" at a supermarket checkout wondering how to pay for "a few pounds of hamburger" when up walks a "strapping young buck" (all "strapping young bucks" are black, of course) with a pile of T-bone steaks, which he pays for with food stamps.

House Speaker Thomas P. "Tip" O'Neill denounced Reagan as "cruel," and "mean" to poor people, but Reagan dismissed him and other critics as "sob sisters."

What I will never forget or forgive is that Reagan had no minorities of consequence inside his campaign team. His cabinet had only one black man in it, and he was embarrassing. And worst of all, Reagan went eight years refusing to talk to any civil rights leaders. When I asked him why, in 1988, he invited me to lunch, where he said, "They criticized me upon my election, so I just said, 'To hell with 'em.'"

That reaction alone caused a deterioration in race relations that fair-minded Americans have not been able to reverse till this day, because presidential hostility weakened the NAACP, the Urban League, and every facet of the civil rights movement.

The added tragedy is that most white Americans now want to remember only the handsome, impish, grandfatherly Reagan — especially now that he is afflicted with Alzheimer's disease — but I cannot forget how he wiped out the flowering goodwill of the 1960s and 1970s and set in motion the corrosive hatreds that seem to be everywhere today.

The 1980 Reagan campaign produced the ultimate lurch toward making U.S. presidential elections a referendum on the level of racism in America. In September the newspaper of the Invisible Empire, Knights of the Ku Klux Klan, declared Reagan its favorite candidate, asserting that "the Republican platform reads as if it were written by a Klansman."

Reagan ran proudly on that platform and, once in office, began executive branch sabotage of all the programs enacted by Congress at the behest of Kennedy and Johnson. The Klansmen and other haters quickly got the message, and began to crawl from under rocks from Mississippi to Montana.

Every white supremacist figured that his time in America had come again, and the bigots had a field day that lasted all of Reagan's eight years.

George Bush will be remembered forever as the candidate who showed that he could go Reagan one better in playing the race card. He rode into the Oval Office in 1988 on demagoguery about Willie Horton, a fearsome-looking black man who had been convicted of rape and murder while on furlough — this supposedly being proof that Democrats were "soft on crime."

Even after his election, Bush continued to play the race card — shrewdly, it seemed for a long time. As the election year of 1992 approached, his popularity rating was higher than the best of Eisenhower and Reagan. It turned out, however, that this was because of his vilifications of Iraq's Saddam Hussein and the quick American victory in the Persian Gulf War.

But Bush was creating such an economic mess that even neutral commentators were referring to him as "the second Herbert Hoover." The number of Americans living in poverty had risen from 29.3 million in 1980 to 33.6 million in 1990. Bush tried to blame this on "welfare recipients," which in the minds of his Republican constituents meant blacks and Hispanics. In May 1992, I wrote of this Bush gambit:

"Bush knows enough not to return to the scene of a [Willie Horton] crime. So this time around he has chosen to run against the unfortunate women and the sick and hungry children who live on welfare. . . .

"Welfare goes to people who live in poverty. . . . Surely Mr. Bush knows why the cost is high when he helped to put another 4.3 million people into poverty."

In his efforts to fan the flames of the nation's "hate the poor" syndrome, Bush also gave new leadership to the nation-searing tirade against affirmative action.

The race card turned out not to be trumps on election day. Blacks gave 82 percent of their votes to Clinton, 7 percent to Ross Perot, and just 11 percent to Bush. Hispanics gave 62 percent of their votes to Clinton, 14 percent to Perot, and 24 percent to Bush. Clinton defeated Bush by just over five million votes, with Perot winning nineteen million ballots.

Bush left Washington a broken man, often expressing fury at the very voters he had slandered and ridiculed.

The tragedy is that, with Colin Powell refusing to run on what polls say would be a winning ticket, Bob Dole seems to think he has no way of winning except to play the same race cards that worked so well for twelve years but failed Bush in 1992.

It is now very clear that no Democrat can win the South with such a margin that he need only break even in the big urban centers of the North and West to win the presidency.

It is noteworthy that only one other southerner, Bill Clinton of Arkansas, could match Carter's feat of winning enough southern states to have a fair shot in the North and West and win the presidency.

In 1996, we were immersed in a presidential campaign in which passions over race were at the forefront — and in unique and curious ways.

Early in the campaign we saw the worst of America. At the winter 1993 meeting of the Republican National Committee, Gingrich, then the House minority whip, offered a drastic program for combating crime. He said the country should go on a "wartime footing" and build "stockades . . . without television or air conditioning" in which to lock up criminals.

Gingrich wasn't running for President. His negatives in the polls were higher than a polecat's stench at a garden party. But the leading GOP candidates all had similar "solutions" to America's problems. Pat Buchanan proposed saying, "No way, Jose," and building a wall to keep Mexicans out. He became so offensive he was frightening, and made Dole look acceptable.

All the candidates railed against "reverse discrimination," and some offered "un-American" solutions to the crime problem.

Every Republican idea seemed to carry a subtle or brazen appeal to racism or ethnic bigotry.

Incredibly, Republican voters and leaders looked at their candidates and said, "None of the above." They cried so loudly for retired general Colin Powell to run that Powellmania swept the nation. I looked with a jaundiced eye at the cries for the immensely popular black general to run. I was certain that the other candidates would never step aside and let Powell be drafted. And I had my doubts about how many of the whites clamoring for him would actually vote for him in the secrecy of the voting booth. But I shall deal with the Powell phenomenon later in this book — especially the obvious question whether Powellmania indicated the racial enlightenment of enough white Americans to forestall any drift into a race war.

# Chapter 3

# The Hatemongers

Human history is scarred by the power-grabbing rhetoric of demagogues who talked their way into great power and then committed horrendous acts. The first name to pop into most minds is that of Hitler, followed perhaps by that of Joseph Stalin. But in modern times we have seen the sweeping power and ruthlessness of Iran's Ayatollah Khomeini, Nigeria's Sani Abacha, Cambodia's Pol Pot, Iraq's Saddam Hussein, and assorted "lesser" dictators in Africa, Asia, and the former satellite regimes of the former Soviet Union.

In the United States, men longing for dictatorial power have burst upon the political scene often, but our long history of democracy combined with widespread education has always thwarted them. Impassioned rhetoric over slavery, and righteousness over economic injustices, or man's inhumanity to man, did drive the people of this land into a gruesome Civil War. But since then we have heard the rabble-rousing of Ku Klux Klansmen and, as a nation, rejected them. We have heard the fear-inspiring talk of Senator Joseph McCarthy and delivered him to shame. We have seen the House and the Senate, and the statehouses of America befouled by the rhetoric of racists, anti-Semites, Catholic-baiters, haters of foreigners, and assorted other bigots, and over their protestations we have for the most part enacted sane laws.

But now we see and hear in America perhaps the widest array of polarizers and hatemongers that this country ever has known. We have people, groups, militias, that hate each other and almost everyone else, including their government and all that they can label "part of the establishment." These are the people and groups that are fueling the drift toward a race war. Our only protection against their destructive influence is to ensure that most Americans know who the hatemongers are, what motivates them, and what they seek to achieve.

In 1996, the two most publicized and most dangerous of a small army of American hatemongers were Minister Louis Farrakhan, leader of the Nation of Islam, and Patrick J. Buchanan, candidate for the Republican nomination for the presidency of the United States.

Farrakhan is an African American who embraces, in his way, the Koran and the Islamic faith, whereas Buchanan is a Caucasian and a devout Catholic. But in many respects there is an eerie sameness about them. Both are great entertainers with that certain demagogic magnetism that draws large crowds. Buchanan consistently outdrew Senator Bob Dole and the other candidates throughout the primary contests, even though many in his audiences eventually voted for someone else. Farrakhan once outdrew a World Series game in Atlanta when he spoke not far from the baseball stadium. He surprised the world by attracting an immense throng of black males to the Million Man March of October 1995.

Both men are notorious for saying outrageous things. They thrive on insulting what they call "the establishment." They play upon the grievances, the sense of being cheated, of their followers, constantly promising to deliver justice to "the little guy" (Buchanan) or the racially oppressed (Farrakhan). Both have gotten rich, Farrakhan more than Buchanan, by peddling bigotry at great profit.

Farrakhan is far blunter than Buchanan in stating his hatreds. He is clearly anti-Semitic and anti-Caucasian. Buchanan is transparently anti-black and anti-Jew, although he works to be clever when expressing his prejudices publicly.

These two men are the spear carriers in America's rush toward violent racial conflict, so it is wise for us to examine what drives them to such evil zealotry.


## Louis Farrakhan

Louis Haleem Abdul Farrakhan has lived a life that would give nightmares to any psychiatrist trying to identify the forces that shaped him. He was born in 1934 in the Bronx to Mae Clark, a West Indian woman who he says tried futilely to abort him on three occasions.

He was christened Louis Eugene Walcott, the name he went by during the Great Depression years when his mother, alone, raised him and his brother in Boston. So as a young man, Louis knew all the forces of urban poverty that shape the lives of millions of young black males in America. He went to church at his mother's insistence, like most young African Americans of that era, and fell under the influence of Nathan Wright, the priest at St. Cyprian Episcopal Church, a man variously described as "militant," "fiery," "angry to the core." Wright was no more or less a firebrand than any of at least a million black men of that time, but he had influence.

After two years at a small college in North Carolina, Louis dropped out and married his high school sweetheart, Khadija, who immediately began to bear his string of nine children. Louis, who had become a fine violinist and calypso singer, earned a modest living as a night club performer known as "The Charmer." He often performed before whites whom he despised — for example, on the rich, white North Side of Chicago, where no one would provide him a place to live.

Louis Walcott learned early and often the pervasiveness of racism in the United States, and he admitted early that it had created "hate in me."

A great change occurred in Louis's life in 1955 when he met a rising young star in the Nation of Islam, Malcolm X. At that time I was a reporter for the *Minneapolis Tribune,* and I remember that the American media were just becoming fascinated with the Nation of Islam and its paramount leader, Elijah Muhammad. This small sect got lots of publicity because Elijah was quoted and quoted and quoted as making statements that white people were "blue-eyed devils," and worse. The "Black Muslims" quickly became, for white journalists, the new fearsome force.

Malcolm X talked Louis Walcott into joining the Nation, changing his name to Louis X, and installing him as minister of a new mosque in Boston. Some five years later Louis X changed his name to Louis Farrakhan.

Malcolm brought Farrakhan into some of the most tempestuous years known in this small Muslim slice of black America. Malcolm presided over the largest mosque in Harlem, often assailing whites and traditional black leaders in terms that got him plenty of publicity and a national following. It also got him the attention, and enmity, of FBI director J. Edgar Hoover, who used wiretaps, bugs, and every means available to try to stay abreast of developments, especially personal enmities, within the Nation of Islam. Hoover knew before most Muslims did that Elijah Muhammad was outraged when Malcolm X violated his order not to comment publicly on the assassination of President Kennedy. *Washington Post* reporter Karl Evanzz has secured FBI documents showing that on December 2, 1963, Elijah suspended Malcolm for saying that the assassination was "God's punishment" of Kennedy for allowing the CIA to assassinate Third World leaders.

Evanzz has written that on March 19, 1964, the FBI recorded a telephone call from Elijah to "Minister Louis X of Boston" in which Muhammad said that Malcolm was spreading stories that Muhammad had impregnated many teenage secretaries, and that Malcolm had to be silenced before he revealed other scandalous secrets.

Documents show Farrakhan used the fake byline "Minister Lewis" over a December 4, 1964, article in *Muhammad Speaks* to say that "if any Muslim backed a fool like Malcolm in building a mosque, he would be a fool himself. Only those who wish to be led to hell, or to their doom, will follow Malcolm. The die is set, and Malcolm shall not escape. . . . Such a man as Malcolm is worthy of death."

Just over two months later, on February 21, 1965, Malcolm X was shot to death in the Audubon Ballroom on 125th Street in Harlem.

Other members of the Nation of Islam were convicted of this crime, but suspicions persisted that Farrakhan was also involved. Farrakhan has made statements suggesting that he may have been. For example, in a 1993 sermon in Chicago, he said, "I loved Elijah Muhammad enough so I would kill you . . . yesterday, today, and tomorrow. . . . We don't give a damn about no white man's laws when you attack what we love." Farrakhan was cleverly murky in meaning. He deflects scrutiny of his role in the death of Malcolm X by asserting that it was a plot of the U.S. government.

In this respect, Farrakhan shows that he learned the art of getting the national limelight well from Malcolm X and Elijah Muhammad. Attack the most powerful people and forces around and you get the most headlines and the most devoted following. The more Farrakhan insults and defies whites, the more ordinary angry blacks, who only wish they could get in the faces of "Whitey" the way Farrakhan does, like him. Black college students find him witty, brilliant, and extremely entertaining, even though many say quickly that they do not endorse Farrakhan's views.

It is mostly students, however, who have given Farrakhan and his aides the platforms for the speeches that have created monumental controversies and caused great grief to other black Americans. The most sensational of Farrakhan's speeches was the one in which he said Judaism is "a gutter religion," Israel is "an outlaw state," and Hitler was "a great man" — a term he later revised to "wickedly great." Farrakhan's handpicked "spokesman," Khalid Abdul Muhammad, regularly insults almost everyone, including non-Muslim black leaders.

When Muhammad spoke at Kean College in Union, New Jersey, on November 29, 1993, he referred repeatedly to "Columbia Jew-niversity" and "Jew York City." He said that Jews were "the bloodsuckers of the black nation." He said, "Everybody always talks about Hitler eliminating six million Jews. But don't nobody ever ask, 'What did they do to Hitler?' . . . In Germany, they usurped, the way they do everywhere they go. . . . My leader [Farrakhan] tried to reason with you [Jews]. But you disrespected him. And then you lied on him. And so now you have to face us, and we will eat your behind alive."

Muhammad cited a man named Steve Cokely, who charged that Jewish doctors inject the AIDS virus into black babies, as "one hundred percent right."

After ridiculing black leaders such as the Reverend Jesse Jackson as "Uncle Toms," and assailing gays and lesbians and women who don't stay home and raise children, Muhammad blasted Catholics. He referred to "the old no-good pope — you know that cracker. . . . Somebody need to raise that dress up and see what's really under there."

This "minister and representative of the Nation of Islam" then urged black South Africans to kill all whites in that country. "We kill the women," he shouted. "We kill the babies. We kill the blind. We kill the cripples. We kill them all. We kill the faggot. We kill the lesbian. We kill them all. . . . When we get through killing them all, we go to the fucking graveyard and dig up the grave and kill them a-fucking-gain because they didn't die hard enough."

Muhammad's performance was part minstrel show and part pure bigotry — an act of utterly shameful hatred and stupidity. But blacks on the Kean faculty either dismissed it as vaudeville or accepted it as an accurate portrayal of what was going on in America and the world. Not one adult black at Kean condemned Khalid publicly.

In fact, everyone at Kean danced around that speech as though it were radioactive poison. It became a national issue only weeks later when the Anti-Defamation League (ADL) learned of it and printed excerpts from it in newspaper ads. A nationwise storm erupted.

Jesse Jackson told the *New York Times* that Muhammad's speech was "racist, anti-Semitic, divisive, untrue and chilling." Roger Wilkins, a professor of history at George Mason University, wrote that "in avoiding swift and forceful condemnation of Mr. Muhammad's bilious diatribe, the black faculty members failed their students, failed their obligations as members of a civilized community and failed to uphold the best traditions of the black struggle." Then-representative Kweisi Mfume, chairman of the Congressional Black Caucus (now president of the NAACP), called the speech "vicious" and demanded that Farrakhan clarify Muhammad's remarks.

The black members of Congress held three secret meetings

with Farrakhan before concluding that they could never work with him. Representative Major R. Owens, a Brooklyn Democrat, stated publicly on February 4, 1994, that the Nation of Islam was "a hate-mongering fringe group" that was spreading "dangerous poison" and had to be repudiated.

Just a day earlier, Farrakhan had told a packed news conference in Washington that he found Muhammad's Kean College speech "vile in manner, repugnant, malicious, meanspirited, and spoken in mockery of individuals and people" and he was dismissing Muhammad as an aide and a spokesman for the Nation of Islam. However, Farrakhan said, he stood by "the truths" that Muhammad had spoken. Then Farrakhan launched into a tirade against the ADL, declaring that the Jewish group and the federal government were in a conspiracy to divide black people and to destroy the Nation of Islam.

As fate would have it, three weeks later Khalid Muhammad was to speak in the nation's capital — at historically black Howard University, at an event arranged by a Howard law student, Malik Zulu Shabazz.

Muhammad was, considering the fact that he was a ranting ignoramus and unconscionable demagogue, on relatively good behavior when he spoke to more than one thousand people (only about half were students or faculty) at Howard. Shabazz provided the fireworks in a pre-Khalid speech:

"Who caught and killed Nat Turner?" he shouted to the crowd.

"Jews," most of the audience shouted back.

"Who controls the Federal Reserve?"

"Jews."

"You're not afraid to say it, are you?"

"Jews, Jews."

"Who controls the media and Hollywood?"

"Jews."

"Who has our entertainers, our athletes, in a vise grip?"

"Jews."

"Am I lying?"

"No," the crowd yelled.

Enter now one of the worst of the sophisticated polarizers, Richard Cohen of the *Washington Post*, the self-designated protector of Jews from black people. On the basis of secondhand notes, Cohen wrote that "Washington had a little Nuremberg rally last week." After quoting Shabazz, he wrote:

> Howard University, federally funded and sometimes called the Harvard of the traditionally black colleges, clearly has itself a problem. The *Post* estimated that two-thirds of the audience that night was composed of students. Howard's dean for student life, Raymond Archer, says fewer than half. I say, who cares? The fact remains that several hundred students acted like extras in a Leni Reifenstahl movie. Moreover, the student government association that night donated $500 to Khalid — which is to say the Nation of Islam, a white-hating, Jew-hating, gay-hating, Catholic-hating group. It's sort of the United Way of bigotry.
>
> The acceptance or toleration of anti-semitism by a new, college-educated generation of black leaders is not, as some would have it, "interesting." It is downright chilling. Farrakhan represents a variant of American fascism. His organization is authoritarian, his message dead-end demagoguery and his dope the bracing narcotic of hate. That Howard University audience, brimming with ignorance and led by Pied Pipers of racism, is going down the sucker's road to nowhere. They are not the leaders of tomorrow, they are the chumps of yesteryear.

Despite the many prominent blacks who had denounced and renounced Muhammad — and Farrakhan — Cohen wanted more. Virtually the entire Howard University community was outraged by the arrogant, condescending tone of Cohen's column. Faculty, students, and administrators were infuriated by Cohen's not so subtle notation that Howard was federally funded and could lose money. Here was a case of a Jewish polarizer making a bad situation much worse.

Shortly after that Cohen column was printed, I appeared on a panel at the Freedom Forum to discuss "the crisis" at Howard — especially noises from Congress about cutting the university's federal appropriation as punishment for allowing Khalid to speak there. I confronted Cohen with a list of all the universities where Khalid had spoken. They were with rare exceptions overwhelmingly white institutions. The room, and Cohen, became quite tense when I asked why he had never tried to punish one of these white colleges for giving Muhammad a platform and even paying him as much as $20,000.

After seething for days, Cohen wrote another column on July 19, 1994, saying Howard had "been slow to understand the implications of both racism and anti-semitism" — things, of course, that only a superior intellect like Cohen could fully comprehend. He went on to say:

> Howard feels so beseiged that some on campus fear that Congress will punish the university by cutting the $193 million in federal funds it's supposed to get next year.
>
> If I had my way, Congress would withhold a symbolic $1 — not a dime more — as an expression of disgust.

By this time General Colin Powell had given the commencement speech at Howard, saying, "African-Americans have come too far, and have too far yet to go to take a detour into the swamp of hatred. . . . We as a people who have suffered so much from the hatred of others must not now show tolerance for any movement or any philosophy that has as its core the hatred of Jews or hatred of any other group. . . . There is evil, there is danger in the message of hatred, of condoning violence, however cleverly the message is packaged or entertainingly it is presented."

It seemed that no number of blacks of any status could satisfy Cohen to the point that he would stop his self-defeating efforts to portray blacks as "the chumps of yesteryear."

By the summer of 1994 it was clear to almost all blacks that Farrakhan and his followers were anti-Jew, anti-white, and anti-integration, and were deliberately driving Americans into separate warring camps. Those who doubted saw abundant enlightenment in the *Time* magazine issue of February 28, 1994. Under the placid circumstances of an interview with a black journalist whom he had known for years — Sylvester Monroe — Farrakhan revealed a lot about his personal attitudes toward Jews and his personal relationships with other black American leaders.

Farrakhan set himself up with his own questions: "Am I really anti-Semitic? Do I really want extermination of Jewish people? Of course, the answer is no."

Then he proceeded to describe Jews in ways that would lead all but his most craven followers to conclude that he is pathologically anti-Semitic. He said:

> Now I'm going to come to something that may get me in a lot of trouble. But I've got to speak the truth. What is a bloodsucker? When they land on your skin, they suck the life from you to sustain their life.
>
> In the '20s and '30s and '40s, up into the '50s, the Jews were the primary merchants in the black community. Wherever we were, they were. What was their role? We bought food from them; we bought clothing from them; we bought furniture from them; we rented from them. So if they made profit from us, then from our life they drew life and came to strength. They turned it over to the Arabs, the Koreans and others, who are there now doing what? Sucking the lifeblood of our own community.
>
> Every black artist, or most of them who came to prominence, who are their managers, who are their agents? Does the agent have the talent or the artist? But who reaps the benefits? Come on. We die penniless and broke, but somebody else is sucking from us. Who surrounds Michael Jackson? Is it us?
>
> See, Brother, we've got to look at what truth is. You throw it out there as if to say this is some of the same old garbage that was said in Europe. I don't know about no garbage said in Europe.
>
> But I know what I'm seeing in America. And because I see that black people, Sylvester, in the intellectual fields and professional fields are not going to be free until there is a new relationship with the Jewish community, then I feel that what I'm saying has to ultimately break that relationship.
>
> Just like they felt it necessary to break my relationship with the Black Caucus, I feel it absolutely necessary to break the old relationship of the black intellectual and professional with the Jewish community and restructure it along lines of reciprocity, along lines of fairness and equity.
>
> TIME: How much does this black/Jewish controversy actually wind up hurting black people?

FARRAKHAN: I did not recognize the degree to which Jews held control over black professionals, black intellectuals, black enter- tainers, black sports figures; Khalid did not lie when he said that.

My ultimate aim is the liberation of our people. So if we are to be liberated, it's good to see the hands that are holding us. And we need to sever those hands from holding us that we may be a free people, that we may enter into a better relationship with them than we presently have.

So yes, in one sense it's a loss, but in the ultimate sense it's a gain. Because when I saw that, I recognized that the black man will never be free until we address the problem of the relation- ship between blacks and Jews.

This is vintage Farrakhan. He states what is visibly true: many, even most, high-profile black entertainers and athletes have Jewish managers, or agents, or directors, or writers. Then he leaps to what is not true: an assertion that the Jewish man- agers "suck the life" out of the black artists "to sustain their life." Farrakhan does not tell gullible blacks what the Jewish agent does for the black person, who often cannot get a foot in- side the entertainment world, or cannot protect himself in an era of colossal football, baseball, and basketball contracts by himself. Farrakhan cons blacks into believing that the Jewish agent "reaps the benefits" while "we [blacks] die penniless and broke."

When are Bill Cosby, Oprah Winfrey, Michael Jackson, Michael Jordan, Denzel Washington, Whoopi Goldberg, Bryant Gumbel, or any other of a thousand top black professionals and intellectuals going to "die penniless and broke" because of ex- ploitation by some Jewish agent?

Farrakhan establishes a tiny, harmless truth and glues a big, destructive lie to it. And thus he fuels a great racial–class divide that imperils this nation.

Farrakhan vacillates between the unconscionable sociopath and the seeker of mass recognition, if not approval, as a "great black leader." That *Time* interview revealed what gnaws at the edges of his brain when he told Monroe:

"I don't have a personal relationship with any black civil rights leader. Rev. Jackson is the only person I have socialized with, been in his home, sat at his table. Every other civil rights leader I have had occasion to meet, I have an acquaintance with. I don't pick up the phone and call any one of them."

Farrakhan finally found a so-called black leader who would cozy up to him in the Reverend Benjamin Chavis. Chavis had been fired as executive director of the NAACP, in part for pledging $334,000 in NAACP funds as "hush money" for a female employee, Mary Stansel, at the end of what she called their "adulterous relationship."

Chavis was also using the NAACP's meager funds for lavish and unofficial outings, and to purchase personal clothing, toys for his children, and more. He was barely ousted before his mentor, William Gibson, was ousted as chairman of the board of the near-bankrupt NAACP for misuse of NAACP funds. The organization's flirtation with Farrakhan was a major reason why moneyed people and groups, Jewish and non-Jewish, had ceased giving to the nation's oldest civil rights group.

Black America was shocked when it was announced that Farrakhan had tapped Chavis to be his lieutenant in an ambitious undertaking called the Million Man March on Washington. Many speculated about which man had lost his mind, Farrakhan or Chavis. I figured early that neither had gone nuts — that they would make a perfect team, with Chavis getting his hands on some money and Farrakhan possibly getting some respect in mainstream black America.

Those of us who were involved in the civil rights movement of the 1960s, and who knew the impact of the 1963 March on Washington, where Dr. Martin Luther King, Jr., made his historic "I Have a Dream" speech, felt certain that Farrakhan and Chavis could never match the drama or move the nation in the same way.

There was just no way that Farrakhan and Chavis and their followers could provoke the Congress to pass any laws remotely comparable to the Public Accommodations Act of 1964, or the Voting Rights Act of 1965, or the Federal Aid to Higher Education Act of 1965. Organizers of the Million Man March wisely emphasized the best things about the Nation of Islam — its emphasis on the family, the need for men to respect their wives and support their children, and its counsel against premarital sex and the use of illicit drugs. When the organizers talked of the need for jobs, and law and order, within black America, I knew

that few black men would disagree. It didn't matter that Farrakhan was preaching a destructive brand of black separatism
in which black men and families supposedly would find prosperity and salvation in a separate black nation within the United
States.

I noticed that neither Farrakhan nor Chavis said much about
the money-raising aspects of this march. Insiders called me to
say that the leaders had set up an incredible marketing scheme
in which march participants were asked to pay $11 to register,
and the great masses were expected to buy T-shirts, books, and
a wide array of other products.

What strange irony that the biggest moneymakers were supposed to be caps and T-shirts extolling Malcolm X, Farrakhan's
old enemy and alleged victim!

I wrote a column before the march that made these three
points:

1. I could never, in good conscience, walk behind a man who
spread racial hatred, anti-Semitism, anti-Catholic bigotry as
venomously as Farrakhan did.

2. I felt certain that only Farrakhan and Chavis would benefit
materially from the many millions of dollars that people would
pour into the march.

3. Even if Farrakhan did not use the occasion to deliver a
wicked harangue against "Jewish bloodsuckers" and "white
devils," he would use the occasion to posture as the great black
leader who truly represented the mass of African Americans.

I was not alone in expressing reluctance to follow Farrakhan
anywhere, or in my concerns about the ultimate result of this
great demonstration. Colbert I. King, a discerning black columnist for the *Washington Post,* noted that at the Congressional
Black Caucus banquet on September 23 the crème de la crème of
black luminaries engaged in an orgy of glitz and sequins, back-
slapping and schmoozing, that suggested "black folks don't have
a care in the world. . . . But for black women and kids on welfare, times could not be worse." King was provoked to ask:

Does the march make sense beyond the symbolism of unity?
Time, not turnout, will be the ultimate test of that. If, say, a year
from now, reconciliations and marriages — yes, marriages — are
up, crime and incarcerations are down, there are fewer kids in

foster care and moms on welfare, more fathers are at home helping to raise their children, there is mutual respect among African
Americans across income and class lines, and we are putting
more money into good causes and less on our backs, then Oct. 16
will have been the transforming phenomenon the sponsors hope
it will be. If, however, things remain pretty much as they are, the
march, as with last weekend's soiree, will be just one more of
those high-octane, emotionally gratifying, political, social and
culturally must-do and be-seen-at events that black folks — despite it all — manage to pull off so well.

In many ways, the march did matter beyond the symbolism
of black unity. It showed me that Farrakhan has great
charisma, raw drawing power for black laborers and intellectuals
who feel alienated from an America essentially as racist as the
worst of Farrakhan's diatribes. They still argue in Washington
about whether four hundred thousand or a million black men
gathered on the Mall that bright October day, but there should
be no doubt anywhere that they shared a sense of desperation
that will make them angry and willing soldiers in any race war
to come.

Many of these black men, groping to find an honorable place
in the land of their birth, saw the searing meaning of thousands
of white men and women staying away from their jobs so as not
to get too close to the Mall that day. Assemble a million black
men and you supposedly invite a million muggings or rapes.

The only thing criminal on that Mall was the length of the
speeches by Farrakhan and a few others.

Yet, as I wrote in a column soon afterward, there was an importance in Minister Farrakhan's remarks that transcended
everything else:

"God brought the idea through me . . . my people have validated
me today!"

Those words by Farrakhan did not surprise anyone who saw
the hundreds of thousands of African-American men who showed
up for the Million Man March.

In those historic moments, with the world watching and listening, it surely was intoxicating to Farrakhan.

Clearly, he believed that all those black people had come,

many with their sons, to declare him the paramount black leader, the man to whom they can forever look for political, economic and spiritual guidance.

But everything that I saw told me that the black throng gathered not for the coronation of Farrakhan, but in a desperate search for hope and for economic, political and social justice in a society that is mired in meanness born of deepening racism.

The blacks in that solemn gathering were not "validating" Farrakhan as the leader with the workable solutions for the woes of black America. No! Thousands of those men will not be back in their hometowns before they realize that Farrakhan gave them some advice that is unassailable as well as a lot of advice that, followed literally, would doom them and their children to deeper failures and sorrows.

Get 8 million unregistered black people eligible to vote in 1996! Black men, stop killing each other! Black men, go home and make your communities prosperous and peaceful places! Black men, confess, feel contrition and stop being a slave to drugs and whiskey! Who is going to argue with that part of Minister Farrakhan's formula, even if implementing any part of it is a million times harder than his saying it?

"Freedom can't come from white folks or this great government. Freedom can come only from God." Those desperate men who were on the Mall knew that their pipeline to God wasn't as direct as Farrakhan claimed his is. They cannot and should not forget that "this great government" sustains a decent life, and even sponsors wealth, for most groups in this country, so it would be folly for blacks not to demand some of the jobs, scholarships, crop supports and corporate welfare that benefit all other citizens.

He threw out the truth that millions of white Americans are crazed with notions of white supremacy — this to justify his assertion that "there is no way we can integrate into white supremacy and hold our dignity as human beings."

Blacks who embrace Farrakhan's separatism, his glib rejection of all hope of an integrated society, would be left with the snare and delusion he offers of poor blacks becoming wealthy just by trading with other poor blacks.

As the new year rolled around, more and more blacks were seeing that I was correct in predicting that only Farrakhan and

Chavis would benefit financially from the march. When asked by marchers or newsmen what happened to the millions of dollars raised through registration fees, Chavis said simply: "That's none of your business." Later Chavis and Farrakhan reported that the event had lost money.

It seemed at the end of 1995 that Farrakhan had made fools of almost all his critics and proved himself to be a reasonable man, a true leader — the only American, in fact, who could have drawn a million black men to Washington, D.C., or any other place. There weren't even a million black men across America who could name the leaders of three of the major civil rights organizations. No one at the NAACP, the Urban League, or at any other organization in black America came close to equaling Farrakhan's crowd appeal, even though it was something else to compare ideological acceptance, or the ability to get blacks to accept an agenda for the future. Afraid of losing what public support they had, most of the leaders of civil rights groups were loath to criticize Farrakhan personally and publicly. Even the brave black preachers and others who had done so got lockjaw after the Million Man March.

Then, early in February 1996, Farrakhan went on a twenty-seven-nation tour of Africa and the Middle East in which he reverted to his indefensible form, squandering whatever respect and goodwill he had gained through the Million Man March. From Libya came word that he had been offered a billion dollars by dictator Muammar Qadhafi to support the Nation of Islam, the implications being that Farrakhan would use the money to influence the U.S. elections of 1996, thus increasing dramatically the political power of black citizens of the United States.

Then, in dizzying bomb bursts, news of Farrakhan's antics reached American ears. Randall Robinson and other members of the highly respected lobbying group Trans-Africa nearly had strokes when they learned that Farrakhan was giving aid and comfort to the brutal Nigerian regime of General Sani Abacha in Nigeria. For Robinson and most other black Americans, it was more than unconscionable that Farrakhan would become an apologist for a regime that had destroyed all current hope for democracy by locking up or murdering any Nigerians who spoke for liberty, or who dared to ask about the brazen theft and corruption that had denied to the people the blessings of Nigeria's oil wealth.

Farrakhan went on to Iraq to cozy up to Saddam Hussein, whose forces had invaded Kuwait, and against whom Colin Powell and other Americans had fought a war.

Then, in Iran, homeland of the ayatollahs who thought their words were Allah's laws, and who had fomented the great Islamic revolution, Farrakhan delivered his harshest assaults on the United States. Americans who remembered that Iran had held Americans hostage for 444 days were furious. Some became livid when Iranian news agencies quoted Farrakhan as saying that God would give Muslims the honor of destroying the United States.

That created a firestorm of criticism of Farrakhan within the U.S. Congress and the media, which again raised questions about the U.S. Muslim leader's sanity.

But Farrakhan mixed that message with a dose of megalomania in which he repeated his occasional charges that the U.S. government was out to assassinate him. He said the success of the Million Man March had left him "a marked man."

"I am a Jesus," Farrakhan shouted. "I am a Messiah. I am a Deliverer." Then, stricken by a burst of modesty, he said he was not comparing himself with "*the* Jesus," who he said works through him, Minister Farrakhan.

Farrakhan's personal fantasies have no basis in the reality of black people seeking a just tomorrow in a country bedeviled by the historic curse of racism. During his trip I wrote:

For the broad mass of black Americans who struggle for justice and full citizenship, he is a curse that just won't go away.

In his constant grubbing for money and publicity, Farrakhan continues to do and say the things that make it easier for bigots and racists to play the race card and gain broader political power in America.

Throughout America's great wars and tribulations, black Americans have stayed remarkably far from acts of sabotage and treason. Farrakhan's trip has raised the specter of masses of blacks making cause with the Muslims who might engage in the bombings of buildings, tunnels, bridges and other things that might cause the destruction of America. Thus Farrakhan has spread calumny upon the integrity and loyalty of black America that is more damaging than the worst propaganda of the neo-Nazis and the Aryan Nation demagogues.

Farrakhan gets richer as he intensifies the spirit of racial warfare in America.

What is worse is that he undermines the legitimate cries of Americans who still face egregious discrimination in almost all aspects of their lives.

The pity is those blacks to whom America's leaders and power-brokers ought to be listening can rarely get a fair hearing. Farrakhan can burp into a hailstorm and find the press all around him.

I said all this and more in my *Chicago Sun-Times* column, provoking a rash of threats from the headquarters of the Nation of Islam. My assistant in Washington, Pam Paroline, was told by telephone that "Rowan will get his — when his car blows up."

In August 1996, in the midst of the Democratic National Convention, Farrakhan formally asked the U.S. government to allow him to accept the billion dollars from Libya — plus a personal "humanitarian award" of $250,000. The government said no. Farrakhan said he would sue.

It is almost impossible to overstate the magnitude of the push that Farrakhan, and other blacks with a Farrakhan-type mentality, are giving toward a race war. There is no room for any efforts to mute the noisy hatreds that dominate race relations in America today as long as the Farrakhans hold the stage. Yet, I know that for every Farrakhan who riles and poisons black America, there are twenty white bigots who seek to take us into organized murder and mayhem. One such hatemonger was a candidate for the presidency of these United States.

Patrick J. Buchanan

Americans will come to bless the day when Patrick Joseph Buchanan decided to go all out to win the presidency of the United States, because in his bigoted, divisive campaign, Buchanan showed just how vulnerable the United States actually is to a candidacy based on phony populism and full of racism and anti-Semitism.

Most Americans came to see that however offensive Farrakhan might be, Buchanan was much more dangerous to the American commonweal. Farrakhan still has relatively few followers in his secretive Nation of Islam — estimates range from only ten thousand to a hundred thousand. Buchanan consistently drew about one-fourth of the votes in the Republican primaries. Farrakhan sought power and glory — and money — in his own little separatist world; Buchanan wanted to be chief executive, with veto powers, of the greatest nation on earth, and commander in chief of its awesome military forces, including its nuclear arsenal.

Buchanan began to rouse Republicans to the reality that a race war and a class war were more than possible in the United States after he won primaries in Alaska and Louisiana, almost caught Dole in Iowa, and then finished ahead of Dole by 27 to 26 percent in New Hampshire. Emboldened, Buchanan began to talk like a half-mad would-be dictator. In New Hampshire he boasted that he would "send Bill and Hillary back to wherever they sent poor Joycelyn Elders," and ranted against "the transnational corporations" that he said were "sending the jobs of American working men and women overseas." Buchanan's staple speech was laced with one-liners against Jews ("I am against a Supreme Court that imposes Justice Ruth Bader Ginsburg's agenda on the American people") and blacks ("Colin Powell will not be my running mate") and Mexican immigrants ("Listen, Jose, you're not coming in this time") and the Japanese ("Mr. Hashimoto, . . . we're going to start with tariffs on your manufactured goods of 10 percent").

No matter how many groups — working women, homosexuals, AIDS victims, or blacks — Buchanan baited and insulted in his stump speech, he always left room for attacks on "Fortune 500 companies, Wall Street bankers, and the K Street lobbyists" in the nation's capital. He made a point of blaming the woes of "working people" on "Citibank, Chase Manhattan, and Goldman Sachs" and other companies he implied were led by Jews.

By attacking the rich and politically generous corporations, Buchanan was driving a dagger into the heart of the Republican party as it had existed for generations.

Lamar Alexander, former Tennessee governor and a fading GOP presidential candidate, said Buchanan would be "a terrible burden on our party." New York's Republican mayor, Rudolph W. Giuliani, said he could never vote for Buchanan. General Colin Powell, courted by millions as the GOP candidate who could win, put Buchanan down in similar words. So did William Bennett, former secretary of education, who accused Buchanan of "flirting with fascism."

Buchanan raised the question "Who speaks for the Euro-Americans?" and quickly indicated that he did. Okay, everyone needs a spokesperson. But Buchanan put a racist cast on this. He expressed worry that Euro-Americans might soon be a minority, adding, "By the middle of the next century, the United States will have become a veritable Brazil of North America."

One of Buchanan's informal campaign advisers, Samuel Francis, a columnist and editorial writer for the *Washington Times*, picked up on this theme in the fall of 1994, saying: "Whites must assert our identity and our solidarity, and we must do so in explicitly racial terms through the articulation of racial consciousness as whites." Francis was forced to resign from the *Washington Times*, a fate that, ironically, Buchanan refused to force upon other campaign aides and advisers whose views about race in general and American blacks in particular were highly inflammatory.

The Anti-Defamation League said Buchanan's policies were "defined by prejudice and rancor, if not outright hate." Buchanan responded by saying the ADL was waging an "orchestrated smear campaign" against him.

"He's the Irish Catholic George Wallace, though he is less anti-black and more anti-Jewish than Wallace," said Leo Ribuffo, an expert on twentieth-century American politics at George Washington University.

Knowing Wallace, and being the first newsman to record his sickbed expressions of regret that he defended "segregation forever," I disagreed with Ribuffo, feeling certain that Buchanan was more anti-everything and anti-everybody than the former Alabama governor ever was.

I had never needed a Rorschach or any other test to conclude that Pat Buchanan was a racist — in fact, the most dangerous kind, because he was of a level and class to make plausible denial of his racism. I didn't doubt that he had denied it to himself a hundred times.

I remembered the Buchanan who once called Dr. Martin Luther King, Jr., "immoral, evil and a demagogue."

I knew that in the Nixon White House, Buchanan was foremost in advocating resistance to the Supreme Court decision outlawing racial segregation in public schools. He encouraged Nixon to do nothing more than the law specifically required, which meant to "hold off" and give communities "freedom of choice," although *Brown v. Board of Education* supposedly had wiped out freedom of choice on the issue.

Part of Nixon's expressed sorrow for white southerners was inspired by Buchanan, who once went to Tupelo, Mississippi, to place flowers on the grave of one of his slave-owning ancestors and brag about how his relatives were "rabid secessionists." Even Nixon interpreted Buchanan's views as saying "segregation forever."

Buchanan had written Nixon a memo opposing the racial integration, of schools or anything, in which he said: "The ship of integration is going down; it is not our ship; it belongs to national liberalism; and we ought not to be aboard." White House staffers often wondered how much Buchanan influenced Nixon and Agnew.

Buchanan was also rabidly opposed to the Voting Rights Act and the delivery of meaningful political power to black Americans. He lashed out against what he called "the democratist temptation, the worship of democracy as a form of governance." When he assailed "the one-man, one-vote Earl Warren system," Buchanan clearly meant that one black man ought not necessarily have the same one vote as a white man.

Buchanan was no less the racist firebrand when he joined the Reagan administration in 1985. Reagan's press secretary, Larry Speakes, wrote in his memoir, *Speaking Out:* "I hadn't encountered anyone like Pat since I had to deal with the White Citizens' Councils in my days as a Mississippi newspaper editor."

Ron Walters, a political scientist at Howard University, told *USA Today:* "As an African American, when I listen to Pat talk . . . it scares the hell out of me."

In his book *Standing Firm* former vice president Dan Quayle said of Buchanan: "There's a firm line between the political cutting edge and what is objectionable. All too often, Pat crossed it."

As he came to believe he really had a chance to get the Republican nomination, Buchanan struggled to recognize that line. He resorted to code phrases, believing that if he ranted against criminals or welfare recipients, his constituents would know he meant blacks; if he talked about a fence to keep immigrants out, everybody would know he was talking about Mexicans, not Englishmen and Scotsmen. But the venom of racism was so deep within him that he just couldn't help throwing out a few gratuitous lines about "Zulus," or "bongo drums" played in Washington, or a "No way, Jose" immigration policy.

Buchanan also had been a pretty effective intimidator with his column and his television shows. Few of his journalistic peers or his political foes would say truthfully what they thought about him. John Sweeney, the new AFL–CIO president, was gutsy in saying at the union's winter conclave in Bal Harbour, Florida, "Buchanan is a racist, he's anti-Semitic, he bashes women's rights along with labor and immigrants, and he's a believer in supply-side economics. We are none of these things."

Whether Buchanan was racist and anti-Semitic became the most passionate debate of the primaries.

Oliver North, the infamous former Marine and now radio talk-show host, portrayed Buchanan as the savior of "the overworked, underpaid, God-fearing, much-maligned, oft-criticized, rarely commended, unappreciated, sexually harassed, reverse discriminated, censured, chastised, condemned and demeaned American hard-working family."

I don't know whether his early losses to Buchanan or the wicked TV comedians provoked Dole to decide that he had to fight Buchanan for "the heart and soul of the Republican party." I am sure, though, that the impact was great when David Letterman said on CBS that Buchanan was "going to take a couple of days off after the New Hampshire primary and then invade Poland" . . . and when Jay Leno declared on NBC that Buchanan's campaign was generating the most heat, "mostly from burning books and crosses."

Buchanan's early success caused his immediate demise when the media was provoked into taking a closer look at him. What they found seemed to justify Leno's *"Sieg Heil"* salute to Buchanan on nationwide TV.

Suddenly, out of Buchanan's campaign woodwork came crawling a chilling assortment of haters and screwballs.

It was revealed that one of Buchanan's campaign managers, Larry Pratt, had attended meetings of and spoken before neo-Nazi and white-supremacist groups. At one gathering Pratt did not leave when another speaker said, "Your enemies are pumping all the Talmudic filth they can vomit and defecate into your living room that they can." Buchanan said on ABC's David Brinkley show: "This man [Pratt] is under savage attack for two reasons. He's a devout Christian who happens to be very strong in favor of gun ownership, and he's standing with Pat Buchanan. That's why the dogs are on him."

So Buchanan would not fire Pratt — he let him take a leave of absence.

Buchanan's talk about a "devout Christian" who favors gun ownership raised questions about his attitudes toward Jews, Hindus, Muslims, and even agnostics who own weapons.

But there was other evidence that Buchanan's campaign was actively racist. Senator Gramm said Buchanan had defeated him in Louisiana in part because Pat's people distributed a leaflet attacking the Texas senator for his marriage to an American of Korean descent. "Conservatives will not vote for Gramm," the leaflet said, "due to his interracial marriage. He divorced a white woman to marry an Asiatic."

Buchanan denied that his campaign had anything to do with the leaflet.

After the exposure of confirmed racists in Buchanan's campaign apparatus, columnist George Will asked Buchanan on "This Week with David Brinkley": "What have you done to generate such enthusiasm among the Nazis?"

After a rancorous exchange, Buchanan ducked the questions, saying: "George, . . . I don't care who comes and supports my position. Jesse Jackson supports me on NAFTA. . . . Ralph Nader supports me on a number of positions."

Buchanan had written a zillion mean-spirited speeches for Spiro Agnew and Richard Nixon; columns in which he attacked powerful Democrats and defended alleged Nazi murderers. He had written outright lies, some about me, provoking me to tell my (and his) lecture agent that I would never share a platform with him.

Who or what made him what he seemed to be? His father? His siblings? The Blessed Sacrament elementary school that Buchanan attended? Or the Catholic church itself, along with

Gonzaga High, the Catholic school that he attended in Washington, D.C.?

Some investigators traced Buchanan's "problem" back to Father Charles Coughlin, the Irish-Catholic priest who is called by some "the white Louis Farrakhan of the 1930s." Father Coughlin gained a remarkable following with radio broadcasts in which he attacked communism and blamed Jews and their "interlocking conspiracies" for everything he thought was wrong with Franklin D. Roosevelt, the New Deal, and the international banking system.

Numerous publications have reported that Pat Buchanan's father, William, always "Pop" to his nine children, was devoted to the Coughlin broadcasts. Whether the message was anticommunism, anti-Jews, or love of Senator Joseph McCarthy, foreign dictators, and the Confederate flag, Pop Buchanan passed his and Coughlin's far-right convictions along to his children.

Pop set up a punching bag in his Bethesda, Maryland, home so his sons would learn to fight anyone who disagreed with the gospel according to Father Coughlin.

About ten years ago, long before anyone imagined Pat would win Republican convention delegates, my Jewish dentist told me of his going to a lot behind Gonzaga High for a pickup basketball game — one of the few places in then Jim Crow Washington where blacks and whites could play together. One day, he recalled, Pat, about eleven, and his older brothers showed up and said: "All niggers and kikes off this field."

"The Buchanan boys had such a reputation as brawlers that we normally would have fled in fear," the dentist recalls, "but one of our players was a priest at Gonzaga. He went over and talked to the Buchanans, and they walked away without a fight."

It seems that everything said by Father Coughlin and by his accountant father seeped deep into Patrick's brilliant mind and questionable soul.


## Bob Grant, Rush Limbaugh, G. Gordon Liddy, and Others

Who else is promoting, willingly or unwittingly, a race war in America? Many others besides the obvious merchants of hate like Farrakhan and Buchanan. Our airwaves are full of racial polarizers, such as hosts Rush Limbaugh, Howard Stern, Oliver North, Bob Grant, and G. Gordon Liddy, and guests such as the Reverend Al Sharpton. Liberals barely survive on talk radio, and blacks get a ghostly chance only if they are conservatives with no clout who are satisfied with the worst air times and very low audiences. No ethnic or political group has a monopoly on the abuse of radio and television to spread divisiveness and hatred, but the American reality is that if you are a reactionary with a mean tongue and you can make bigotry funny, you can make it in talk radio.

The result is that talk radio and TV feed the paranoia and open hatred that roil workplaces, destabilize every neighborhood, and cause us to distrust each other.

Look at the most celebrated of talk-show hosts whom I've mentioned above — Limbaugh, who by his own admission is "an entertainer" who not only spreads misinformation himself, but who professes no journalistic obligations to his audience. On December 26, 1993, he said to David Brinkley on ABC:

"My show is one of the most tightly screened shows. You've got to pass a lot of tests to get on the air. Based on the fact that I don't have guests, every call has got to make me look good — because I'm the show. . . . Nobody ever says, 'Man, I listen to Rush Limbaugh because I love those callers.' Now this is not to put them down, but the caller has to do one of two things — has to be entertaining on his own, or inspire me to be. And I take whatever call is going to do that."

Brinkley noted that when serious journalists interview Limbaugh, and he starts cracking his wicked, often bigoted, jokes, they immediately feel he has "disqualified their credibility." Limbaugh rested on his view of himself as "a harmless, lovable little fuzz ball."

This nation never had a more destructive fuzz ball.

Columnist Ben Wattenberg deplored Buchanan's stance on democracy, writing in his column, "Buchanan declares that America was wrong to go to a one-man-one-vote system. He salutes and applauds a Pakistani dictator, a Filipino dictator, the sultan of Brunei, the king of Saudi Arabia — specifically because they are not democrats. And he asks, 'What have the democracies done for America lately?' He announces that 'conservative principles do not sanction democracy worship.'"

Mary Matalin, the manager of George Bush's losing presidential campaign, has dismissed Howard Stern as a cretin. He is that and worse, but I can never dismiss anyone who Arbitron, the audience-measuring service, says has four million listeners during several hours of daily broadcasting, and who claims he has sixteen million listeners. Nor can I dismiss any broadcaster who says on air that Los Angeles cops "didn't beat this idiot [Rodney King] enough."

There is nothing so tasteless that Stern won't do it, nothing so mean-spirited or racist that Stern won't say it, and nothing so demeaning of the entire broadcast industry that Stern won't spread it across the airwaves — often incurring huge fines from the Federal Communications Commission that his employer, Infinity Broadcasting, must pay.

Limbaugh ingratiates himself with piggish men when he says, "I love the women's movement, especially when I'm walking behind it." Stern's idea of intellectualism is to talk disgustingly about his wife's miscarriage, and both consider it a public service to crack jokes about black people.

Still, their audiences grow, Limbaugh's by 50 percent a year in the last two years, he claims.

## Bob Grant

A lot of the blood of America's race war victims will be on the hands and bloated bodies of Rush Limbaugh and Howard Stern. But there are others, some well known and some hardly heard of nationally, who daily yank the chains on the beasts of bigotry in America. You may never have heard of Bob Grant, known in New York City as "the Pat Buchanan of local radio."

Grant committed one of a myriad of outrages in March 1996 when he plumped for a May conference in Louisville of a bunch of white supremacists called the Renaissance Conference. That outraged *New York Post* columnist Jack Newfield (who is white), who deplored Grant's previous coziness with racists, including neo-Nazi leader Tom Metzger.

Newfield wrote in the March 8 *New York Post:*

> Grant's recent free advertising for the white-supremacist conference is consistent with his new role as the Air Traffic Controller of Hate. . . .

Bob Grant must take responsibility for what he puts out over the air.

Grant is not some neutral mirror reflecting public opinion.

He screens his calls. He decides who gets free publicity. He decides who can give out their telephone numbers and to be able to recruit from his listeners.

He lets his callers rant and rave about oiling guns and shooting blacks, and he doesn't reproach their racism.

He puts members of David Duke's hate group on the air. . . . He promotes a conference of known white supremacists like Michael Levin.

Bob Grant is a civic arsonist in a tinderbox time. It's time for WABC's new owner, Disney, to evict this Dumbo.

Newfield got his wish in mid-April when ABC Radio zipped the lips of bombastic Bob. The slur that finally moved the station to can him apparently was Grant's broadcast wish that Commerce secretary Ron Brown had not survived the crash of his plane in Croatia.

I know that Grant, Limbaugh, Liddy, and Stern are foremost among hundreds of radio jocks who have played a major role in polarizing racial and ethnic groups in America. They have wiped out civility to the point where there is no mannerly discourse in American politics. Their broadcasts feed the paranoia of the Freemen in Montana, the Aryan Nation, the violent skinheads and other white supremacists, as well as the militia movement that has grown across America.

People screamed that Grant was "a dirty little cancer" among American opinion-makers because he persistently called American welfare mothers "maggots" and "brood sows" who should be sterilized; referred to blacks as "savages"; attacked illegal aliens as "bilge"; accused Representative Charles Rangel (D-N.Y.) of having a "pygmy mentality," and described former mayor David Dinkins as "the men's room attendant."

He remains a *big* cancer. Grant is a venomous bigot who, with a handful of other hatemongers, has succeeded in putting Americans at each other's throats.

But there is no solution in firing him or the other strident racists on our radio and television stations. They express and reflect Hitlerian views that are shared by millions of other Americans. Grant quickly found another platform on New York's WOR because his views cannot be effectively suppressed. The public appetite for bigotry is insatiable.

The answer always has been to open the airwaves to people who can effectively correct the lies of Limbaugh, rebut the fulminations of Grant, and expose the fallacies of the jailbird rantings of Liddy and the foul mouthings of Stern.

But we have gone through a decade in which the people controlling radio and TV stations — and the op-ed pages of newspapers — have felt that "liberalism" was dead.

So right-wingers, especially the whites-first flamethrowers, became the ideal talk-show hosts. Blacks could break into the fraternity only if they professed to hate affirmative action and could meet the litmus tests on abortion, prayer in public schools, publicly financed vouchers for private schools, the death penalty, and more.

WABC's firing of Grant follows the unconscionable act of ousting lawyer Alan Dershowitz after the latter, on air, called Grant "a racist, a bigot" — a statement of truth. ABC must be told that the firing of Grant does not atone for the ousting of Dershowitz.

There will always be millions of Americans who will call the Reverend Jesse Jackson "Reverend Jerkson," as Grant did. Or who will rant against "fags" and "faggots," as Grant did. Or who will suggest, as Grant did, that the solution to the Haitian boat crisis is to let the Haitians drown. I see no salvation for anyone in taking their programs away.

I say to the radio and TV networks, Give the people now being slandered and cheated a voice. The national war over affirmative action is at fever pitch partly because you have not given blacks, Hispanics, and women the same voice on this issue that you are giving the Grants and Limbaughs and other "angry white males" every day. I'm not asking you to hire some blacks and Hispanics to mimic the incendiary and irresponsible behavior of Grant and Liddy; just some responsible, well-informed, articulate Americans who can give people an alternative to anti-black, anti-poor demagoguery and blind hatred.

If ABC and the other major networks — and Infinity and the other radio chains — would open the airwaves to the people being scapegoated, I would take to the streets tomorrow to ask ABC to return to Grant his fetid platform.

But the bosses of the airwaves and the op-ed pages will never do what I suggest. So this problem will probably worsen.

Look at the top one hundred radio talk-show hosts in the United States. Only five or so are black, and of those all but one or two are nouveau right-wingers. If you are white, you can be a disgraced former marine colonel, Oliver North; a former political burglar and convict, G. Gordon Liddy; or a rejected politician, Buchanan. But if you are black, the airwaves are closed off unless you are willing to espouse causes that are inimical to the uplifting of black and poor Americans.

The situation is almost as bad in the area of syndicated columnists. Editors and publishers will pay dearly for a black writer who will play dummy to troglodyte ventriloquists. But they panic if someone puts the label "liberal" in front of the by-line of a black writer.

If we are to avert a race war, editors and publishers will have to open up the dialogue on the nation's op-ed pages to every stripe of opinion.


Howard Stern

The *Chicago Tribune* has said of "the shock jock," Howard Stern: "He talks about sex and race in ways that others only whisper. . . . To some, he's a nightmare: a threat to our morality; his radio show a damaging feast of crude, racist and sexist comments."

I know of no one who doubts that Stern is crude, rude, and lewd — the most offensive man in American broadcasting. His employer, Infinity Broadcasting, paid the federal government $1.7 million in fines, imposed partly because Stern talked on and on, on air, about having a guy play the piano with his penis.

He is appalling and titillating, boring and amusing — enough of the latter to earn some $7 million a year playing to an audience of middle-class white people. But is he a menace in the sense that he foments racial hatred?

"I don't feel I have a racist bone in my body," Stern told the

*San Diego Union-Tribune* in 1995. "But because there are so many racists in our society, if you even talk about race, if you talk about how sick it is that we're all at each other's throats because of the color of our skin, people misconstrue that and think I'm a racist."

Well, poor misunderstood Stern! One aspect of his destructiveness is that he trivializes every effort to wipe out virulent racism in America. "You know what the sweetest fruit of the civil rights movement was?" he writes. "We all know what the prize was. *Porking White Babes!* And you know who enjoyed this benefit the most? Superstar black athletes."

And that gives Stern an excuse to go on and on about black athletes fornicating with white women — an essay that he knows will enflame his white audience.

It isn't the cavalier way that Stern throws the word "nigger" around that is so damaging; it is the fact that, no matter what he is discussing, he makes black people wretched caricatures of human beings. He justifies unconscionable violence and police misconduct when he says of Rodney King, "They didn't beat this idiot enough. He should be beaten every time he reaches for his car keys."

Stern says, "People take me too seriously. I'm an entertainer."

Filipino listeners weren't very entertained when Stern talked about them. One wrote the station to complain that Stern had said, "Filipinos are the most depraved people in the world and probably worse than people from France. . . ."

Stern replied:

"I never said that. I was talking about a segment of the Filipino population that caters to horny Americans by selling off their women. . . . I never said the Filipinos were worse than the French . . . the French are the worst."

Stern expects credit because he is an equal-opportunity insulter.

He did apologize for his remarks after the immensely popular Mexican American singer Selena was shot to death in Corpus Christi, Texas, in March 1995. Stern mocked Selena and her mourners, saying, "Alvin and the Chipmunks have more soul. Spanish people have the worst taste in music. This is music to dance around flies and maggots."

When the National Hispanic Media Coalition asked the Federal Communications Commission to revoke the licenses of the stations that carried those Stern comments, the shock jock apologized.

Some of Stern's defenders say he can't be a real racist if he keeps a black woman, Robin Quivers, on his show. His critics say she is a shameful sellout who endures Stern's racial insults just for the money.

In 1995, in Fort Lauderdale, Quivers faced the criticisms directly:

"I've been criticized and disowned by the black race," she told the *Sun-Sentinel* newspaper. "But they didn't make me a member of the club, so they can't put me out.

"People tell me, 'You shouldn't sit there with him.'" Well, where should I sit? Where there won't be racism? It's everywhere. . . . You think the only time I hear the word 'nigger' is when I'm with Howard? I hear it all the time.

"Critics take my role and the show too literally. It's a show. It's entertainment. It's not social commentary. It's comedy. We're performers."

That, of course, is what was said by whites who used to blacken their faces and put on minstrel shows around America. They finally learned that more people were crying than laughing because of this cruel kind of racism, so they put an end to the minstrels.


G. Gordon Liddy

G. Gordon Liddy personifies both the right-wing bent of talk radio in America and the public taste for right-wingers. Liddy's great claim to fame is that he is a convicted felon; yet he is syndicated on some 250 radio stations.

In 1995, at the very time that most Republican politicians were raging against paroles, shouting, "If you do the crime, you do the time," or warning, "Three strikes and you're out," the GOP announced that it would honor Liddy at a fund-raiser labeled "A Salute to Talk Radio."

Honor Liddy? The man who spent five years in prison for

masterminding the Watergate burglary? The Republican party honor the man who pulled off that juvenile attempt to steal the presidency for Richard Nixon?

Somehow Republicans like New York senator Alphonse D'Amato, who proposed the honor for Liddy, seemed to believe in rehabilitation of human beings, and giving them second and third chances. At least, rehab was OK if it was for a troglodyte soul brother.

Trouble was, someone asked what Liddy had brought to talk radio. Everybody remembered that he had made headlines by saying on air how he thought citizens should respond if federal agents were coming into their houses to make arrests.

"Head shots! Head shots! Kill the sons of bitches," Liddy screamed.

He denied a clamor of charges that he was "fueling the lunatic fringe," asserting that he only advocated shooting firearms agents "in self-defense."

Millions of Americans think Liddy *is* the lunatic fringe. He once boasted that on a gun range he put up the faces of President and Mrs. Clinton as targets and began to shoot more accurately. He admits that he once tried to get newspaper columnist Jack Anderson assassinated.

Liddy's strong suit is not in the hurling of racial insults. His style is to give aid and comfort to Americans like the Viper Militia, who were arrested in Phoenix after they amassed weapons with which to blow up several federal buildings in Arizona. He has admitted to illegal buggings and other unlawful activities, and to feeling no respect for the U.S. Constitution.

Liddy is paid handsomely to mouth the views of the members of the eight hundred militias in which those claiming to be alienated from America have adopted his slogan, "Kill the sons of bitches!"

Newt Gingrich

This country is afflicted by the willful hatemongers, the polarizers who pretend not to know that they are divisive forces and the politicians who, blinded by ambition and a lust for power, don't much give a damn about how much their words and actions tear the fabric of American unity.

Because the leading members of the Congress have great power and visibility, and command media attention every day, they contribute to an American dialogue that is imbued either with mutual respect for all of our people or with contempt and combativeness.

No politician has burst upon the American scene more dramatically in this generation than Representative Newt Gingrich of Georgia, the first Republican Speaker of the House of Representatives in forty years. Let's look at what Gingrich has brought to the pre–race-war psychosis of America:

In June 1995, Newt Gingrich got up at a breakfast meeting sponsored by *National Minority Politics Magazine,* a new black-owned conservative publication, and said: "There is real prejudice in America. . . . I don't believe we live in a color-blind society. . . . It is harder to be black and American. It is more difficult to acquire wealth as a black American. If you're black, you have to work hard, and if you're black and poor, you have to work twice as hard."

Had he stopped there, listeners might have concluded Gingrich was an enlightened politician — and a superenlightened Republican. But out of the other side of his glib mouth, he said that the problem blacks face isn't just white racism — that as a "historian" he thought poor blacks' "habits" were partly to blame for their failure to achieve, and that the civil rights movement had become more interested in filing grievances than in promoting economic opportunity.

Gingrich said the Republican party was interested in finding ways to help people "who are financially and culturally deprived," but was opposed to what he called "genetically based patterns or grievance-based patterns" of assistance. In other words, the GOP didn't like affirmative action programs.

In the long, bloody annals of racial bigotry in America, the state of Georgia has produced its share of villains: the Talmadge brothers, Eugene and Herman; former governor Lester Maddox, who brandished ax handles to keep blacks out of his restaurant; and others.

I am sure that Newt Gingrich, the Georgian who serves as

Speaker of the House and who is clearly one of the most powerful men in America, does not consider himself in that league of
racists. And I wouldn't accuse him of spewing the same vicious
venom and hatred as Pat Buchanan or the Reverend Louis Farrakhan.

But when talking about minorities and their aspirations for
equal opportunity, Gingrich, with his self-righteous hypocrisy,
good-guy-bad-guy double-talk, "historical" declarations — and
most of all, his singleminded dedication to the destructive, unfair Republican Contract with America — may be just as dangerous as the old gallus-snapping, wool-hat racists ever were,
and just as much a polarizer as the worst of today's lot.

In the legislative program of the Contract, in his book *To Renew America,* and elsewhere in speeches and writings, Gingrich
fuels the smoldering fires of social conflict and racial divisions in
America.

"He has the slaveowner mentality," charged Representative
Charles Rangel, a black Democrat from New York, after Gingrich's statements at the breakfast meeting.

That same incident prompted Roger Wilkins, a history professor at George Mason University, to label Gingrich "a weak
historian" and say that his comments were "either bigoted, stupid, duplicitous or a combination of all three." Wilkins noted
that on one hand Gingrich said he was for providing opportunities for blacks, but on the other, he appeared to blame them for
their own problems.

In naming Gingrich its Man of the Year for 1995 — the person who had the greatest impact on American life, for better or
worse — *Time* magazine noted that there was a "Good Newt"
and a "Bad Newt." In fact, the words and phrases used to describe Gingrich and his actions in the *Time* article illustrated the
dichotomy. On the positive side were "brilliant," "amazing,"
"forceful," "revolutionary," "effective." And on the negative
side: "scary," "obnoxious," "ruthless," "arrogant," "militant."

*Time* praised Gingrich's achievements in streamlining operations in the House of Representatives and pushing his Contract
with America through the House in record time. But it noted
that the problem is "not just what he's done, but how he's done
it." To which I would add — and what he's said while doing it.
(Columnists Jack Germond and Jules Witcover have asserted

that Gingrich doesn't seem to realize that "words have consequences.") As a result, Gingrich has undermined his own
goals — most of the Contract is hopelessly ignored now by Congress — and he has added to the anger and fear and disappoint-
ment that threaten to rip this country apart.

Doris Kearns Goodwin, a Democrat and author of books
about Presidents Franklin D. Roosevelt and Lyndon B. Johnson, offered this view of the Gingrich enigma:

"I thought his state-of-the-Speaker address [in January 1995]
was remarkable. He talked about cities, racial problems, the
need for opportunity. But since that time, he has shown little of
that large-heartedness. He seems like such a contradiction because he has such big ideas. Yet he has fallen prey many times to
petty mishaps that seem to emanate from part of his personality. You cannot brush off such incidents as just tiny mistakes."

Gingrich's dealings with blacks are a good example of that
first-year roller-coaster ride. When it looked as if Colin Powell
might enter the presidential race, Gingrich publicly urged him
to run as a Republican, not an independent, and said he'd fit in
just fine as a "fiscal conservative with a social conscience."

But Gingrich raised doubts about his own conscience after
columnist Robert Novak criticized him for not saying anything
about affirmative action in his book *To Renew America*. Instead
of welcoming the Novak column as a compliment or just ignor-
ing it, Gingrich apparently felt his conservative credentials had
been challenged, so he wrote a letter to the editor of the *Washington Post:*

"As a speaker, each time I have been asked about this issue, I
have responded that it is clear where Republicans stand on the
issue: We're not backing off on affirmative action, and this Congress will address it. . . . Affirmative action, a bureaucratic approach to assisting minorities and women, stems from the same
misguided impulse that created our nightmarish welfare state.
Just as we ask what will replace the welfare state, we can also
ask what will replace affirmative action. The answer to both is
the same — an opportunity society."

That brought another rebuttal from Roger Wilkins, in his
own letter to the editor. "Gingrich's choice is clear. He can use
his enormous power to help Americans learn what their real
problems are and work on honest solutions, or he can continue

the course of political profiteering that insults blacks and divides the nation. If he continues his current course, he and others like him will keep on disgracing their party by pushing our country farther and farther away from Martin Luther King's 'Someday.'"

Gingrich's double-talk and hypocrisy are not new. In 1984, after campaigning for Congress on family values and calling his opponent a home-breaker, Gingrich went to the hospital where his first wife was recuperating from a cancer operation and demanded that she agree to his terms for divorce.

This same righteous man, who engineered the fall of Democratic Speaker Jim Wright in 1989 because of a shady book deal, has himself been caught up in a highly questionable book deal and is the object of a House Ethics Committee inquiry. A special counsel is investigating whether Gingrich improperly used tax-deductible contributions to fund a college course he taught.

Gingrich verbally beats up on welfare mothers who he says are ripping off taxpayers, but his district in the suburbs of Atlanta is home to large numbers of companies, including the Lockheed Corporation, that are collecting welfare for the rich.

Streaks of pettiness and name-calling have emerged: Gingrich described the Clinton administration as "the enemy of normal Americans," called the President and his wife "counterculture McGoverniks," and asserted on a talk show that up to one-fourth of the White House staff had used drugs in the last four years before they came in. Gingrich offered no names, no evidence, no sources.

Statements like those hit a sore spot with A. Leon Higginbotham, an African American who had a distinguished career as a federal judge and later became Public Service Professor of Jurisprudence at Harvard University. Higginbotham wrote an open letter to the Speaker in which he complained.

"Because of political spins and distortion, you and your colleagues have often branded the critics of your Contract as irresponsible liberals detached from the real America. . . . Liberals are now typecast as some non-normal, almost diseased Americans. [George] McGovern, the son of a Republican Methodist minister, has been married to the same woman for 51 years. He flew 35 combat missions in World War II. It is absurd that his patriotism is disputed or that he is branded as "counterculture" by a person who never served in the military and whose own family history can hardly be called exemplary."

*New York Post* columnist Jack Newfield was a little more colorful in his reaction. Gingrich, he wrote, "is the Tonya Harding of politics. If he disapproves of you, he will try to break your knees."

More than once, Gingrich has tried to turn tragedy into political capital. After Susan Smith drove her car into a lake and drowned her two young children, Gingrich said: "How a mother can kill her two children . . . in hopes that her boyfriend would like her, is just a sign of how sick the system is, and I think people want a change. The only way you get changes is to vote Republican."

Previously, he tried to link Democratic policies with Woody Allen's courtship of his ex-lover's adopted daughter, and he charged that eight hundred babies a year were found in Dumpsters in Washington, D.C. — an unsubstantiated attack on welfare mothers in a predominantly black city.

After a bizarre killing in Chicago, in which a mother and two children were killed and an unborn baby was ripped out of the dead woman's body, Gingrich came up with a way to blame welfare.

"What's gone wrong," he said, "is a welfare system which subsidizes people for doing nothing, a criminal system which tolerates drug dealers and an education system which allows kids not to learn. We end up with the final culmination of an underclass with no sense of humanity, no sense of civilization and no sense of the rules of life in which human beings respect each other."

To which the *Louisville Courier-Journal* pointed out in an editorial: "Crime did not begin in this country with the creation of the Great Society."

Gingrich, of course, is free to criticize, to interpret things as he wants to. But at the very least — which is really the very most in these tension-filled times, when the smallest verbal spark can ignite an explosion — Gingrich's words are dangerously incendiary.

He may not be totally oblivious of that. In *To Renew America,* he writes, "I want to encourage you to be a little anxious. . . . I want to encourage you to turn that anxiety into energy."

Of all the Speaker's words and actions, however, the ones that worry me the most are those that involve the Contract with America and the rest of the Republican legislative program.

Gingrich was the father of the Contract, and it reflected his feeling that most of the blame for society's ills rests on "liberals" and their policies of affirmative action, the redrawing of voting districts, entitlements for the poor, taxes on the rich. In earlier years he had pushed to use the Contract as a national platform for GOP congressional candidates, but he didn't achieve that goal until the 1994 election.

When the Republicans took control of Congress for the first time in four decades and installed Gingrich as Speaker, he figured he had a clear-cut mandate. His goal was nothing less than to rewrite the social contract between Washington, the states, and the American people for the first time since Lyndon B. Johnson's Great Society programs of thirty years ago and Franklin Roosevelt's New Deal of sixty years ago.

He would sharply alter welfare, health care, the tax code, and government support for education, environmental protection, and much more. Crime fighting would take a scary "lock-'em-all-up-or-execute-'em" turn. College scholarships would be cut for middle-class youngsters. Over the next seven years, government spending would fall by roughly $1 trillion and taxes would be cut by more than $245 billion. Welfare, Medicare, Medicaid, food programs, would not only be slashed, but would be turned over to states to run, and the once-sacred idea of absolute entitlements for poor people would be ended.

Newt & Company rammed most of these measures through the House of Representatives and might have imposed them on the nation were it not for a more cautious Senate and a President who finally found his backbone and a veto pen. Mr. Clinton cast the budget battle as a test of America's fairness — "a choice between a society where winner takes all or a society where everybody's got a chance to win."

For my part, what I find most frightening is that this legislation — together with the rhetoric from Gingrich, his number one aide, Representative Dick Armey of Texas, and others — is the raw meat that feeds both the anxieties of an underclass unable to rise out of poverty and the angers of the middle class troubled by stagnant wages, a bloated federal bureaucracy, and educational woes. As such, it will divide even more this already-splintered nation.

I wish I could believe that the Newt Gingrich who speaks approvingly about "an integrated America" would ever boldly withhold tacit approval, even rabid support, of this dangerously divisive campaign of government shrinkage.

But then I see passages in Gingrich's writings like this: "[American] civilization is based on a spiritual and moral dimension. It emphasizes personal responsibility as much as individual rights. Since 1965, however, there has been a calculated effort, by the cultural elite, to discredit this civilization and replace it with a culture of irresponsibility that is incompatible with American freedoms as we know them."

That may not be the in-your-face bombast of a Pat Buchanan, but it surely wouldn't sit well with someone like twenty-three-year-old Araceli Cobarrubias of San Diego, a single mother who's been struggling, far from irresponsibly, to get the job training that will enable her and two children to escape from welfare.

What is happening in America is arousing the poor and down-trodden. These people don't know about a study which found that over the last two decades the poor had become more likely to stay poor while the affluent were more likely to stay affluent. But they do see America' opportunity gap widening. They know their salaries, if they still have them, aren't going as far.

The poor are keenly aware that their children don't get the food to keep them nourished, the medical care to keep them healthy, the shelter to keep rats and lead poisoning at bay, the schooling to give them a chance at a better job.

Kids who are starved before and just after birth are not simply at greater risk of educational failure. They are more susceptible to the kind of "rage" that is being imputed to subway killer Colin Ferguson, or to young blacks who cheer the rantings of Louis Farrakhan.

Labor secretary Robert Reich has noted that the moral core of capitalism, the faith that if you work hard you can get ahead, is being eroded. This could strain the nation's social and political fabric, he warns. "Young Americans who are poor or ill-educated increasingly know that they will occupy a place in society in which inequality works against them. We face a great danger if the time comes when they refuse to accept that inequality."

All of which brings me back once again to that open letter that Leon Higginbotham sent to Speaker Newt Gingrich, for it is as clear and ringing an expression of indignation and alarm as you'll find.

". . . I fear that some aspects of the recent legislative program have awakened *the worst forces of our nature* and have set them loose. These forces overshadow the lives of the poor, the weak and the powerless, and threaten to beat them down, back to the great miseries of the Great Depression," wrote Higginbotham.

"It seems that in order to win the white male vote, you and your colleagues have formulated a conciliation policy for white males that says, 'Poor people to the rear and minorities take care of yourselves.' It may be a successful political formula for the moment, but ultimately this country will pay a heavy price for those unwise diversions. The weak and the poor will not long tolerate programs that give persons earning $200,000 a year tax breaks, while school lunches, food stamps and other programs for the needy are cut back with block grants that have tens of billions of cuts. There is no moral or economic justification to dismantle and replace federal entitlements with unaccountable state block grants. The retrogression that your Contract has set loose will not only beat down the poor, it will, in time, engulf us all, leaving no safe haven for either the enforcers or the victims of their inequitable Contract With America."

## Richard Cohen

Perhaps you have noticed that I have not lumped Richard Cohen, the *Washington Post* columnist, in with Limbaugh, Liddy, and the other flagrantly provocative hatemongers and polarizers. That is because Cohen is profoundly different from them, and more respected by other journalists than all of them combined, though he may be as destructive as any one of them.

Grant, Liddy, and Limbaugh are full-time cannon blasters, so predictable and incessant in their hate propaganda that only myopic fools can fail to see them for what they are. Cohen is more a sniper, firing away at strategic times to anger blacks, and most often further poison relations between blacks and Jews. Between such snipings, he passes fairly well as a sort of semi-liberal.

I've written earlier about his role in the controversy over Khalid Muhammad's stupidly bigoted speech at Howard University. It is instructive to note that former congressman William Gray, now president of the United Negro College Fund (UNCF), denounced Khalid's diatribe as "poison." Yet, because of Cohen's columns advocating a cut in the federal appropriation for Howard, some Jews concluded that they ought to punish the UNCF. Gray had a very difficult time getting the truth out.

In 1986, Cohen was involved in a confrontation with the black community in Washington, D.C., that seems to have colored his writings about African Americans ever since.

In September of that year Cohen wrote a cover article for the brand-new *Washington Post Magazine* about how white merchants at jewelry, clothing, and other stores either refused to let young black males in or quickly shooed them away. Citing complaints that this was unfair, racist behavior, Cohen wrote:

"As for me, I'm with the store owners. . . ."

This article, in a million copies of the magazine, provoked a tornado of protest. Black broadcaster Cathy Hughes denounced the article as "an indictment of all black males in the metropolitan area between the ages of eighteen and twenty-five." She said a coalition of more than fifteen powerful community groups would take their magazines to the front of the *Post* threatening to make a bonfire of them.

Donald Graham, the *Washington Post* publisher, spent hours with Hughes on her radio station, WOL, trying to placate the black community — a fact that had to be both galling and embarrassing to Cohen.

It was probably a Pyrrhic victory that Hughes and other black protesters won, because Cohen has continued to write for the *Post* and many other newspapers, and he has been sticking it to black Americans ever since.

On the critical issues, he is probably a more effective enemy of black people than the flamethrowers such as Grant and Liddy. Here is a sampler of vintage Cohen:

On affirmative action:

> After 30 years of affirmative action, it's time to limit its application — maybe only to instances of recent discrimination. I say that with reluctance, and with full appreciation that racism endures and racists will cheer, but with the overwhelming conviction that the program has outlived its usefulness. Whatever good it has done, it violates the American creed that we must be judged as individuals, not on the basis of race or sex — a group membership over which we have no choice. The civil rights era is over. The civil liberties era must begin.
>
> But even here at the *Washington Post* affirmative action has produced "racial strife." The *Post*'s announced goal is to have minorities make up 25 percent of its new hires and women 50 percent. To that end, it has established an operation within the newsroom that, among other things, is responsible for recruiting minorities and women. The *Post* is adamant that its goals not be perceived as quotas, and, as with Ford, quality remains job one.
>
> Still, to a white male a message has been sent. He feels himself operating under a quota system, and no amount of assurance that goals are not quotas is going to ameliorate the emotional impact. Somehow, a goal feels like a quota, and a quota feels unfair. The *Post* insists its standards have not been lowered. Okay. But for white males, a barrier appears to have been raised.

On illegitimacy:

> The public's frustration with welfare is understandable, not to mention justified. It really does seem to have funded a permanent underclass, underwriting illegitimacy itself. (In 1991, about 30 percent of all births were out of wedlock.) Moreover, too many of the children of welfare mothers wind up either as welfare recipients themselves or as true menaces to society, the criminals who turn cities into ghost towns once night falls. Nevertheless, the fact remains that welfare is by and large a successful program. Most recipients sooner or later manage to get off the dole. It's the ones that don't who are the problem, and it is their children who are the dilemma.

The few blacks with unfettered voices in the media are no match for either the open hatemongers or the many Richard Cohens. The most dangerous elements in America count on the purveyors of hatred every bit as much as they count on their stashes of ammonium nitrate.

I detest the very idea of censorship. Who at the Federal Communications Commission, in Congress, or anywhere else is so wise or fair as to have the right to decide whether I or G. Gordon Liddy or the worst of the radio and TV hatemongers should be silenced?

I am not naive enough to believe that I could silence all the race-baiters on the airwaves, even if I were inclined to do so.

So am I praying for some introspection that will cause the verbal flamethrowers to repent and refrain from their collective poisoning of America's social bloodstream? Hardly. If I had that kind of optimism, I would not be writing this book. I know that Al Sharpton will never admit that his rhetoric provoked the burning of that store in Harlem. Liddy and Grant are not likely even to say that the militia movement is a menace, let alone that their rhetoric has provoked the spread of gun-toting paranoids over much of the country. Limbaugh isn't going to stop milking his money cow, vituperation. Gingrich seems to have cooled his rhetoric a trifle in the face of a strong challenge for his seat in Congress, but this wily leopard isn't going to change his spots. Cohen will go on spewing sophisticated bilge, thinking he has a whole nation fooled.

So the searing rhetoric will continue, as will the maimings and killings that flow from it. Lord, how far will it go?

**Chapter 4**

# Abandoning Affirmative Action — and Justice

O ne of the most inflammatory confrontations in the coming race war has been building up for years, and on many battlefields. Americans are brandishing hand grenades over "affirmative action." And some who throughout their lives practiced or tolerated the most egregious racism and discrimination are now waging conflict over their assertion that the victims of three hundred years of white racism are now the undeserved beneficiaries of "reverse racism."

In October 1977 the U.S. Commission on Civil Rights defined affirmative action as a term which broadly "encompasses any measure, beyond simple termination of a discriminatory practice, adopted to correct or compensate for past or present discrimination or to prevent discrimination from recurring in the future."

This time the war is not over cotton or slaves, but over which and how much of the benefits and blessings of American life may be enjoyed by the grandchildren of those who picked cotton, and for centuries were abandoned and almost forgotten.

In the precincts of America that were already supercharged with rage, the feelings of hopelessness have grown exponentially. The long deprived believed more and more that justice was forever beyond the reach of those whom the white man had decreed to be an underclass that was to hew the wood, draw the water, and do the dirty work of the capitalist elite.

In Memphis, Detroit, Birmingham and almost every city in America, where total bans on blacks were recently commonplace in the fire and police departments, or where blacks were limited to mostly entry-level jobs, furious legal warfare rages over efforts to hire and promote in ways that make up for some of the past injustices.

Even where white city officials have *admitted* to past racial discriminations in hiring and firing, and have *asserted in court consent decrees* that there is a compelling state interest in rectifying the effects of long-entrenched bigotries, whites are going back into court to argue, incredibly and with some success, that the remedial actions violate the rights of white men under the Fourteenth Amendment.

Disgruntled, whites are turning upside down the Equal Protection Clause of the Fourteenth Amendment to the Constitution, the 1964 Civil Rights Act, the 1991 Civil Rights law, and every other law designed to free black Americans from slavery and its residual discriminations. Whites argue that these laws forbid any government use of racial classifications, however benign, in trying to remedy injustices of the past or present.

On the set of my television show, "Inside Washington," in hundreds of letters responding to my newspaper column and radio show, in the audiences where I have spoken, for more than two years I have been told to beware of the "angry white male." The most strident white men have written to me saying that "we are goddamned mad at incompetent blacks taking what belongs to us, and we ain't gonna take it any fucking more." The more polite white men deal in anecdotes, telling how they lost their jobs, or were refused a job, at some California university or somewhere because "the slot was being reserved for some dumb, fat broad, or some black jigaboo," as one writer put it.

I have read thousands of these letters, many even more nasty and racist than the above, and I have understood and felt sorry, in my way, for the writers. I did not write off all the white man's anger to paranoia, even though he was blaming black men for his own weaknesses, his own incompetence.

I know that there was a time when if the white man said,

"Pick cotton!" my great-granddaddy picked cotton. There was a more recent time when if a white man said, "Boy, you can't come in this library," I didn't go inside the only public library in McMinnville, Tennessee. If a white man said, "Niggers can't shoot craps or play poker in their homes," we left that privilege to white men, and shot craps and played poker in the shelter of the weeds along the Barren Forks riverbank.

Even the lowliest of white men was a lord in the presence of the most accomplished black man. Well, no longer! The changes of the last half century must have wounded the psyches of millions of American white men. All of a sudden, it's a black cop who's arresting him; a black female giving him his TV news; a black "Colin Powell" he's saluting; a black judge to whom he's saying, "Yes, Your Honor"; a black doctor ministering to his injured child in the hospital emergency room. His world is scary, because black people he once abused, or dismissed as lowlife jokes, have moved with some authority into what once was his Caucasian-dominated world.

Sometimes white men notice these changes only subliminally — until a real bigot mentions them: his alma mater is now fielding an all-black basketball team; the "all-state" football team picked by the "white" newspaper is overwhelmingly black; and, what's worse, the newspaper publisher is now black.

I know how painful it is for a white man to get a female supervisor, and how a "twofer" — a black woman boss — puts a strain on his manhood. He almost never whines openly about his plight, but he cannot escape the fact that this contributes in inexplicable ways to his anger.

But it isn't just the workplace. The white men who indicate they're ready to fight someone also used to be kings in their families. They were the sole breadwinners, which made them admired — and feared — by their wives and children. Untrained or disinclined to enter the job market, women treated white males as gods. But now hosts of wives "bring home the bacon" in bigger slabs than their husbands do. A new independence for women permits many of them to say, "Get lost!" to their husbands, and get divorces, and that has brought a terrible measure of insecurity into the lives of white males.

It is now impossible for them to drive women out of the labor force, so they direct their anger at black males.

The "angry white males" don't seem to comprehend the fact that black men suffer more than they do because independent women now represent a huge portion of the work force. Because black men are still so cheated that they "bring home the bacon" in tiny strips, they find it harder to sustain a marriage with an intelligent, working black woman. So the trauma, the breakdown of the black family, is incrementally larger than that of the white family.

Under the rules of scapegoating, the white male gets to believe fervently that he has to pay for the collapse of black families — for their crime, their welfare babies, their failures in the workplace and everywhere else. The "angry white male" is the worst scapegoater in the land, blaming someone else at home and abroad for the fact that he doesn't feel as manly as he once did.

I've heard thoughtful white men suggest that angry white men resent bitterly the evidence that black men enjoy more sexual freedom than they do. They see black men impregnate black girls without suffering any consequences. And black males are now fornicating with white girls, and daring white men to try to stop what black men boast that white women really want.

The white American male's ego and self-esteem have taken a terrible beating. He now comes home and watches his children singing the songs of black superstars, doing black dances, sporting black hairdos, and popping black slang.

In his anger and fear, the "angry white man" forgets that it is mostly white men who get rich off rap music and "black" clothes and the filthy-mouthed black comics his kids watch on HBO. This troubled white man forgets that he still holds all the levers of economic power in America; that all American children go to schools where the white man's literature and history and culture are taught. There may now be a black college president here, a black bestselling author there, a black cabinet member here, and a black opera star there, but there is not a single sign anywhere that African Americans are taking over any major element of American business or cultural life.

Sadly, millions of whites do believe that the leaders of their government have embarked on "social engineering" and federal giveaway policies that will cheat whites and waste American resources on masses of blacks and Hispanics who are both undeserving and incompetent.

A special White House panel chaired by Christopher Edley, Jr., reported to President Clinton in 1995:

> The longest-standing federal affirmative action program has its roots in World War II. The Executive Order banning discrimination in the federal government and by war industries was issued by President Franklin Roosevelt. . . .
>
> The current scope of affirmative action programs is best understood as an outgrowth and continuation of our national effort to remedy subjugation of racial and ethnic minorities and of women.
>
> But affirmative efforts did not truly take hold until it became clear that anti-discrimination statutes alone were not enough to break long-standing patterns of discrimination.

Richard Nixon had said, "A good job is as basic and important a civil right as a good education." Republican vice presidential candidate Jack Kemp has been adamant in arguing that this society must make economic opportunity available to its poorest communities through special tax-supported programs, such as the creation of urban enterprise zones.

I should say here that I do not contend that all, or even a great majority, of American white men and women want a race war. Most know the risk of violent eruptions in all American cities. Most know that the legacy of slavery and more than two centuries of racial oppression is still a cruel chain upon the minds and ankles of 33 million black Americans, and a blight upon the consciences of millions of white people.

The Edley report to President Clinton states:

"The available evidence, from court and administrative litigation, refutes the charge, based on anecdote, that equal employment opportunity goals have led to widespread quotas through sloppy implementation or otherwise. EEOC and court records simply do not bear out the claim that white males or any other group have suffered widespread 'reverse discrimination.'"

A report prepared by Rutgers Law Professor Alfred W. Blumrosen for the Office of Federal Contract Compliance Programs shows there is *"no widespread abuse of affirmative action programs in employment."* It also shows there are *"only a small num-*

*ber of reported reverse discrimination cases by white males* — a high proportion of which have been dismissed by federal courts."

Still, there remain enough craven politicians and mean-spirited, selfish, and often ignorant whites to light the fuses on all the powder kegs they have planted in the recesses of their minds.

I hasten to say that social tragedy would arise from any legislation or public policies designed to placate these angry white Americans. For one reason, because there are equal armies of raging blacks and furious Hispanics who would go ballistic over effectuation of the proposed campaigns to roll back the meager gains that nonwhites have made in America during a cruel century.

Of all the issues that must be better understood by those Americans who truly want to avoid a race war, affirmative action heads the list. This issue was expected to be the most explosive of the 1996 presidential campaign. Many responsible Americans argued that it would be nation-demeaning for voters to choose the President who would take us into the twenty-first century without understanding the issue that really sets the candidates apart. But by midsummer Dole was trying to hide the differences by turning silent on the issue.

In a cabinet meeting in January 1995, President Clinton had declared that his Republican opponents' demagoguery would use "affirmative action" to define him as the "quotas" President. The word "quotas" now carries the connotation of vicious discrimination. Among Jews especially, the word draws forth memories of bankers on Wall Street and in Nashville and Minneapolis, saying that their quota of Jews would be one, or perhaps none. For blacks a "quota" meant that even where people wanted integrated neighborhoods, the limit would be two black families, else the neighborhood would go to hell. "Quota" meant a policy of either absolute exclusion, or inclusion at the lowest feasible level. Blacks have always argued that affirmative action did not *exclude* anyone; it was a program of *inclusion.* But many white Americans believed that any preference based on race, in any way or form, was "Un-American." People who had never lifted a finger to achieve a "color-blind society" cried unctuously that affirmative action was an affront to the concept of a society in which skin color is meaningless.

It was clear that while Bill Clinton had eked out a victory in 1992 with promises to appoint a cabinet that "looked like America," by 1995 he had lost all willingness to fight Republicans on a playing field called "race." A couple of cabinet members, including Henry Cisneros, the Hispanic secretary of Housing and Urban Development (HUD), warned the President that if he got weak-kneed on affirmative action he would surely be challenged for the Democratic nomination. But for months, the President refused to walk away from his early assessment that America was growing more and more opposed to federal spending on programs designed to benefit minorities, or even women, and wanted an end to affirmative action. Clinton was correct in his reading of most white Americans' attitudes, but he lacked the slightest conviction that he, with the bully pulpit of the presidency, could change it.

It became obvious that the white Americans who formed the political action committees that lavished money on candidates, and even the middle-class whites who had more clout than any collection of minorities, did not want a cabinet that "looked like America." They wanted policymakers who looked like themselves, if they could not actually be policy architects themselves. They wanted *their* children to get the college scholarships, and to be taught by professors who looked like them.

Diversity became a bad word, like *liberal*. Opposition to affirmative efforts to do justice and produce workplaces and learning centers of diversity suddenly became a bigoted ritual of white solidarity. And nowhere more so than among journalists who eat the regurgitations of scribes they consider their intellectual soul brothers.

So Irving Kristol writes in the *Wall Street Journal* that "as a result of administrative decision and judicial intervention, affirmative action has imported racial quotas into American life, and the racist ideal has acquired a new lease on life."

That's a powerful, though inaccurate and absurd claim.

Affirmative action introduced racial quotas? Hell, I remember that the quota for black kids who could read in my hometown library was zilch. The quota for blacks who could enroll in the University of Tennessee was zero. The quota for Negro commissioned officers in the U.S. Navy was "none."

Kristol sounds the same alarm I do about a future of tragic

conflict. The great difference is that he thinks those striving for diversity have "imported" racial quotas into American life.

Kristol dispenses quota crap. But there's hardly a Jewish journalist who dares to differ with him. I personally want to vomit when I read Kristol saying, "It took us a century to recover from the curse of slavery. How long will it take us to recover from the tragic error of affirmative action?"

When did Kristol decide that this country had recovered from the curse of slavery? There is not one black man in America, however rich, however prestigious, however lionized by the likes of Kristol, who has recovered from the curse of slavery. The greatest curse of slavery was that one group of people would try to use a group of black-skinned human beings as mere beasts of the field sentenced by God to deliver comfort and riches to white people.

We haven't "recovered" from the arrogant, evil assumptions of slavery. They are alive and virulent in every Kristol diatribe against affirmative action.

The question now is, "How long will it take us to recover from slavery if the Kristols make successful war on the affirmative action programs that unlock the last shackles of slavery?

An army of little media dogs is sniffing behind Kristol, inhaling such fetid droppings as the following: "The upshot is the Balkanization of America. Racial tensions and ethnic tensions in American life have increased, instead of decreasing. Under the flags of 'multiculturalism' and 'diversity' we are moving deliberately and desperately away from being a color-blind or ethnic-blind society."

Kristol is right about the desperate move away from a color-blind society. What he refuses to see is that he is energizing that move, thus setting the stage for a race war in which former allies will maim each other.

I know that Kristol, Charles Krauthammer, George Will, Mona Charen, Bruce Fein, and many other columnists and editorial writers wear blinders that prevent them from seeing America as it has been and is, but I do not believe any one of them thinks this is or ever has been a "color-blind or ethnic-blind society."

We are going to be at each other's throats, and in more physical and deadly ways, until those white Americans who think they can write away reality crawl out of denial and admit that racism is deeply entrenched in this society. From the moment a black child is conceived, throughout the months spent in a generally undernourished womb, through the formative childhood years of myriad deprivations, racism hovers over and around the lives of black children like the smell of greasy chitlins cooking in an open pot.

For years now the American media, especially newspapers like the *Wall Street Journal,* which caters to Wall Street fatcats, and astigmatic right-wing columnists who pretend also to love color-blindness, have harrumphed the line that "preferences" based on race are destroying America. One result is that editors almost everywhere have caved in and gone along with those who want to couch the debate in words that make affirmative action seem anti-white, even anti-American, on its face. You can hardly find a newspaper or magazine article on the subject in which the headlines, the lead, the core of the article, are not loaded with words such as "reverse discrimination," "unfair preferences," "race-based," "quotas" and other terms that have become unerasable parts of the campaign against even the most elementary efforts to take white racism and bigotry out of the dispensing of opportunity, jobs, advancement, in America.

There has not been any sane dialogue about affirmative action in the American media for years. That's because there is no societal agreement on what affirmative action is. And there is incredible ignorance about the ways it is put into practice, whom it benefits, and whom it victimizes.

The tragedy is that blacks do not control, or have a real voice in, enough of the media to make the point that encrusted white discrimination, not wise white efforts at affirmative action, is polarizing America to the point that open racial warfare seems inevitable.

I am personally appalled, often offended, that my white journalist colleagues will not walk away from demagogic bombast about affirmative action and tell Americans some facts about the need for, and extent of, our government and others giving goodies to minorities.

The ugliest, most venal, most destructive part of the affirmative action debate is the drumbeat of baseless assertions that blacks and other minorities are getting things for which they are either unqualified or less qualified than white males vying for the same job or opportunity.

Perhaps the poisonous impact of the anti–affirmative action campaign by the press and politicians was captured best by a woman in Goodridge, Illinois, who wrote me in January 1996 to say:

> Quota systems aren't fair. Why should a person who isn't qualified for a job get it because of race, gender, etc., and push a more qualified person out of the way. Nonsense!
>
> So the median income of whites is more — maybe they're more stable and qualified — also better educated. I taught a lot of black children who never did their homework and spent the whole day causing trouble. A lot of black teenagers turn their noses up at jobs that white kids take. They'd rather make big money hustling drugs.
>
> I'm sorry to hear about more black babies dying than white ones and more black women dying of cancer than white women, but that's not the fault of the superior (so-called by you) white race.
>
> Mr. Rowan, you, as a writer, could do so much for *all* the children of the world if you would just teach love, not hate, and the truth, not lies. We are all members of the human race and unless we all realize that we can catch more flies with honey than vinegar the next generation will be lost.

This woman, whom I read to be honest, honorable, and very troubled by the situation, had spelled out our tragic dilemma. She had swallowed whole the baseless propaganda that affirmative action means "quotas" for people who don't qualify for a job. She typified the white American notion that black children are also an inferior species, preferring to "hustle drugs" rather than study. She implies that we blacks who support affirmative action are preaching hate when we could do so much for all the children of the world if we "would just teach love." I can't preach enough "love" to rectify the war-inviting fact that too many black teenagers, however much they do their homework and resist the blandishments of drug dealers, cannot get even a two-bit job in America. Our own government tells us the dismaying truth monthly, but most Americans don't read it. Month after month, 30, 40, 50 percent of black teenagers in the labor force are unable to find a job — while only a third as many white teenagers are denied the chance to make a dollar for college, or to learn about our capitalist world of work, of profit, of wealth.

Aside from the argument that perhaps blacks, Hispanics, women, and others are not qualified and don't deserve jobs or promotions, there is the argument that nevertheless they are salting away the goodies of American life.

Just what have minorities been getting that is so unfair to Caucasians? Most white families would shout, "College scholarships!" A few years ago a national stink arose after a black man, Michael L. Williams, head of the Education Department's Office of Civil Rights, said race-specific scholarships were illegal because they drained money from white students' education. Congress ordered the General Accounting Office (GAO) to determine whether minorities were getting an unfair share of scholarship money.

In January 1994 the GAO reported that almost two out of every three American colleges targeted scholarships at minorities, but that minorities got only 4 percent of total scholarship money. In law, medical, and other professional schools, minorities got 10 percent of the money — still far below minority representation in the population.

Wayne Upshaw, the assistant director of the GAO, who supervised the college survey, said, "We found a lot of programs, but they accounted for relatively little money."

That provoked Senator Paul Simon (D-Ill.) to say that scholarship programs for minorities "ought to be expanded." Education secretary Richard W. Riley, a white South Carolinian, said: "I believe race-based scholarships can be a valuable tool for enhancing a diverse educational environment for the benefit of all students."

There is grim irony in the fact that while the clamor grows to deny college scholarships to blacks and other Americans, colleges are recruiting foreign students as never before. The Institute of International Education reports that twenty years ago 154,580 foreigners were enrolled at U.S. public and private universities and colleges. In the 1992–93 school year that number had risen to 438,620.

Despite these facts, the foes of affirmative action have carried out a withering attack designed to wipe it out on the college level. It is as though they don't know the Jim Crow histories of the University of Maryland or the University of Texas, where they have provoked federal court decisions that some see as the death knell of affirmative action in education.

If blacks and Hispanics cannot get redress for the educational abuses and denials of the last two hundred years, there will be no chance of avoiding the conflicts that will benefit no one and hurt everyone. So it is essential that all Americans know the shameful legacy that made affirmative action necessary on every campus in the land.

As I detailed in my biography of Justice Thurgood Marshall, the University of Maryland embraced for many generations Jim Crow statutes, policies of bigotry, and almost every imaginable ruse to prevent a single black person from enrolling in that tax-supported institution. It was Marshall who sued to get the first black student, Donald Murray, into the Maryland law school.

But University of Maryland and state officials threw up barriers to the admission of blacks in every school, undergraduate or graduate, for a generation after the 1954 *Brown v. Board of Education* Supreme Court decision outlawing racial segregation in public education. In 1970 Maryland and thirteen other states were sued by the NAACP Legal Defense Fund to force them to end policies of racial exclusion.

By 1978, top officials at the University of Maryland chafed at being viewed as the Neanderthals of higher learning. They knew that they were despised by Maryland's black intelligentsia. They knew that they were obligated, not by the courts, or any concept of "affirmative action," to bring bright black teachers and students to the university's campuses if Maryland were ever to compete with, or be respected by, other institutions that generations ago walked away from raw racism.

In 1978 University of Maryland officials decided that to restore their own reputations, and to make their campuses true learning places, they would have to make a conscious effort to show bright black people that they were truly welcome. So they decided to name about thirty scholarships in honor of Benjamin Banneker, the eighteenth-century black scientist and inventor who helped to lay out the nation's capital, and reserve them for high-achieving black high school graduates.

This tightly administered program at Maryland's College Park campus drew hundreds of applications from top-level black high school seniors. It was so successful that the university's Baltimore campus created the Meyerhoff Scholarship Program for African Americans interested in earning doctorates in engineering and the sciences. The University of Virginia set up a similar program, as did other once Jim Crow institutions.

The program rolled along magnificently. "Having these students on campus serves as a kind of magnet to attract other African American students," said university spokesman Roland King. "It also helps to dismantle the stereotypes a lot of society has about African Americans. It's very positive and reinforcing."

But no matter! In the mid-1970s the idea had arisen that whenever a member of a racial minority got a scholarship, a job, or anything else worthwhile, some white person who deserved it more was being cheated. Suddenly, when the issue was reparations, recompense, making amends for three centuries of brutalizing black people, white lifelong racists rose up to demand "a color-blind Constitution."

University attempts to "do the right thing" from one end of America to the other were enshrouded in controversy when a white man, Alan Bakke, sued the regents of the University of California, arguing that he should have gotten one of the slots for medical school that had been given to a black applicant.

The Supreme Court's ruling in this case revealed great divisions — something destructively different from the unanimity that the Warren Court had shown in *Brown v. Board of Education*. Many of the nation's white people asked rhetorically whether *any* past injustice justified *any* race-based remedy.

In the Bakke case, Justice Harry Blackmun of Minnesota wrote these words:

I suspect that it would be impossible to arrange an affirmative-action program in a racially neutral way and have it be successful. To ask that this be so is to demand the impossible. In order to get beyond racism, we must first take account of race. There is no other way. And in order to treat some persons equally, we must treat them differently. We cannot — we dare not — let the Equal Protection Clause perpetuate racial supremacy. In fact,

applying strict scrutiny to the benign use of race-conscious affirmative action, which seeks to alter employment patterns shaped
by past racial discrimination, comes perilously close to nullifying
the amendment as it pertains to persons of color.

*Bakke* and other affirmative action decrees were decided in a
time when leaders in the White House, the Congress, and most
other places saw merit in healing the wounds of slavery and brutal Jim Crow — even by giving African Americans opportunities
that might rankle whites who would see some of their lifelong
special privileges vanish. That was a time when a Republican
"conservative" chief justice, Warren Burger, would write in
*Swann v. Mecklenberg,* a North Carolina school desegregation
case:

> All things being equal, with no history of discrimination, it
> might well be desirable to [engage in solely race-neutral employ-
> ment policies]. But all things are not equal in a system that has
> been deliberately constructed and maintained to enforce racial
> [discrimination]. The remedy for such [discrimination] may be
> administratively awkward, inconvenient, and even bizarre in
> some situations and may impose burdens on some; but all the
> awkwardness and inconvenience cannot be avoided in the in-
> terim period when remedial adjustments are being made to elim-
> inate [our racially-sullied past].

But lawyers who didn't give a damn what Burger or Blackmun had said insisted in 1990 that Maryland was violating the
constitutional rights of a Latino student, Daniel J. Podberesky,
when it refused to give him a Benjamin Banneker scholarship.

In May 1995 there were 139 Banneker scholars on the College
Park campus, making up only 5 percent of total black enrollment. But the Banneker students were almost invariably campus leaders, because in order to get those prestigious grants they
had to write essays about race, civil leadership, and other issues
that would make it clear to other black — and white — students everywhere that the Banneker program was drawing in
students of class and of nation-leading potential.

It was clear to me, and presumably to all fair-minded people,
that the Banneker program was not depriving others, of what-

ever race, of anything. In the pursuit of racial harmony, the university had created a $700,000 program to send 460 white students to four historically black colleges, and allocated some $2.3 million to allow 969 black students to study on seven predominantly white campuses.

Furthermore, of the 20,799 nonblack students enrolled in May 1995, 11,489 received financial aid; and of the 2,925 black students, 2,743 were given financial assistance. To talk about "reverse discrimination" at the University of Maryland was an absurdity. That is, until Podberesky and his lawyers decided he wanted one of the Banneker scholarships. Not one of the many other scholarships available to him, but a Banneker! Podberesky thus put in peril a university effort to walk away from a long, shameful history of cruel and sometimes outrageously laughable racism.

U.S. district judge J. Frederick Motz first heard the case, observing that "few issues are more philosophically divisive than the question of affirmative action. It strikes at our very souls as individuals and as a nation. It lays bare the conflict between our ideals and our history."

Judge Motz upheld the constitutionality of the Banneker program. Maryland, Virginia, and other once-racist schools continued their programs to do justice by setting aside scholarships for blacks. Podberesky's lawyers appealed to the Fourth U.S. Circuit Court of Appeals in Richmond, Virginia. On October 27, 1994, three judges of that court stunned the academic community by ruling that the Banneker program was unconstitutional because it was not "tailored narrowly enough" — that is, limited as to who could benefit — to merely make up for previous discrimination at Maryland.

That ruling produced the rare spectacle of white educators who had admitted to perpetrating egregious injustices upon black students for decades shouting angrily that the courts were preventing them from doing what was morally right.

"This court decision reflects an unfortunate mood in this country," said William E. Kirwan, president of the College Park campus. "Rather than a mood that brings us together, we seem to be splitting apart."

"Brit" Kirwan, a white man who is a dogged fighter for racial justice, told the university's lawyers to appeal to the U.S.

Supreme Court. Thus the mostly conservative members of the country's high tribunal had to bicker through much of 1995 over a ruling that they all knew could bring on a measure of lasting peace or a terrible amount of urban violence.

On May 22, 1995, just forty-one years and five days after the anniversary of *Brown v. Board of Education,* the Supreme Court dominated by Justices William Rehnquist, Clarence Thomas, and Antonin Scalia made a nondecision of letting stand the Fourth Circuit view that constituted a dagger in the hearts of all who believed that no sane court could find the Banneker program an affront to the U.S. Constitution. But the high tribunal caused the *Baltimore Sun* to write: "Swiftly and with no sign of dissent, the Supreme Court scuttled yesterday the University of Maryland's 17-year-old program giving top-flight blacks special scholarships to enroll on the College Park campus."

"A disservice to students of all races everywhere," *USA Today* said, adding prophetically: "Disturbing side effects are inevitable. Nervous college officials will become more cautious about scholarships helping minorities, wondering if they'll be next to be sued. Those who oppose race-based aid will be emboldened to launch new challenges based on the Maryland result — a head-in-the-sand approach."

From time to time I see a column so brilliant in concept, or so courageous in content, that I say to myself, "I wish I had written that." On May 30 I saw such a column written by Garry Wills, debunking the notion that if the Supreme Court hadn't thrown up a monstrous roadblock to affirmative action, blacks would take over American universities. Wills said:

"There's only one group you can discriminate against now — white males." That has become a regular statement on campuses.

Some who feel victimized talk about being crowded out by women or Asians, but their special animus is reserved for blacks. According to a 1992 Martilla and Kiley survey, 20 percent of American whites claim to have been penalized for not being black, and 43 percent are certain that others have been penalized. "They're taking over" is another thing one hears.

This is a miraculous takeover. About 2 percent of the nation — young black males eligible for school or jobs — has supposedly cowed the majority culture, changed school curricula, distorted the electoral system and shoved whites aside on the job market. For 2 percent to do this to 20 percent means that all of these superblacks are holding 10 jobs previously held by whites.

No wonder whites fear the superblack — him, since female blacks play little role in this imagery.

This historical miracle is not much adverted to because most Americans are unaware how small a minority is bringing them to their knees.

The entire black population is only 12.5 percent of the U.S. population. Yet one-half of the whites (55 percent) think blacks make up from 25 percent to 51 percent of their fellow Americans — two to four times their actual number.

Twelve percent of whites — roughly the size of the entire black population — believe that blacks are a majority of the American population. Obviously blacks occupy a huge amount of psychic space, no matter what their actual numbers are.

Black males as a whole make up only 6 percent of the population. Discounting those who are underage or over working age, those who are in the military, in prison, in gangs or unemployed, those available for college or starting jobs come to 2 percent at the most. Do we really want to exclude them from the discipline of an education or a job?

Apparently we do, according to those who say "they have been given enough breaks." The learned liberal Christopher Jencks, the John D. MacArthur Professor of Sociology at Northwestern University, says that blacks who have been admitted to college perform below whites, prompting whites to racist conclusions and undermining black self-esteem.

By this reading, white racism will be diminished if not cured, and black self-esteem will be advanced, if blacks are just kept out of school. This is a seductively easy way to fight racism.

It is not only white students who feel picked on. Employers complain that they are being forced to hire unqualified or less qualified black workers — even though black employment has not increased during the period of affirmative action.

The noted black economist Thomas Sowell used this fact to argue that affirmative action does not work. Whatever one thinks of his argument, it certainly weakens the claim that blacks are "taking over."

Some professors feel that blacks have undermined the education they are incapable of receiving, substituting "Afrocentric" curriculum they can absorb. The political scientist Abigail Thernstrom — whose work was cited by Justice Sandra Day O'Connor in the decision that struck down a black congressional district created in North Carolina — believes that efforts at getting blacks into political office have led to the subversion of the Constitution. She claims that the Voting Rights Act of 1965 violated the constitutional provision that states should regulate their own elections. Others complain that blacks have imposed their culture on our popular media, making TV shows too "politically correct."

All in all, if blacks could really do what people are claiming, they would be superhuman, and we should yield to them as our natural leaders.

The federal courts had surrendered to racist mob psychology as cravenly as any law officer ever did in the Reconstruction South under pressure from a lynch mob. Suddenly, mass bigotry was more dominant in the so-called halls of justice in 1995 than it had been in 1955.

So what did the politicians and closet hatemongers do to parry cries of "shame" when they snatched financial aid from the Banneker kids? They told us that they would have supported these youngsters happily if they had been poor. They wanted to make scholarships and other educational grants a new "poverty" program, even as they ridiculed and tried to destroy the old poverty programs.

The *New York Times* of June 17, 1995, carried an Associated Press article headlined "Affirmative Action Should Focus on Poor People, Gingrich Says."

Speaking to a group of blacks, mostly journalists, the House Speaker had said that Republicans were interested in making "preference programs work for the poor," but there was a growing Republican consensus against "helping people solely because of their race or sex." He added that "the trouble with affirmative action" was that it was "backward-looking, grievance-looking" and misled people so "they wind up spending their lives waiting for the lawsuit, instead of spending their lives seeking opportunity."

Probably no one in that audience recognized the glib nonsense, the dismaying falsity, of Gingrich's words faster than Wade Henderson, head of the Washington bureau of the NAACP, whose lawsuits lay behind almost every advance of blacks, other minorities, and women in America over the last eight decades. Henderson bristled when Gingrich said the black poor needed "to learn new habits;" he later told the Speaker that it was not the victims, but the perpetuators of bigotry, who had to learn new habits.

"Our Contract with America is the United States Constitution," Henderson said to Gingrich. "We expect the nation to live up to its commitment to all its citizens."

Few things infuriate me more than the "only help the poor" argument. Restrict scholarships to the poor, however incompetent, and when poor blacks flunk or fail in other ways, the Gingriches can say, "I told you *they* weren't ready."

I also know that when white people and corporation and government officials say to a youngster, "I can get you into college if you are black and needy, but I can't help you if you're just black, smart, and dedicated," black ambition, pride, and self-esteem are destroyed.

I've heard that line from officials at Harvard, Swarthmore, and other Ivy League and "highbrow" universities and colleges since 1987, when I established my scholarship program, Project Excellence. Since the days of *Bakke*, it was frighteningly obvious that the nation's campuses were becoming premier battlegrounds when any issue of race arose.

You can get a scholarship for almost anything but being a black victim of three hundred years of American racism, and nobody will sue you or the scholarship giver.

Cases involving college admissions and scholarships have aroused great emotions. Some astute observers feel that passions over the dwindling supply of good jobs, and over even the "worst" jobs, as in the nation's police and fire departments, produced the greatest threats to national tranquillity and unity. Few people are aware of the depth of hostility that cases involving hiring, firing, and promotions in these departments have provoked within the nation's courts. In late 1994 a decision came out of the Sixth U.S. Circuit Court of Appeals, seated in Cincinnati, that embodied all the legal arguments that matter, plus all the personal anger that sets black judge against white judge.

This case (*Aiken et al. v. City of Memphis*), in simple terms, involved a white policeman, Russell Aiken, and other white policemen and firemen who claimed that affirmative action consent decrees entered into by Memphis officials (all of them white) subjected them to reverse discrimination, denying them their constitutionally guaranteed equal protection of the laws.

Note that a "consent decree" means that all parties involved have agreed to the facts — in this case, that blacks in Memphis had been discriminated against egregiously — and on a remedy for that discrimination, and the judge had ordered the remedy put into effect.

The genesis of this case was a lawsuit filed by the U.S. Department of Justice against the city of Memphis in 1974 accusing the long–Jim Crow city of race and gender discrimination in hiring and promoting city employees.

Memphis officials denied the charges of deliberate discrimination filed by a black man, Freddie Eason, but admitted that "certain past practices" of the city might have created "an inference" of unlawful discrimination. So the city entered into a consent decree "to insure that blacks and women are not placed at a disadvantage by the hiring, promotion and transfer policies of the City, and that any disadvantage to blacks and women which may have resulted from past discrimination is remedied so that equal employment opportunities will be provided to all."

In this and subsequent "consent" decrees the city agreed that the long-term goal was to have the percentage of black and female employees approximate "their respective proportions in the civilian labor force" of Shelby County, of which Memphis is the dominant community. All the decrees cautioned that they should not "be construed in such a way to require the promotion [of] the unqualified or the promotion of the less-qualified over the more qualified as determined by standards shown to be valid and non-discriminatory."

During 1988 and 1989 some white policemen, Aiken among them, were denied promotions to sergeant while promotions went to black patrol officers who the whites claimed ranked below them based on the old criteria. Aiken and other whites sued, complaining that their rights under the Equal Protection Clause of the Constitution had been violated. The U.S. district court held that, in the face of the consent decree, their complaint was without merit. Hence the Aiken appeal to the full Sixth Circuit.

On October 6, 1994, the rancorously divided appeals court overruled, 11 to 4, the district court for Western Tennessee. Well, sort of "overruled," because the opinion by Judge Ralph Guy was really a strained search for some reason to declare that the Memphis remedies for past discriminations were not "narrowly tailored." Guy spent a lot of time writing about the Tennessee requirements that policemen and firemen be high school graduates, free of convictions on felony charges, and have "a good moral character."

The implication was that since blacks had lower levels of education, more troubles with the law, and more evidence of bad moral character, the percentage of "truly qualified" blacks in Shelby County would be reduced greatly. Thus the courts might find it legally justifiable that blacks got far fewer jobs than their sheer numbers might suggest were due them.

In remanding the cases to the district court, Guy wrote that "the [lower] court should consider the City's failure to utilize or even develop validated procedures for promotions in the police and fire departments. Additionally, the court should ascertain as best it can the racial makeup of the qualified labor pool for the positions at issue, so that it can determine whether the decrees' hiring and promotion goals have caused black representation in the relevant higher ranks to be greater than that representation would have been if no discrimination ever occurred."

In plain words, the district court was supposed to decide whether black ignorance, criminality, and immorality — not discrimination — was the actual reason for denying jobs and promotions to blacks.

Here was an explosive suggestion. Yet, apparently Guy had not articulated it strongly enough to suit chief judge Gilbert Merritt of Nashville, who for a few days had been on President Clinton's "short list" for appointment as a U.S. Supreme Court justice. In a concurring opinion, he wrote:

"The 1990 census shows that 85% of whites in Shelby County graduated from high school. Only 60% of blacks over 24 years of age are high school graduates and only 68% of blacks between 18 and 24 are high school graduates. Thus there is a substantial difference in the general labor pool and the qualified labor pool for fire and police officers. If the consent decree remains in effect, this difference must be either taken into account in hiring and promotion or a valid reason must be given for discarding it."

This infuriated the judges on the court who knew that for generations, Shelby County had been as Jim Crow, as racially repressive in education policies, as any county in neighboring Mississippi. They saw Merritt suggesting that blacks, who were less likely to graduate from high school because of the legacies of slavery and cruel Shelby County bigotry, should now accept as their due a lower percentage of the good jobs available in Shelby County.

But Merritt would go further and argue that because of population and political changes in Memphis, the consent decrees might have become a threat to white people. He wrote:

The general population and the voting population of the city of Memphis is now predominantly black and African-Americans hold the levers of governmental power. The Mayor, the police chief and the majority of high level administrative officials of the city are black. Accordingly, there is a substantially greater risk that the continued use of racial hiring goals which greatly exceed the qualified labor pool in question will discriminate against whites. That is what the plaintiffs claim. We may not assume in such a situation that the required employment ratio is benign. History and common sense tell us that it is possible for blacks to discriminate against whites as well as vice versa. The court has an obligation to ensure that the decree is not being used to prefer the majority race in the city, whether black or white.

Careful and intensive scrutiny should be required in communities where it is claimed that the race which controls the governmental machinery is placing the minority race at a clear disadvantage in hiring and promotion. It may well be that a trial will show that racially based hiring under the consent decree should now be terminated. The Equal Protection Clause does not allow the majority race in a city to use its governmental power to

prefer its race over the minority race except in the most unusual
and compelling circumstances. To hold otherwise would be to re-
institute racial discrimination, the constitutional wrong that the
parties and the court below were seeking to remedy when the decree was originally entered.

Circuit judge Nathaniel R. Jones, the former chief counsel of
the National Association for the Advancement of Colored People
(NAACP), wrote a dissent joined in by another distinguished
black jurist, Damon J. Keith of Detroit, and two white judges.
Jones lashed into what he called "the benighted concerns" of
Judge Merritt, especially his fear "that the remedial plans will
be abused because Memphis is now predominantly black."
Jones then dealt with a fact that fuels so much hopelessness
and rage even in the loftiest levels of black America: nothing is
ever fully won for blacks or other minorities. Some white males
are always trying to take gains back, either with a gun or with a
gavel. Jones concluded:

> We write at considerable length, because today the majority in-
> validates Memphis's laudable attempt at racial healing and erad-
> ication of the present day effects of racial discrimination. In so
> holding, the majority takes yet another premature step toward
> the illusory concept of a color-blind Constitution. This repre-
> sents a repudiation of the good faith that attended the unifying
> purpose of the consent decree. The undeniable fact is that this
> nation has yet to fully confront its racist history. Until this pre-
> liminary hurdle is surmounted, the rejection of race-conscious
> remedies, under the guise of promoting color-blind justice, sim-
> ply maintains a status quo premised upon the subordination of
> minorities.
>
> The majority today opts to sidestep the lingering and indis-
> putable vestiges of past discrimination by reversing one city's
> commendable effort at healing, as it struggles to come to terms
> with the sins of its past. I concede that for many persons dealing
> with racial injustice and remedies is painful. The easier course is
> to marginalize the issue or pretend that color blindness forbids us
> from directly confronting the problem. This ill serves our nation,
> and is in contravention of sound remedial principles and prece-
> dent.

The depth of the racial divide in Memphis and on this court was manifest, but not in the brutal dimensions that were illustrated in the raw dissent of Judge Keith, an NAACP Spingarn Medalist and one of the most honored, respected black men in the land. "I write separately," he said, "to address the unfortunate inaccuracies and misconceptions articulated within Chief Judge Merritt's separate concurrence.

There is no support for the assumption that Blacks in positions of power will discriminate against whites as their white predecessors discriminated against Blacks. It saddens me deeply to read this political button-pushing in what should be a legal opinion.

Although the population of Memphis has become "majority" African-American within the past ten years, this fact — largely a result, I assume, of white flight — does not erase the past discrimination within the city and within the fire and police departments. The consent decree was enacted to remedy this past discrimination in an attempt to put African-American officers on a realistic promotional track. Where departments historically refused to hire African-Americans until forced by court order, and where promotional requirements included a seniority factor, no realistic hiring or promotional opportunities for African-Americans exist without this remedy.

The fact that a minority race — I assume all will concede that African-Americans are still a minority race in America — assumes a numerical "majority" within a city's limits changes nothing. The history of the discrimination against African-Americans and denials of opportunities to African-Americans within the City of Memphis ensures the "minority" white race will never be at a disadvantage there. Certainly the "minority" white population will never experience the legally segregated and underfunded education of their children, the denial of access to housing in "majority" neighborhoods, the indignity of having to use the "minority" only water fountain at a department store or the double indignity of "minority" employees having to use the back door of the Peabody Hotel in order to serve "majority" patrons.

All the affirmative action programs we could possibly dream up can not change the color of one's skin. This fact renders the likelihood of legalized racial discrimination against a white "minority" preposterous. The appearance of this proposition in legal discourse, especially considering the history of Memphis, is insulting and saddening.

Here, delineated by a distinguished white judge and a black one, was the heart of a conflict. Neither of the men speaking so forcefully, even angrily, would ever do violence themselves, or even advocate it. But they personified the rise of racial hostility and the decline of civility in America. They showed us why what once was unspeakable conflict is now more than just possible.

## Black Jobs, White Jobs, No Jobs

Justifying minority set-asides of contracts that involve taxpayer dollars is the most difficult aspect of affirmative action to defend, because the public has been steeped in the mistaken assumption that in all circumstances the lowest bidder gets the government contract. There have in fact been many exceptions, based on what the courts still recognize as a "compelling government interest." Several Presidents — Kennedy, Johnson, Nixon, Carter, and even Reagan have seen a compelling national need to bring long-oppressed, cheated groups into the mainstream of the American economy.

The 1995 federal report to President Clinton said, "Apart from securing individual fairness, these programs reflect a need to build a stronger economy by tapping the entrepreneurial talents and drive of all segments of the population — that means affirmative efforts to open mainstream opportunities to underrepresented groups."

Set-asides were created, in part, because even though America had changed dramatically in population patterns and otherwise, the old white-male network still controlled all the contracting, and handed out subcontracts mostly to those who looked like their brothers.

The federal government tried giving rewards to contractors who would subcontract to minorities. Then it flatly mandated 5 percent set-asides.

It seemed patently unfair that millions of competent Americans, even in predominantly minority urban areas, could not share in the largess of federal contracting with their tax dollars, guaranteeing that urban areas would become and forever remain pockets of poverty, welfare, and crime.

On June 12, 1995, the Supreme Court issued a decision that intensified passions over affirmative action and lifted the level of fear and anger in black America.

The justices voted 5–4 that government set-asides of contracts and jobs for minorities — a virtual guarantee that blacks would get some $10 billion in federal contracts to do work that sustained black families all across the land — violated the Constitution. The issues in *Adarand Constructors v. Pena* at first seemed clear, and the court decision an obvious setback for minorities. In fact, on the day of this decision the Reverend Jesse Jackson told *USA Today:* "It is a setback. While we react to those wearing white sheets, it is those who wear black robes who take away our protection."

Specifically, the case involved a contract to build a guardrail on a federal highway in southern Colorado. A white-owned firm, Adarand, had submitted the lowest bid. But with a cash bonus at stake for giving a subcontract to a minority firm, the main contractor, Mountain Gravel & Construction Company, gave the guardrail contract to a Hispanic-owned firm, Gonzales Construction Company. Adarand sued.

It is noteworthy that the white justices' opinions were split 4–4, with Reagan-Bush appointees William Rehnquist, Antonin Scalia, Anthony Kennedy, and Sandra Day O'Connor opposing the set-asides, and John Paul Stevens, Stephen Breyer, Ruth Bader Ginsburg, and David Souter favoring them. So the lone black member of the court, Clarence Thomas, would break the tie and tilt in myriad ways the national conflict over affirmative action.

Thomas not only condemned the specific set-aside in Colorado, but seized the occasion to rail against affirmative action in general. He wrote:

> That these programs may have been motivated, in part, by good intentions cannot provide refuge from the principle that under our Constitution, the government may not make distinctions on the basis of race. As far as the Constitution is concerned, it is irrelevant whether a government's racial classifications are drawn

by those who wish to oppress a race or by those who have a sincere desire to help those thought to be disadvantaged.

These programs stamp minorities with a badge of inferiority and may cause them to develop dependencies or to adopt an attitude that they are "entitled" to preferences.

Black leaders, who had long before declared Thomas an outcast and in their views a quisling, a traitor, reacted angrily. Jesse Jackson said, "Clarence Thomas has betrayed the very social justice movement that made his opportunities possible. Without the laws we worked for, he couldn't have gone to Yale, couldn't have gone to the EEOC [Equal Employment Opportunity Commission], and he couldn't have gone to the Supreme Court."

The *Baltimore Sun* said, "The Supreme Court yesterday dealt what may be a fatal blow to affirmative action by the federal government." The *Wall Street Journal* said, "With or without yesterday's decision, it's clear that affirmative action as we know it is heading for a change." The *Washington Post* said, "It is still possible that this form of affirmative action can be justified. But, in fact, it will be very difficult to sustain."

True, affirmative action programs would be "difficult to sustain," but not just because of the high tribunal's decision. Other politicians from California to New York would soon help the country lurch toward a virtual civil war over jobs and promotions. An earlier *New York Times* headline read: [New York City mayor] GIULIANI IS HALTING OR SCALING BACK AFFIRMATIVE ACTION EFFORTS. In California, Governor Pete Wilson, in an ego spasm, envisioned himself as President of the United States, and for one humiliating period declared himself a candidate who would win because of his opposition to affirmative action.

Few things were rarer in America than a GOP presidential candidate who would publicly support affirmative action. Republican presidential candidate Bob Dole summed up the conventional screams of "angry white males" when he introduced the so-called Equal Opportunity Act of 1996, a proposed law to wipe out all "preferences" based on race. Dole said:

For too many of our citizens, our country is no longer the land of opportunity, but a pie chart where jobs and other benefits are often awarded not because of hard work or merit but because of someone's biology.

Now I have an admission to make. While I have questioned and opposed group preferences in the past, I have also supported them. That's my record, and I am not hiding from it.

But many of us who supported these policies never imagined that preferences would become a seemingly permanent fixture in our society.

In fact, there weren't many Democrats who advocated programs of deliberate, out-reach racial fairness. Evidence was piling up that President Clinton was about to fall out of the camp of affirmative action supporters — if at heart he ever was in it.

Mr. Clinton had long been an enigma on the issue of race, especially when the stakes became high, or a high-profile job was involved. Black Americans would never forget how he left a brilliant black woman, Lani Guinier, twisting and dying in the political winds of Washington, when some senators opposed her confirmation as head of the Civil Rights Division of the Justice Department. I personally had said on TV that Mr. Clinton seemed to be a "yellowbelly," an Arkansas term for a male who lacked a strong backbone.

As is almost always the case where a leader is not dominating, Clinton's aides engaged in wars to tilt every major decision or policy dispute their way. In early and mid-1995 the newspapers were full of leaks about what President Clinton would do about federal policies that supported affirmative action in education, scholarships, federal and private hiring and promotions, and particularly contract set-asides. In March 1995, the *Washington Post* carried a story headed, CLINTON AIDE URGES SHIFT ON AFFIRMATIVE ACTION and claiming that Stanley Greenberg, the pollster for Mr. Clinton and the Democratic party, advocated an anti–affirmative action stance in order not "to continue losing male voters." Eleven days later the *Washington Times* declared, CLINTON AIDES BACK AFFIRMATIVE ACTION.

In April 1995, front pages carried stories suggesting, PRESIDENT MAY APPOINT PANEL TO STUDY PREFERENCE PROGRAMS; CLINTON TO ADDRESS "SET ASIDES." The President himself inspired stories that he would support affirmative action in concept, but responded to the national clamor by declaring certain kinds of affirmative action "unfair." He expressed a certain unspecified understanding of the emotions of "angry white men."

Many people, I included, were waging a pretty hot war for President Clinton's mind. I wrote in the *Chicago Sun-Times*:

Before President Clinton turns "scaredy cat" and abandons federal and other affirmative action programs, I hope he will reject the myths and learn some facts about what affirmative action does, and does not do.

The President obviously has been "spooked" by cries that "angry white men" have been cheated, and that he must pacify them before the 1996 campaign for reelection begins. . . .

Does this President, frightened by rhetoric by Republicans such as Sen. Phil Gramm of Texas, want to wipe out a set-aside program that makes "the American dream" come true?

If we ever are to achieve economic justice where welfare is replaced by work, the federal government *must* use set-asides and other methods to give the long-cheated "a piece of the action." Mr. Clinton will understand this if he notes that the Supreme Court decision in *Croson v. Richmond* sent minority contracting plummeting from [38.5 percent to 2.2 percent] of the business. So many blacks who were becoming stable, middle-class citizens were pushed back into dependency and despair because with no pressure from federal and state governments, or the courts, white contractors simply refuse to subcontract with minority companies.

I know that most white males realize that they still control almost everything, and that allowing a relative handful of blacks, Hispanics or even females to get "a piece of the action," as Mr. Nixon put it, is no threat to them.

We have armies of white male failures in America who feel compelled to blame their lack of achievement on blacks, or women, or someone else who got opportunities the whites thought belonged to them simply by virtue of their "race." They push the pitiable cry that in a "color-blind" America they would be at the pinnacle. What self-delusion!

I don't believe that President Clinton, however embattled, is going to side with, or give comfort to, these "angry white men" who are pumping deadly poison into the social bloodstream of America.

I was informed privately that President Clinton was stung by the criticism of people like me. I was told to "be alert" when, on July 19, he would report to the nation on the results of his aide Christopher Edley's full review of federal affirmative action programs. He was to speak from the rotunda of the National Archives, giving probably the most important civil rights address by any American since President Johnson's appeal for passage of the Voting Rights Act before a joint session of Congress.

*USA Today* on July 18 advised Mr. Clinton, in a lead editorial, that it was time for him to tell skeptical Americans that affirmative action represented "a high principle the nation cannot afford to abandon."

Then Mr. Clinton learned the strength of support by not just black leaders, but white corporation heads, the educational community, and especially the American Bar Association (ABA) for affirmative action programs.

The ABA said:

The current debate regarding affirmative action is based in part upon the misperception that discrimination no longer exists, or that even if it does, simple legal prohibitions against discrimination will suffice. The perception, while perhaps understandable, is inaccurate. Notwithstanding the substantial gains made by women and people of color to date, largely through enforcement of the civil rights laws and use of programs such as those described above, discrimination remains a stark reality in most spheres of American life.

Continued support for affirmative action principles is imperative. Not only the direct beneficiaries, but governments, institutions, communities, and the private sector all have benefited from affirmative action programs. Conversely, abandoning affirmative action principles would jeopardize progress made to date, and certainly would restrict future gains, by women and people of color, their families, and the nation in all areas affected by affirmative action programs. More fundamentally, however, abandoning affirmative action will not move us toward our desired goal of a color-blind and gender-neutral society — and may well divide us even more into a society of "haves" and "have nots." The Association must make clear its unequivocal support for a

policy that embodies this nation's promise of equal opportunity
for all.

The Labor Department told the President that all the talk
about "reverse discrimination" was hokum — that in looking at
more than three thousand discrimination-case opinions in federal district courts from 1990 to 1994, there had been fewer than
one hundred cases in which "reverse" bias against whites was at
issue.

Of those "reverse" discrimination claims found, Rutgers law
professor Alfred W. Blumrosen said that many were brought by
persons "found by the courts to be less qualified for the job than
the chosen female or minority applicant." Anyone who looked at
the anti–affirmative action spasm in California could see that
some of its initiators were ne'er-do-wells and social misfits who
sought glory in blaming some minority, or female, for a lifetime
of failures.

The President said a lot more than that. Millions of less-than-
privileged Americans applauded when he said:

> The purpose of affirmative action is to give our nation a way to
> finally address the systemic exclusion of individuals of talent on
> the basis of their gender or race from opportunities to develop,
> perform, achieve and contribute. Affirmative action is an effort
> to develop a systematic approach to open the doors of education,
> employment and business development opportunities to quali-
> fied individuals who happen to be members of groups that have
> experienced longstanding and persistent discrimination.
>
> Let me say that affirmative action has also done more than
> just open the doors of opportunity to individual Americans.
> Most economists who study it agree that affirmative action has
> also been an important part of closing gaps in economic oppor-
> tunity in our society, thereby strengthening the entire economy.
>
> I also want to emphasize that the Adarand decision did not
> dismantle affirmative action and did not dismantle set-asides. In
> fact, while setting stricter standards to mandate reform of affir-
> mative action, it actually reaffirmed the need for affirmative ac-
> tion and reaffirmed the continuing existence of systematic
> discrimination in the United States.
>
> What the Supreme Court ordered the federal government to

do was to meet the same more rigorous standard for affirmative action programs that state and local governments were ordered to meet several years ago. And the best set-aside programs under that standard have been challenged and have survived.

Let me be clear: Affirmative action has been good for America.

Affirmative action has not always been perfect, and affirmative action should not go on forever. It should be changed now to take care of those things that are wrong, and it should be retired when its job is done. I am resolved that that day will come. But the evidence suggests, indeed, screams that that day has not come.

With all the conviction I could muster, I wrote:

In an eloquent and courageous speech to America about affirmative action Wednesday, President Clinton issued one of the greatest statements ever about race in America.

In his gutsy truth-telling about bigotry in America, and his firm assertion that "affirmative action has been good for America," this son of once-Jim Crow Arkansas gave an address that ranks with Lincoln's Emancipation Proclamation, Martin Luther King's 1963 "I have a dream" address, and President Lyndon Johnson's 1965 commencement speech at Howard University.

Mr. Clinton's ringing defense of government and private programs to give equal opportunity to all Americans was especially remarkable because he delivered it in an atmosphere of intense racial demagoguery, especially by the Republicans who seek to oust him from the presidency in 1996.

That address was of enduring greatness because of what Mr. Clinton refused to do:

- He would not accept strident arguments that affirmative action has been a blight on the nation, or justifies the assaults of "angry white men." In fact, he asserted that politicians — such as Gov. Pete Wilson of California and Sen. Bob Dole of Kansas — are shamefully trying to make many Americans believe that affirmative action is the cause of their economic distress.

Noting many deep problems, the President said, "Affirmative action didn't cause them and won't cure them, and wiping out affirmative action won't cure them."

- He did not accept the pretenses that racial discrimination in the job market, in education, in government contracting, or in the granting of business and housing loans has been erased to the point that affirmative action programs are no longer needed. In eloquent ways, some personal, Mr. Clinton acknowledged the painful and shameful truth that racism still permeates all aspects of American life.

I got a copy of that Clinton address with a handwritten note from the President saying, "To Carl Rowan, with appreciation and respect . . . Bill Clinton." Later I got a note from him suggesting that he really had figured out where justice lay, and would not waver in the future.

For a couple of days I felt a little guilty, concerned that I might have been co-opted by a politician whom I could not afford to have sway me by giving one speech, or sending me notes on his speech, or other massages of my ego. Then, reading the full text of Mr. Clinton's speech again, I sensed that its content justified my praise and was a rebuke to those who believed that he had sold out to the racists of America.

But how much could even a President with renewed religion influence a society that was entranced by notions of racial superiority?

I want to be specific and clear here in stating that I do not lump all white Americans together as producers and protectors of a new form of slavery. Just as white Americans were divided at the time of the war between the states, brothers versus brothers, so whites are divided today. The anti–affirmative action clamor today, which threatens tragic violence, is led mostly by conscienceless politicians, publicity-seeking bigots, whites with individual gripes who find it easy to make trouble in a litigious society, and a handful of blacks who harbor doubts about their own intellectual merits and have found that these days the route to fame and wealth is to drift along with the conservative tide.

Many white business leaders are firmly committed, financially, intellectually, and morally to the concept of affirmative action. These leaders know that it gives them a leg up on the competition when they tap new pools of talent.

Most team owners know that the game of baseball, for one, became better, and infinitely more profitable, when black Americans and Latinos were allowed to become part of the talent pool. And when millions of nonwhites were motivated to spend their money at a baseball game.

Sane Americans of all races may harbor memories of a bigot, Ty Cobb, but they don't yearn for an era of baseball when there could be no Jackie Robinson, Willie Mays, Henry Aaron, Roberto Clemente, or Frank Robinson.

Race-baiting politicians will cheer black sports heroes, wangle to get their pictures taken with them, exploit them in any way imaginable, but they will not stop playing the powder-keg political game of telling their constituents that there is something anti-white about leveling the playing field in all other areas of American life.

Few Americans go beyond the anecdotes to see what is being said by the government leaders and the corporate CEOs and personnel officers who live and die by worker productivity and the bottom line of profits.

In 1996 the private nonpartisan Citizens' Commission on Civil Rights reported on the views of corporate leaders, and on the impact of affirmative action programs within such great corporations as General Motors, Du Pont, Mobil, Corning, Hughes Electronics, Motorola, Kaiser Foundation Health Plan, Philip Morris, Baltimore Gas & Electric, and Hoechst Celanese.

This report gives, in the words of corporate executives, the answers to all the critical questions about affirmative action within the corporate workplace. For example:

The commission found that huge American corporations embraced the concept of affirmative action. It quotes Edgar Woolard, Jr., the chairman of Du Pont, writing in *Du Pont World* in July/August 1995:

> While the number of senior management positions has shrunk by more than 40% since 1985, the number of women in these positions increased 10 times to about 9% of the company's population at these levels. Over the same period, the number of minorities in senior management positions increased 4 times to about 7% of the population at these levels.

General Motors reported in 1994:

In 1993, 21% of the company's U.S. employment was minority, including 16% of GM's white-collar and 23% of its blue-collar workers. Women represented 19% of all workers, 28% of white-collar workers, and 17% of blue-collar workers. The company reports that its workforce has proportionately more blacks (17%) than the U.S. workforce overall, and is the largest private employer of blacks in the U.S., accounting for nearly 2% of all black wages and salaries in the country.

Corning CEO Jamie Houghton said in a New York address:

Since 1987, the company has doubled its number of women and black employees. 29% of managers are women, up from 17%. Black employees hold 8% of management jobs, up from 5%.

Motorola said:

So we started the effort in '89, September of '89, when we had two women vice presidents and six people of color who carried that mantle of Vice President. Today we have 33 women vice presidents and 40 people of color.

Philip Morris reported:

In 1995, in its domestic operations, people of color accounted for over one of every four employees (or 26%) and women accounted for over one of every three employees (or 34%). Women accounted for 30% of professional/managerial employees and people of color accounted for 17%. Women accounted for 15% of vice presidents and people of color accounted for 10%.

Aside from the corporations mentioned in this survey, I can speak personally about the Gannett Company, the nation's largest media company. As a member of its board, I watched proudly as its chairman, John J. Curley, said:

We are committed to building a Company whose people reflect the true diversity of America.

Gannett employees are hired, promoted and rewarded on the basis of talent, performance and dedication.

A company in the information business cannot continue to be successful if it ignores any segment of its audience. . . .

Workplace diversity is strength and it makes sense. It broadens our reach and it puts our Company in a strong position for the competitive years ahead.

For Gannett, equal employment is not just the right thing to do — it is the smart thing to do if we are to be as successful in the future as we have been in the past.

The corporations cited here are among the best managed, most profitable in America. Have they achieved this by cheating white males? Have the top executives of these companies embraced affirmative action under pressures from a federal government that has put the wooing of minorities and women above the national interest?

The issue of affirmative action is ripping America apart because most Americans don't know what it is, why it was begun, what its effects have been, or whether and why it is still needed. Craven politicians and the lemmings of the media have exposed Americans to myriad anti–affirmative action anecdotes (in *Adarand* the low white bidder on a highway project "loses to a Hispanic firm," or a black teacher in Piscataway, New Jersey, is chosen over an equally qualified white teacher because the school board wants a black presence on the faculty, or the University of Texas Law School gives a preference to black and Hispanic applicants over whites with higher LSAT scores).

We have had two major efforts to go beyond the anecdotes and gather empirical evidence about affirmative action in government, and in the business places of this nation. We have the July 19, 1995, report to President Clinton, and three reports by the Citizens' Commission on Civil Rights.

Several corporate leaders pointed out that affirmative action has raised stock values of their companies, bringing great new wealth to shareholders, foremost among them being white males. Du Pont's chairman Woolard said "affirmative action is not only good business, it is also part of being a good corporate citizen — working to the benefit of the companies themselves, all of their employees (including white males), and the nation as a whole."

The Hughes spokesman said, "[Overcoming the good old boy network] has served us well whether we're white or minority. . . . Affirmative action has opened doors all up and down the employment spectrum. . . . Because of affirmative action we have looked at it and you know what that has done? That has affected white males in a positive manner probably more so than it has affected minorities or women."

The statements of corporate executives about the job gains of minorities and women make it clear, by simple math, that the overweening dominance of white males in corporate America has been eroded. But every empirical study shows that the effects on white males have been marginal and not unfair. "We don't hire unqualified individuals," said David R. Barclay of Hughes Electronics. "It doesn't make business sense."

"No one has ever asked anyone in this organization to hire an unqualified person," said a Kaiser Permanente executive. "To be able to hire an unqualified workforce on the basis of some gender or racial preference . . . it just makes no sense. It flies in the face of sanity."

I know anecdotally, and the empirical evidence shows, that thousands of incredibly incompetent white males have held important posts simply because their Old White Boys' Club connections got them the job and then protected their tenure for years.

While serving as director of the U.S. Information Agency (which had thirteen thousand employees), as a senior State Department official, and as a director of Gannett, I have dealt with white males in high ranks who were incompetent bullies and frauds, pitifully inferior to many of the white and black women secretaries, and less qualified than many of the black males relegated to jobs as messengers. Yet the crony system sent many of the incompetent white males to crucial overseas posts, or top corporate jobs.

It is this truth, I am sure, that caused Chairman David M. Lawrence of the Kaiser Foundation Health Plan to write to President Clinton saying that "for us, Affirmative Action is both a basic moral imperative and a significant, dynamic and compelling element of our business strategy." And in turn, it is why Mr. Clinton said in July 1995 that "affirmative action has been good for America. . . . It is a moral imperative, a constitutional mandate, and a practical necessity."

The country got a stunning example of the need for affirmative action last spring from an unexpected source — Hollywood.

Only one black was nominated for an Academy Award and *People* magazine came out with a hard-hitting cover story entitled HOLLYWOOD BLACKOUT that detailed the dearth of African Americans in the film industry — from top to bottom, on and off camera — calling it "a national disgrace."

"Despite the widespread perception — fueled by the rise of big-draw talents like actors Denzel Washington and Whitney Houston or directors Spike Lee and John Singleton — that blacks are enjoying a boom in Hollywood, a shocking level of minority exclusion remains," said *People*.

For African Americans, the article noted, "breaking into Hollywood can be like climbing a mountain of marbles. In the union ranks, rampant nepotism and byzantine work rules mean it may take longer for a black aspirant to become a makeup artist than a heart surgeon. As for the higher strata, about the only black faces getting near Hollywood's executive suites are studio security."

After conducting an "exhaustive" four-month investigation, *People* reported that exact figures were hard to come by, but that "there was ample evidence that the film industry, for whatever reasons, continues to resist the inclusion of African-Americans, on screen and off."

Noting that blacks make up about 12 percent of the total U.S. population and 25 percent of movie audiences, *People* listed these figures on black employment and representation in Hollywood:

— Only one of the 166 Academy Award nominees was African American — and that was for live-action short-film direction. (She did not win.)

— Of the 5,043 members of the Academy of Motion Picture Arts and Sciences, who nominate and choose Oscar winners, only 3.9 percent — about one out of twenty-five — are black.

— Only 2.3 percent of the Directors Guild members and 2.6 percent of the Writers Guild are black. Blacks make up less than 2 percent of the union that includes set decorators and property masters.

And when it comes to the executive suite, insiders told *People* that the number of African Americans at the level of studio vice president or above can be counted on the fingers of one hand.

As the article noted, more is at stake in this exclusion of African Americans than Oscar statuettes. "Hollywood's creations are the mirror in which Americans see themselves — and the current racially skewed reflection is dangerously distorted," said *People.*

The insidious impact of such distortion was described by Emily Mann, artistic director of the McCarter Theater in Princeton, New Jersey, and author of *Having Our Say,* a play about two pioneering black professional women, Bessie and Sadie Delaney. "The consequence of exclusion by the film industry is cultural apartheid," Mann told *People.* "It's happening now — white America doesn't understand black America. A lot of racist images are made unconsciously, and whites just aren't aware they're doing it. With black writers and producers on the inside, they would be able to call them on it."

One outsider who tried to call the film industry on it was Jesse Jackson. After first threatening to picket the Academy Award ceremony itself at the L.A. Music Center, Jackson wound up leading about seventy-five pickets outside the ABC affiliate in Los Angeles (ABC televised the awards).

Jackson urged African Americans not to watch the awards. "It doesn't stand to reason that if you are forced to the back of the bus, you will go to the bus company's annual picnic and act like you're happy," he said. He also called for a protest at the box office, in order to get Hollywood to increase the number of films featuring blacks and to give blacks a wider range of roles, both in front of and behind the camera.

In the end, a lot of people saw once again — in a new and surprising setting — how terribly divisive the whole issue of job fairness is in America. I hope they realized that what mattered was not just how many African Americans were nominated for an Oscar, or how many were members of the nominating and voting Academy, but the fact that there had been few openings and not much training for blacks to get into jobs of writing, directing, and the like.

I now resort to anecdotal evidence to illustrate what the 8(a) program for disadvantaged minorities has meant. Richard Nixon, Commerce secretary Maurice Stans, and Arthur Fletcher began this program with the idea that you could never lift the level of life of people hobbled by slavery, bound down by generations of poverty, chained down by cruel bigotries, simply by throwing them welfare crumbs. You had to give them at least a chance to show what they could do with opportunities to produce, to build new wealth in America.

I know a black man in suburban Virginia who personifies what Nixon et al. had in mind. In the mid-1980s he started a little company dealing in computer technology and telecommunications. By 1988 it was floundering because big white-owned commercial companies would not believe that black people had anything to offer in this field.

Desperate, this black man turned to the government, got certified under the Nixon-Stans-Fletcher 8(a) plan, and won two federal set-asides. His company performed so magnificently that soon it was doing computer networking for the National Institutes of Health and other federal agencies and doing non-governmental work for our largest telephone companies.

The bottom line is that for eight years this little company has provided steady incomes ranging from $50,000 to $210,000 a year, for some sixty families. And half those families are white!

Now that is "building a stronger economy"!

Set-asides were building a stronger, majority-black Richmond, Virginia, until the Supreme Court outlawed that city's set-aside program in 1989 in *Croson v. Richmond*. The minority share of city contracting dollars plummeted from over 38.5 percent to only 2.2 percent.

After its 1995 review, the affirmative action panel reported to President Clinton that "these [set-aside] programs cause only a minor diminution in opportunity for nonminority firms. In that respect, current programs are balanced and equitable in the large."

Still, the attacks on set-aside programs grow in fury. Ironically, the people opposing set-asides are often the ones screaming for welfare reform, demanding "workfare," insisting that welfare recipients "get a job" even when there are no jobs for them to get.

This kind of Catch 22 drives peaceful people to blind rage . . . and warfare. That warfare is more imminent than most Americans realize.

# Chapter 5

# IQ and Race

Why are we Americans rushing to kill each other over race when none of us really knows what race is in this society?

I can understand Larry Wayne Shoemake of Jackson, Mississippi. He fired over a hundred rounds from two AK-47 assault rifles, a MAC-11 assault weapon, a 12-gauge shotgun, an AR-15 assault rifle and two handguns, all of which killed one black man and wounded ten other black people, before setting an abandoned restaurant afire and dying in the flames.

Shoemake was certifiably crazy with hatred. He had left behind neo-Nazi notes and placed a copy of Adolf Hitler's *Mein Kampf* alongside a copy of the Bible on a bed draped with a Nazi flag.

Shoemake was surely an exponent of the view that God created two classes of people: whites, who are good and born to rule, and all others, whom God relegated to be beasts of the field because they are "subhuman."

Yes, I can understand the murderous behavior of this crazy man. His philosophy was clear: the subhumans should be eliminated. What I cannot understand are the self-styled Christian and Jewish intellectuals and the unthreatened political leaders who are driving this society to a race war even when they cannot answer the question "What is race?" Are these celebrated columnists, talk-show hosts, and supposed statesmen really more enlightened than Shoemake, or the other whites who inspire race murders?

Those driving the divisive anti–affirmative action campaign denounce racial preferences as if they know what they mean by race.

What race am I, or my children? I used to be "a Negro," or "colored"; then I became "black" and am now, presumably, an African American. Somewhere in my slave plantation heritage there was an Irishman or Scotsman named Rowan, which is why I am brown, lighter skinned than many Jews, or "white people" of Louisiana, or Hispanics. Meaning that skin color does not reveal a lot.

My fair-skinned wife, Vivien, maiden name Murphy, has some Irishman, some Cherokee Indians, and someone of African heritage hanging from her family tree. What race is she? A dear late friend, Daryle Feldmeir, once answered that question this way: "What the hell difference does it make? If I say she's white you'll be upset because she's married to Carl Rowan, a supposed Negro. If I tell you she's a Negro, you'll be pacified. Either way, she's the same human being."

And what of three of my grandchildren, whose mother is a Jew, which makes them half Jewish and half whatever their father is, based on whatever I and my wife are. At the synagogue my grandchildren are Jewish, at their politically correct school they are "mixed race," at the Census Bureau they were born "black," as they are designated by the white man's laws in many states.

Now, what the hell are they if the Universities of Maryland or Texas offer them a scholarship? Recipients of "racial preference." Which "racial preference"?

This country always has been preoccupied by "race"; it has endured its greatest pains over race, and it is now about to face a suicidal war over race, that term of great passion but no clarity. A huge majority of the world's cultural anthropologists and at least half of physical anthropologists reject race as a meaningful biological category. They subscribe to the 1972 findings of the Harvard University population biologist who wrote that if you analyze seventeen genetic markers of all the populations of the world, you will find more differences within any one race than there are between any two races. In other words, there will be more genetic differences between me and another so-called black man than between me and the prime minister of Great Britain.

This nation is roiled by the tracts, pamphlets, and books of pseudoscientific whores who talk about "genes" and "Bell Curves" that make or prove one "race" of people superior and others inferior. There would be no war-inviting hassle over affirmative action but for the fact that America's Caucasians, from the brightest to the dumbest, keep swallowing the propaganda that they are at least fifteen IQ points more intelligent than African Americans. This even when they also don't know what "IQ" is, or how it can be applied to real-life decisions.

I have both laughed and cursed over the endless theses that white males deserve the best of everything because God endowed them with superior minds, characters, and other qualities. I laugh only when I recall how talk of racial inferiority and superiority has graduated from the crude and comical to elitist pseudoscientific pretenses.

When I was in Mississippi just before and after the 1954 Supreme Court decision outlawing racial segregation in public schools, the defenders of Jim Crow never talked about genes; "Negro blood" was the feared substance.

A circuit judge, Tom P. Brady, was warning white people against "race mixin'" by asserting that "one drop of Negro blood thickens the lips, flattens the nose, and puts out the lights of intellect."

Brady said that "whenever and wherever the white man has drunk the cup of black hemlock, whenever and wherever his blood has been infused with the blood of the Negro, the white man, his intellect, and his culture have died."

I recall asking others who claimed blacks were inherently inferior how they explained the achievements of Ralph Bunche, Marian Anderson, and Jesse Owens. "Well, they must have some white blood in 'em," was the frequent reply.

I was grimly amused by the contradictory assertions that one drop of "Negro blood" would destroy a white man, yet "some white blood" could lift an inferior black person to greatness.

These crazy "blood" theories were not limited to backwoods

bigots. The Reverend G. T. Gillespie, a leader in the Presbyterian church and president emeritus of Belhaven College, wrote an article in the early 1950s, "A Christian View on Segregation," in which he said that the child of an interracial marriage would be weaker than either parent. He said, "The intermingling of breeding stock results invariably in the production of 'scrubs' or mongrel types, and the downgrading of the whole herd."

Most Americans today would not think that such racist, contradictory, unscientific, even stupid views about "blood" could ever have controlled public policy. But they did. My home state, Tennessee, had a constitution forbidding "the intermarriage of white persons with negroes, mulattoes, or persons of mixed blood, descended from a negro to the third generation." The penalty for such miscegenation was up to five years in prison.

## Who Is "Passing"?

The wording of that old Tennessee law reminds us that in most of America, a person can have 87.5 percent "white blood," but society still considers and treats him as "black," and even as a pariah.

It is no secret that throughout the history of America, miscegenation has been commonplace beyond anything white people would admit. Slave masters made "consensual" love to, or raped, millions of African women. It was not exactly rare for the wives and daughters of slave masters to enjoy that forbidden fruit — a sampling of those allegedly "massive" black penises. Interracial miscegenation statutes have now been repealed or declared unconstitutional.

We have seen a remarkable "browning of America." Millions of "black" people have been "passing," living as whites, in this country for well over a century. So-called mulattoes and octoroons have married the most powerful "white" men in America and, their secret hidden, have become socialites. There cannot be 5 percent of African Americans who have 100 percent "African blood." Probably 95 percent of "white" Americans have some "Negroid blood."

So who the hell in America is black enough to be a target of the eugenicists, the racial purists, the Bell Curvers?

The authors of the book *The Bell Curve: Intelligence and Class Structure in American Life,* Charles Murray and the late Richard Herrnstein, would base all sorts of national policy actions on the supposed lower IQs of "black people." If educational, economic, and other public policies are to be based on the mumbo jumbo in *The Bell Curve,* a book which says, in effect, that it is hopeless to try to lift blacks up to the level of whites, how do we now decide who is doomed as "black"?

## The White Right-Wing Agenda

Americans are apparently ignorant of the fact that over history, all "social scientists" who have made a reputation, or a lot of money, proclaiming the inferiority of some race or group have had a nefarious political agenda.

I recently finished reading a marvelous book, *The Science and Politics of Racial Research,* written by William H. Tucker, associate professor of psychology at Rutgers University. This book, published by the University of Illinois Press, is as enlightening as *The Bell Curve* is dismaying. I believe that after reading Tucker's book, every American who is Irish, Jewish, black, Polish, Italian, Latino, or anything but a "Nordic Super Race" male will ask, "Why am I being suckered into Murray's venal agenda?"

I have seen during almost half a century as a journalist, and it is confirmed in Tucker's brilliant narrative, that the proponents of superrace or inferior-race theories shared an array of arrogant-to-insane agendas.

They all begin by purporting to establish "scientific proof" that some races are of superior intelligence, others of inferior intellect. Naturally, to alleviate their own mental and emotional insecurities, these "scientists" find that their own race is among the most intelligent.

Sexual insecurities seem to drive all the "superrace" theorists, because only the rarest of these "social scientists" has avoided relating IQ to the size of both male and female genitals, or to the alleged "animal passions" of women deemed inferior. Perhaps the only anatomical features getting as much attention as genitals have been the size of the skull and the size of the brain.

Take for example Samuel George Morton, the Philadelphia physician who made his mark with supposedly unimpeachable evidence of the black man's inherent inferiority. Morton had collected eight hundred skulls from around the world, made his strange measurements of their cranial capacity by filling them with pepper seeds, and concluded that a small cranial area means a small brain, which means a small amount of intelligence. Morton's 1839 book, *Crania Americana,* was once hailed by some as absolute proof of the mental inferiority of Africans.

After establishing which are the "inferior," or "undesirable" races, the next step has always been to make them appear to be a drag on and a threat to the dominant, or "superior," race. After the Civil War there was a flood of publications warning whites that Negroes were "outbreeding" white people. In 1883 a sociology professor named E. W. Gilliam wrote that blacks would "overwhelmingly preponderate" in the South by 1980. This produced a flood of cries for the deportation of blacks to Africa or someplace else. Then some white "experts" pointed out that blacks also were dying at a far higher rate than whites, thus blacks would never become dominant in numbers unless whites made the mistake of improving the public health and other conditions under which blacks lived.

But there were other areas in which whites might become contaminated by the near presence of blacks. There was always the danger of miscegenation, with white women being lured by the talk of what great lovers the "savages" with the huge penises could be.

The argument, generation after generation, was that the white man had to pass laws, lynch, and do whatever else was necessary to prevent miscegenation and intermarriage, not just because these things defiled white women, but also because they produced "mongrel" babies that surely would be of such low IQ as to lower the average level of intelligence in America.

Blacks were deemed a public health threat because they got tuberculosis at a higher rate than whites, and because of their proclivity for contracting gonorrhea, syphilis, then AIDS — well, all the diseases associated with promiscuity, a quality some "social scientists" said was a God-given quality of African Americans. Charles Murray would argue in his devious way that the tremendous, worrisome increase in the numbers of young white girls getting pregnant out of wedlock represented some behavioral weakness that they had "caught" from black girls.

Blacks were not by any means the only group cited as a threat to the well-being of the "super" Americans. An Oxford University professor, Edward A. Freeman, toured the United States in 1881 haranguing about the "threat" posed by Irish immigrants. He said "the best remedy for whatever is amiss in America would be if every Irishman would kill a negro and be hanged for it."

Every one of the discoverers of "proof" of inferior races has made central to his policy agenda the "protection of the racial purity" of the group deemed superior. Note that Henry H. Goddard, a renowned psychologist, was at the turn of the century the United States' greatest expert on "feeblemindedness." His agenda was to prevent the entry of "feebleminded" immigrants into the U.S., where they would contaminate the nation's blood with "bad plasma" and drive down the national IQ level. In 1911 he was assigned to Ellis Island to use his tests to screen out undesirables.

Goddard would boast that he wasn't opening the doors wide to any "huddled masses" — that he rejected as "feebleminded" 87 percent of the Russians, 83 percent of the Jews, 80 percent of the Hungarians, and 79 percent of the Italians who came before him.

Even as some advocates of superrace theories were warning of the need to get rid of, or stay away from, the low-IQ and "parasitic" peoples, others were citing alleged inherent inferiority as a justification for the exploitation and abuse of the unfavored peoples. Slavery couldn't be immoral; it was justifiable in the curse that God had put on black people, decreeing that they be the slave class. Not just plantation owners believed this. Aristotle, the great Greek philosopher, had proclaimed some two thousand years ago that "just as some are by nature free, so others are by nature slaves, and for these latter the condition of slavery is both just and beneficial."

Consider briefly just a few of the people who through the generations have pressed so zealously their arguments about race and IQ, and about the need to allow the weaker races to die, or else exterminate them.

Sir Francis Galton, a first cousin of Charles Darwin, had a most provocative agenda: a program that he labeled "Eugenics" under which he and his followers would raise "the present miserable standard of the human race." He wrote about "Hereditary Genius" and the selective breeding of human beings that would spread it, with proper attention paid to the intelligence gaps between "the highest Caucasian and the lowest savage."

Under Galton's "eugenics," only "the few best specimens" of an "inferior race" would be allowed to breed. It was Galton who suggested introducing "the Chinaman" into the struggle for Africa, saying, "The gain would be immense to the whole civilized world if [the Chinese] were to outbreed and finally displace the negro."

Hans F. K. Gunther, Erwin Baur, Eugen Fischer, and Fritz Lenz were the intellectual inspirations for a eugenics movement in Germany that led to brutal oppressions of Jews, including mass sterilizations and the Holocaust. While still in Landsbergam Lech prison, just beginning to write *Mein Kampf*, Adolf Hitler was reading Lenz, Fischer, Gunther, Baur, and other maniacal fomenters of the theory of Aryan supremacy, and of Germany's "Final Solution" to exterminate the Jews, whom they had for decades excoriated as "parasites."

If assimilation is unavoidable, as it is now in the twentieth century, create economic barriers for undesirables. Give the high-IQ rich an excuse to cease giving to charity, and politicians a reason for abolishing government programs for the needy, by telling them that low-IQ people can never be lifted by money, because nature sealed their fate when it made them dumb. Make white racists feel comfortable by telling them that denying jobs and scholarships to members of "inferior races" is not unlawful or immoral discrimination, but an intelligent recognition of the fact that the job or scholarship is better invested in someone white and thus presumed of superior ability to benefit from them.

In his *Origin of Species* and other works, Darwin inspired a group espousing "Social Darwinism" that believed, simply, that the fittest humans should survive while the "weaklings" were left to die. In *The Science and Politics of Racial Research* Tucker writes:

"As a consequence, the Social Darwinists opposed all governmental programs for charity, free meals, or other benefits for the undeserving inferior. Similar reasoning also justified opposition to the regulation of minimum wage and working hours, free public education, and all those other socialistic institutions, which, by improving the lots of the poor, would shield them from the just consequences of their own inferiority and pave the way for society's degeneration."

This generation is as vulnerable to these "superior race" rantings as were people of Darwin's days. Consider the fact that William Bradford Shockley, a Nobel Prize winner (for helping to invent the transistor) was surely one of the two most notable American purveyors of the thesis of black inferiority in history. He was the occupant of a chair in engineering at Stanford University. In the mid-1960s he gave a speech at a Nobel conference on "Genetics and the Future of Man" and spelled out a brutal eugenics program. Shockley's views were simply that the human race was deteriorating genetically, primarily because "inferior races" and poor people were producing offspring in greater numbers than superior white and rich people.

Shockley wanted the government to halt poverty programs that encouraged the inferior races to have babies. He wanted a larger income tax exemption for the children of the rich than those of the poor. He wanted the government to adopt penalties that would discourage "breeding" by the poor.

Shockley held that the intelligence gap suffered by Negroes was primarily of hereditary origin, and thus relatively "irremediable." William H. Tucker observes that "in Shockley's opinion, IQ was a measure not just of intelligence, but of overall human worth — for whites. Blacks he found to be an exception to this general relation between IQ and other 'high quality' traits; even when they were intelligent, their ability was unassociated with these other useful characteristics. For Shockley, this analysis provided a justification for the racial gap in earnings that still existed after controlling IQ. 'An IQ increment for a white,' he explained, 'pulls up with it other personality traits valuable for earning power to a greater extent than does an equal IQ increment for a Negro.'" Thus even when "intelligence" was ruled out as a factor, scientifically derived explanations could justify lower black wages, nicely eluding any taint of discrimination or prejudice.

According to Shockley's "scientific" logic, not only was there no basis for giving a black person a job wanted by a white person with equal or higher IQ, but even if the white person had a *lower* IQ, other "traits" could be cited to justify giving the white person the job. Nature had handicapped blacks in so many ways, Shockley argued, that practicing white supremacy in hiring and promoting was not discrimination, but good judgment.

When some of Shockley's racist views were published in *Stanford MD*, alumni and faculty of the medical school exploded in anger. All seven members of the Department of Genetics, including Nobel laureate Joshua Lederberg, assailed Shockley's claims as the "kind of pseudoscientific justification for class and race prejudice [that] is so hackneyed that we would not ordinarily have cared to react to it."

But Shockley's views were not so hackneyed that millions of Americans did not embrace them, simply because Shockley's political agenda matched theirs. Shockley opposed Medicaid, the food stamp program, and nutrition programs for black women and children. If "inferior" blacks and others were not allowed to die of natural causes, then it was imperative that they be sterilized in mass numbers to keep them from dragging down the IQ level of America. Politicians and people who dared not use the word "sterilization," or appear to adopt the eugenics program of the Nazis, were still happy to join Shockley's call for abandonment of social programs for people who supposedly had been limited by nature to the point of "irremediability."

Arthur Jensen, a psychologist at the University of California, Berkeley, had until recently the most deleterious effect on racial and social views in America. Jensen started beating the drums of racial warfare early in his career, when he argued that the seeming inferiority of blacks probably resulted from the incredible barriers to social mobility that the white majority had erected. This was very personal to me. How the hell was I, or my bright, Jim Crowed schoolmates in McMinnville, Tennessee, supposed to beat white kids on IQ tests when we blacks were not even allowed to read a book in the town's only public library? How was I to compete with the white kids who went to summer camps and other places where they got life-changing experiences, when summer for me always meant mowing white people's lawns, or unloading boxcars of fifty-pound bags of cement mixture for a white builder?

But during the mid-1960s, during a stint at Stanford, Jensen fell under the spell of Britishers and Americans who argued that mental ability is about 80 percent inherited, almost unalterable by environmental factors. Suddenly, Jensen wasn't just arguing that blacks suffered from an inherited IQ gap, but that there was no remedy for it. Thus, he argued, Head Start and other remedial education programs were a waste of money, and the Great Society social programs to produce racial justice were futile, and even destructive for blacks, because the totality of world research showed blacks to be hopelessly inferior. The conclusion Jensen drew was that the U.S. would suffer an overall decline in intelligence if it allowed blacks to breed in numbers significantly greater than Caucasians.

In 1969 Jensen published a nation-jarring article in the winter issue of the *Harvard Educational Review* entitled "How Much Can We Boost IQ and Scholastic Achievement?" He began with an assertion that "compensatory education has been tried and apparently has failed," and went on to expound on his thesis that black slum children were uneducable.

But Shockley and Jensen are not, by any stretch of the imagination, isolated cases. In October 1994 J. Philippe Rushton, a professor at the University of Western Ontario, was still doing "research" by asking strangers in shopping malls how big their penises were and how far they could ejaculate. Rushton, too, concluded that blacks have larger penises, buttocks, and breasts. He told a *Rolling Stone* reporter: "It's a trade-off: More brain or more penis. You can't have everything."

Imagine serious research in which guys in shopping malls get to describe their own genitals. There can't be a penis in Canada that is less than a foot long!

Rushton coauthored a paper with Thomas Bouchard of the University of Minnesota claiming that blacks have a propensity to contract AIDS because nature has given them a "reproductive strategy" of sexual promiscuity. That set me to laughing.

Outrageously silly stuff, I thought. But I had known all my life that white people everywhere had been obsessed with the "scientific" claims that African men and "heirs" descended to the umpteenth generation all had "massive penises." Every white college girl, it seemed, was told that "once you go black, you never go back!" That, people thought, was why Nicole Brown

Simpson married and stayed with O. J. Simpson, even after she allegedly learned that his fist stayed hard longer than his dick.

A million African American teenagers have whipped their penises to the limits of erection and cried out, "God, you didn't give me enough 'black' blood." How cheated to be given a normal-size dick and a complexion that supposedly tells everybody that you have a small brain!

But surely no scientist today believes that black intellectual inferiority can be proved on the basis of Rushton's discredited rantings, which echo those of French anatomist Etienne Serres, who argued that the distance between the belly button and the penis proved the inferiority of black men, or the 1903 "discovery" by W. L. Howard that education could never "reduce the large size of the negro's penis" or "prevent the African's birthright to sexual madness."

Well, perhaps Rushton is no more a crackpot than those "average" Americans whose sexual fears, curiosities and insecurities take over whenever the issue of race is raised — and who are stupid enough to base national policy on such sophistry.

Surprise! Herrnstein and Murray wrote in *The Bell Curve*: "The most abundant source of data that we downplayed is in the work of J. Philippe Rushton, a psychologist who since 1985 has been publishing increasingly detailed data to support his theory that the three races he labels Negroid, Caucasoid, and Mongoloid vary not just in intelligence but in a wide variety of other characteristics."

Those arguing that God made some races smarter than others, and that people of African descent got a deficit averaging fifteen points, have had tremendous influence upon human society. They clearly drove the Third Reich to tragedy while inciting unconscionable violence against Jews. They still color the British attitude toward the people of Northern Ireland. They made South Africa a scourge of humanity for generations, with racism still a grave threat. And their impact is still manifest in almost every nook and cranny of life in the United States.

How to explain why our public and private schools are still, in every practical sense, Jim Crow except for the fact that most white parents believe that black children are inferior intellectually and morally and are thus a drag on, and threat to, white children? How else to explain why housing patterns are so resolutely Jim Crow in just about every city in America? If we are not still absorbed in the belief in white supremacy, why are whites so determined to change rules and boundaries to limit the exercise of black political power?

When Richard Nixon said he favored allowing blacks in the body politic "when they learn to behave," was he not mouthing the language of white supremacy?

A mind-set handed down by Lenz, Fischer, Gunther, and Baur is essential for any American to justify repressive, discriminatory crime laws that enable ruling whites to fill jails and prisons overwhelmingly with blacks, Hispanics, and a relative few poor, low-IQ whites. What powerful white person is to feel guilty when he or she has a "scientific" finding that just as low intelligence is heritable, so is an inclination toward lawlessness, violence, sexual promiscuity, laziness, and whatever else is wrong with people who get incarcerated?

## Banker of Hate

The "social science" frauds have made both white arrogance and white paranoia seem justifiable, if not laudable. I asked myself in 1994 how so many phonies kept getting the money, generation after generation, to publish propaganda that promotes the political agendas of the eugenicists, the neo-Nazis, the skinheads, and other haters. I was amazed, after some research, to learn that the "superrace" psychologists, anthropologists, and others have been financed for more than half a century by a foundation bankrolled by a superbigot.

I learned that the Pioneer Fund has pumped millions of dollars into financing the "research" of Jensen, Shockley, and others who propound eugenics and the idea that anything — from deliberate mass deprivations of the "underclass" to race-based deportations to simple genocide — should be employed to protect the IQ level of the United States.

In 1937 a New England textile tycoon named Wickliffe Draper founded the Pioneer Fund, to promote his goal of "repatriating" all blacks to Africa and to maintain immigration laws that would limit the number of Jews and other "undesirables" who could enter the United States. The Pioneer Fund then became a rich ally of those seeking to preserve racial segregation and later, to thwart the civil rights "revolution" of the 1960s.

On October 20, 1994, *Rolling Stone* magazine published an article asserting that the Pioneer Fund had given Arthur Jensen $1,096,094, J. Philippe Rushton $770,738, William Shockley $188,000 and millions more to others whom the magazine called "PROFESSORS OF HATE."

## Let the "Dumb" Die

The tragedy is that neither Jensen, Shockley, Rushton, nor their like-minded colleagues has written a paragraph about IQ that is of real value to this society. What they have done is propel America toward a race war that no group can win.

The latest, most destructive, contributors to Caucasian madness were two men who put a "scientific" veneer on all the crap of the preceding century and produced a bestselling book.

In 1994 a political scientist named Charles Murray and a psychologist named Richard Herrnstein saw the white man's anguish. The climate was ripe for them to influence American life to a degree that earlier soul brothers William Shockley and Arthur Jensen never could. So they packaged all the old theories about IQ and race into a book that declared a "Bell Curve" tolled for a social and economic dictatorship of the "cognitive elite."

Murray and Herrnstein prefaced their book with an apologia:

"People have shied from the topic [of race and intelligence] for many reasons. Some think that the concept of intelligence has been proved a fraud. Others recall totalitarian eugenic schemes based on IQ scores or worry about such schemes arising once the subject breaks into the open. Many fear that discussing intelligence will promote racism. . . .

"We are not indifferent to the ways in which this book, wrongly construed, might do harm. . . . But there can be no real progress in solving America's social problems when they are as misperceived as they are today."

Still, the Murray-Herrnstein book exploded upon the American social-political landscape almost as dramatically as did the bomb that destroyed the Alfred P. Murrah building in Oklahoma

City. "A flame-throwing treatise on race, class and intelligence," said the *New York Times* editorially, adding: "The concern here is the governmental fallout of a book that aspires to set the agenda of social policy debate for the decade. What gives their sweeping generalities poignancy is an overlay of sophisticated statistical tools that create an aura of scientific certitude sure to intimidate ordinary citizens from challenging the alarmist conclusions."

What Murray and Herrnstein said was that IQ tests are accurate and meaningful; that the average IQ of a black is fifteen points lower than the IQ of a white person; that differences in genes account for 60 percent of the differences in the IQs of children; that low IQs produce poverty and an inclination toward criminal behavior, and that no remedial programs can undo the gap in IQ. The *New York Times* called these unproven assertions "an economic death knell for much of America's black population."

Yet, the *New York Times* review of the book by science writer Malcolm Browne was generally approving. The *National Review* held a symposium at which several neoconservative Catholics swallowed whole Murray's and Herrnstein's "finding." The magazine itself declared "'Intelligence,' vulgarly known as IQ, does exist. It can be measured. It is substantially inherited. It varies among individuals. It also varies, on average, among races."

Black conservatives like Glenn Loury of Boston University, and Thomas Sowell, who more or less share Murray's social and legislative agenda, were in virtual lockstep with the *Bell Curve* authors.

In attacking the book, Jude Wanniski wrote in *Forbes Media Critic:* "I could not find a single essay or comment by a conservative journalist or opinion leader who attacked *The Bell Curve*'s quackery."

Wanniski said *The Bell Curve* was "probably the most important book published in 1994," despite his view that that "does not mean it is worth reading, much less buying. *The Bell Curve* contains a racist message, one that is morally objectionable. . . . Equally important, the message rests on a 'finding' that can only be called quackery."

The danger is that Americans swallowed the quackery, sending the book roaring up bestseller lists. It still constitutes a new "bible" for the white supremacists who spread a message of racist violence from Montana to Mississippi.

The only "progress" *The Bell Curve* would make is to encourage the members of Congress, the other politicians, the "angry white men" who share the political agenda that the late Richard Herrnstein, and especially Murray, have been pushing fanatically for years, to push their views harder.

Murray and Herrnstein knew at the start of their provocative, misleading, and in many ways fraudulent, book that they were likely to do great harm to all Americans but those they refer to as the "cognitive elite" — that is, the white males they expect to see ruling America from fortresses constructed to ward off the angry "permanent lower class." They knew the distastefulness of their project when the Manhattan Institute, which had sponsored Murray for eight years, ceased its financial support upon learning of the impending screed about racial superiority and inferiority. Even their friends protested enough to warn them that scientists of worldwide eminence and unquestioned integrity would question both their research and their motives.

*USA Today* said editorially:

> The attempt to justify racist policies with racial stereotyping is old and common and grubby, not to mention useless. The academic who pities blacks as unable to rise above their genetic station merely invites closet racists to flaunt their bias. Worse, he encourages abandonment of poor blacks who would do just fine with a little help. . . . But of course, no one is hushing the debate, merely denouncing the racism one side of it dignifies. And when it comes to foolishness, which is worse: Respecting one of the basic premises of this nation — that each individual is precious and deserves equal opportunity — or deciding that we will be forever stratified by race and that our social policies should ensure that end? You know that answer, don't you?

*U.S. News & World Report* said, "The authors contend that social policy must be overhauled to account for this: Welfare, education and affirmative action programs aimed at helping the poor should be scrapped because the recipients have limited intelligence and cannot benefit from a helping government hand."

Jason DeParle wrote in the *New York Times Magazine:*

"Murray has something . . . dangerous and inflammatory on his mind: the relationship between race, class, genes and intelligence . . . [his] book argues that I.Q. scores — and their large genetic component — are the key to understanding who gets ahead in America and who languishes in crime, poverty and dependency."

DeParle wrote that Murray "will never be the country's most famous conservative, but he may well be the most dangerous."

No evidence was produced that Murray and Herrnstein were bankrolled by the Pioneer Fund, but it is noteworthy that they relied mightily on the Pioneer professors for "proof" of their most outrageous Bell Bull assertions.

Murray would have people believe that he is merely a courageous social scientist violating a great taboo, trying to educate Americans away from a cataclysm of ultimate polarization when smart, rich people in mansions will be violently assaulted by legions of dumb slum-dwellers. *The Bell Curve* has gone a long way toward making its grim warning a self-fulfilling prophecy.

# Chapter 6

# Undermining the General Welfare

I am sure that the authors of the Preamble to the U.S. Constitution thought they had conjured up a beautiful, lofty goal when they proposed to "promote the general welfare." Which of them could have imagined that "welfare" would become one of the most scarred words in the English language? It isn't used much by anyone as a reference to the general well-being of all the people of America. It is now a word of opprobrium applied primarily to those millions of Americans whose state of well-being is bad, to say the least.

A surly nation, more and more bedeviled, even crippled, by class hatreds and jealousies now uses that word, "welfare," mostly when talking of "queens" and "bums," and in political demagoguery about people the comfortable regard as lazy misfits and "undesirable parasites." The vast majority of Americans now profess to hate welfare, to attach a stigma to receiving it, to blame it for allegedly turning people who might be industrious into pitiful globs of dependency, and to scream alarmingly that it is luring young women — especially young *white* women — into pregnancies out of wedlock. From President Clinton to Newt Gingrich to the least-known, most craven of politicians, everybody wants to "reform" welfare. Yet few seem to know or agree on what welfare is. The *Washington Times*, a very conservative, anti-welfare newspaper recently carried a big headline, HOW TO REFORM WELFARE IF YOU CAN'T DEFINE IT?

## What Really Is Welfare?

The level of bigotry is so high in America today that everyone with two dimes to rub together wants to think, "Welfare is money I'm busting my ass to get and give away to some slut who keeps having babies and eating steaks while I can't take my kid to Disneyland." Or "Welfare is what lazy bitches and sons-abitches get from you and me for doing nothing."

For most Americans, then, their anger is focused on the Aid to Families with Dependent Children (AFDC) program. Brutally maligned AFDC is, in fact, not the costliest part of welfare in America. It cost $22.8 billion (plus $3.2 billion in administrative costs) in 1994. Food stamps cost $26.3 billion, SSI (Supplemental Security Income) cost $25.9 billion, Medicaid $131.7 billion, and Medicare for the elderly $142.9 billion. The various programs supporting farmers cost about $15 billion. Not to mention billions spent by Uncle Sam to promote foreign sales of grain and other merchandise by rich corporations.

The AFDC rolls are composed nationally of 38.3 percent white, 36.6 percent black, 18.5 percent Hispanic, and 2.9 percent Asian. The *New York Times* reported on May 19, 1996, that Southeast Asians had "the highest rate of welfare dependency of any racial or ethnic group."

We now have a food stamp program that feeds 27.4 million people at a cost of $27 billion a year; a school lunch program that nourishes 25 million children at an annual cost of $4.5 billion; a WIC (Women, Infants, and Children) nutrition program that protects 6.2 million at-risk Americans at an annual cost of $3.1 billion; nine federal child-care programs for low-income families that cost $1.9 billion; low-income energy assistance that pays $1.3 billion in heating and cooling bills for more than 6 million households; legal services for the poor that cost $415 million.

Some years ago the Congress created a "Cadillac" version of welfare that was called "aid to the aged, blind and disabled."

This "Supplemental Security Income" protection enabled a lot of white people to disassociate themselves from the huddled masses of minorities and "white trash" who got plain old ghetto–tobacco road "welfare."

But the once high falutin' SSI program has become rife with frauds who would make most "welfare queens" look saintly. Mortimer B. Zuckerman, editor in chief of *U.S. News & World Report*, described it as "welfare's scandalous cousin." Hell, SSI is no "cousin"; it's plain welfare, sometimes at its worst, but at its best, truly useful to millions of Americans.

Zuckerman wrote:

Refugees — a loose term — can begin collecting hundreds of dollars a month the moment they are admitted. Some 700,000 cost us almost $4 billion a year. Thousands have been encouraged by entrepreneurial "social workers" to qualify for SSI by fabricating tales of political and other wartime suffering that has left them too traumatized to hold a job.

Drug addicts and alcoholics can qualify as disabled, making it possible for virtually anyone hooked on dope or booze to get a monthly check, even if he has no other disability. Today the federal government is paying some $1.4 billion annually to 250,000 substance abusers — who often spend the money on the substance, not on treatment. Example: A Denver liquor store owner has been receiving $160,000 to run a tab for 40 alcoholics.

Too many of the incentives of the SSI program are perverse. When recipients receive cash assistance, but no rehabilitation or job training, there is a disincentive to work. When the SSI payments are higher than AFDC payments, parents are egged on to qualify their children as disabled. The system gives cash awards for bringing up children badly. Drug addicts, offered cash for up to three years, have little incentive to conquer the addiction because it means losing SSI benefits. And states have an incentive to support a shift to SSI from AFDC since they bear about 45 percent of the cost of AFDC but none of SSI.

It ought to shock you who read this to learn that in fiscal 1994, federal and state governments pumped $24.5 billion into SSI.

Yet, in the public eye, other programs are far more guilty. Affluent people curse costly Medicaid ($131.7 billion in 1993) because it is means-tested, or medical care for the indigent. But they never bother to learn that 69 percent of Medicaid money goes to help the elderly and the disabled, and that millions of very ill, poor Americans never get real help from this program. The unwavering rule is that the poorer, the hungrier, the sicker the people who got the assistance, the more likely it will be denounced as "welfare."

Who's on the Dole?

People denounce the soaring costs of welfare, and close their eyes to the fact that they themselves may be recipients. The conservative Heritage Foundation and the Congressional Research Service count in the nation's "welfare" bill $23.4 billion in housing programs, which, in fact, props up the nation's housing (read construction/real estate) industry more than it helps the homeless; $6.3 billion worth of Pell Grants that have helped 3,700,000 students who don't think they're on welfare; some $4.7 billion in community development programs that pay the salary of some policeman or librarian who lives next door. Of course, all those stalwart American entrepreneurs whose new day-care centers profit or fail on the basis of money from Uncle Sam never admit to being beneficiaries of "welfare." I won't hold my breath until either the *Washington Times* or the Heritage Foundation totes it up, but Uncle Sam gives billions of dollars of welfare to them, to corporations, to the superrich, to me and my family. Hell, we're all on welfare.

Some of my most pleasant moments came when I spoke before a group of newly rich business leaders. I told them that we never had a welfare system in McMinnville, Tennessee, where I grew up desperately poor, "but I sure as hell went on welfare when they passed the GI Bill."

Though many of the self-styled "Horatio Algers" in the audience would have been loath to think of themselves as welfare recipients, I pushed my argument that the GI Bill was the most successful welfare program the United States ever had. I became particularly offensive when I said, "Now don't give me any crap about how you earned your education. Most of you never saw a

Nazi or a Japanese warrior, and you never fired a shot in patriotic fear or anger. And you'd have had one hell of a time getting good college educations without the welfare help of Uncle Sam. We got the money, and we've paid it back to the nation — handsomely. Which kid out there today is undeserving of our investment of relative pennies in the faith that he or she will also pay it back in multiples?"

I put those ideas in a column and got a wheelbarrow of mail from veterans who objected to being compared in any way with "real welfare people."

The school lunch and school breakfast programs have long been spared the calumny heaped upon the food stamp and other nutrition programs because millions of middle class and even rich white kids eat at their schools at taxpayer expense. Affluent mommas who are spared making peanut butter and jelly sandwiches would erupt with fury if anyone dared to say their children were on welfare. Well-heeled moms and pops showed us which "welfare" is expendable and which isn't in 1994, when they beat back Republican attempts to mangle the school lunch program by turning it over to the states.

Yet, many of these people join Gingrich, Charles Murray, Robert Rector, and others who pretend in other ways to wage a holy war to close down the "welfare" system and rid this society of parasites. Well, don't think that a band of sucker-the-masses politicians is going to produce a society that is devoid of poor, jobless, untrained, sick, desperate people. In January 1995, *U.S. News & World Report* described THE MYTH OF REFORM. It said that "both parties are vowing to get hundreds of thousands of Americans off the dole and into jobs. It may be harder than they think."

I remember a 1970 speech by Donald M. Kendall of PepsiCo before the Whittier, California, Chamber of Commerce. Kendall said he hoped for a welfare program that would double both the number of recipients and the amount of money spent on it. He noted that school-lunch, welfare, and food-stamp dollars go to buy bread, enriching the farmers of Kansas and Nebraska; to purchase milk and butter, keeping dairy farmers solvent; to grocers, supermarkets, mom-and-pop store owners, and bottlers of soft drinks happily ringing their cash registers.

"If we wanted a better prop under the economy, we couldn't

find one," said the PepsiCo chairman, a close friend of President Nixon's.

It is a sad little reed to lean on, but I'm guessing that no matter how much Republican congressmen hate the poor, they will not zap them if it takes billions of dollars away from their country-club pals who are their big campaign contributors.

Yes, many thousands of businessmen have learned what Donald Kendall knew during the Nixon presidency, and they, too, have learned to make the streams of "welfare" money their sources of wealth. But almost none has the guts to say, "Stop these cruel attacks on welfare. These programs keep poor people alive, and they pay for my pads in Palm Springs and West Palm Beach!"

Many of the "welfare" programs of today are as badly needed, and twice as defensible, as they were a quarter century ago. It's just that the Americans who need them most are least able to defend them.

Drawing the Battle Lines

But the country is in a kneejerk orgy about the cost of and the alleged social destruction caused by welfare programs. The magazine of the National Conference of State Legislatures carried a piece in June 1994 about WAGING WAR ON THE WELFARE MONSTER. It traced the origin of AFDC in 1935 as a way to help widows and orphans, Food Stamps in 1966 as a way to distribute surplus government food to needy families, and Medicaid in 1965 to pay for health care for the poor. Excluding Medicaid, the article noted, welfare programs now cost the federal government more than $50 billion annually, with the states kicking in another $15 billion or so. Then the article complained:

> In human terms, the number of people on AFDC or food stamps has risen virtually every month since 1989, approximately 36 percent between July 1989 and December 1993. An unprecedented number of people need assistance: One child in seven nationwide is a recipient of AFDC while one person in 10 is on food stamps.

While fulfilling the original, Depression-era goals of helping the desperate and downtrodden, welfare programs now have burgeoned into complicated bureaucratic systems that are costly and foster dependence instead of independence and self-sufficiency. It's little wonder that states have taken the lead in seeking ways to "end welfare as we know it."

"The public hates it, recipients hate it, politicians hate it, business hates it," says Representative Bill Purple of Tennessee. "We must reward work rather than welfare."

Welfare to work. What a lovely goal. The problem that fans the emotions of racial war in America is that so many Caucasians believe that only they regard work as better than welfare. They believe that blacks and Hispanics are genetically lazy and prefer welfare to any job. They believe that welfare simply guarantees only the "survival of the weakest."

What could be simpler than the fact that if you run your society in a way that leaves many millions of men and women poorly educated and untrained for work, and millions more denied decent jobs because of racial and sexual discrimination, then you are going to have millions of people living in poverty? If you pretend to be a decent, compassionate society that rejects Social Darwinism, then you devise ways — cheap ones, if you can — to prevent members of the underclass from starving, or freezing, or finding death in the myriad tentacles of poverty. We Americans recently have talked of "a safety net" to ensure that none of our citizens fall below a tolerable level of degradation.

Throughout our history our national need to appear caring and compassionate has constantly clashed with the greed that is inherent in capitalism, and perhaps in human nature. Racism, ethnic bigotry, and sexism — things so deeply ingrained in this society — complicate matters further. As a result, this country's efforts to give comfort to the destitute have been at times laughable, sentimental, condescending, cruel — and always controversial.

There was a time when it was politically safe for a politician in America to espouse policies of welfare, of broad-gauged support for the impoverished. Roosevelt was eloquent in 1932 when he scolded Washington pols for pretending that the United States was not populated by millions of people who needed a full meal, decent housing, medicine, and the other comforts of life. "The federal government," he said, "has always had and still has a continuing responsibility for the broader public welfare."

As a boy in Tennessee, during the Great Depression, I remember talk of some program called "Mothers' Aid." My mother never got any of that. It was for "destitute" women, which for the most part meant white women whose husbands had died or vanished. My mother had a husband, and even when he had no job, she did not qualify as "destitute." She could, after all, work as cook or charwoman for white families at one dollar a day. So no "Mothers' Aid" for her or any black women I knew in McMinnville.

There seems always to have been something in the American psyche that opposes giving cash to anyone who hasn't earned it, however needy the recipient. The idea that a "dole" of pure cash destroys character and breeds dependency brought a quick end to Franklin D. Roosevelt's "emergency relief" programs of the mid-1930s. My family occasionally got cans of "surplus" foods, but no cash handouts. I once got $3 a month from the Works Progress Administration, but had to "work" for it — raising and lowering the flag.

During that depression political leaders became aware that a lot of children were growing up amidst terrible need and disadvantage because their "breadwinner" father had died, was disabled, or was derelict and gone. It wasn't fashionable to express concern for the mother, but most in the Roosevelt camp thought it proper for government to give Aid to Dependent Children. This modest program was the forerunner of our current AFDC program. As the ranks of America's poor have swollen and the numbers of Americans benefiting from AFDC have grown, it has become perhaps the most castigated, even despised, of all America's social programs.

I shall not live long enough to forget sitting with Lyndon B. Johnson, in India in 1961, after a sweaty trudge through a village of utterly miserable people, listening to him say what he would do for poor people if he ever became President — and then hearing him say as President in January 1964: "This administration today, here and now, declares unconditional war on poverty."

But since Johnson, we have not had a single President, Democrat or Republican, who has not tried to get political mileage out of assailing "welfare."

Richard Nixon played the race card with welfare, saying things that led Americans to believe that the average AFDC recipient was a slothful black woman with ten illegitimate children, living at taxpayers' expense at a Ritz Carlton–type hotel. His great political ploy was to demand "workfare," but he added a dramatic flourish when he said in 1969: "I propose a new approach that would make it more attractive to go to work . . . and will establish a nationwide minimum payment to dependent families with children."

Nixon never moved to destroy welfare programs, but his idea of giving a cash income tax credit to families where working people aren't paid enough to rise out of poverty became very much a part of the American idea of "workfare" for the underclass. That is, until Newt Gingrich came along to wage war on the earned income tax credit.

Jimmy Carter as President presided over some very hard times when the so-called "misery index" was abominably high. His was a time when he was expected to defend welfare and to reinvigorate Johnson's War on Poverty. But Carter said, in 1977, "The welfare system is anti-work, anti-family, inequitable in its treatment of the poor, and wasteful. . . . We must make a complete break with the past."

His administration never came close to breaking with any part of America's welfare past. He probably added to the paranoia that was rising in middle-class America, where hard-pressed people began to express deep resentments against paying taxes or sacrificing in any other way to help the poor.

Surely no President ever did more to arouse a "hate the poor" syndrome in America than Ronald Reagan. In 1976, as he launched his futile campaign to wrest the GOP nomination away from Gerald Ford, Reagan fired off some incredible rhetoric demeaning welfare recipients. On February 14 he said: "There's a woman in Chicago. She has eighty names, thirty addresses, twelve Social Security cards and is collecting veterans' benefits on four nonexistent deceased husbands. . . . She's got Medicaid, is getting food stamps and welfare under each of her names. Her tax-free cash income alone is over $150,000." That woman was prosecutable under many laws. Oddly, she was never named or hauled into court.

After he was elected President in 1980, in the midst of the worst recession since the Great Depression, Reagan continued to rail against "welfare queens" and to excoriate TV networks that ran features on "some poor family in South Succotash," programs he felt wrongly sentimentalized the poor.

When there was scarcely a job to be found by millions of Americans, some very educated and highly skilled, President George Bush seemed to delight in saying, "Get a job or get off the dole."

And Bill Clinton, trying to prove he is a "new Democrat," promised, "We're going to put an end to welfare as we know it."

Meanwhile, during all these presidencies, all the recessions, and even the "good times," the number of Americans needing help from their more fortunate neighbors has grown, and grown, and grown.

The injustice and impact of poverty is magnified by the fact that the poor have been getting poorer as the rich get richer — until the gap between the two is now a financial canyon that has cut frightening scars on the American political and social landscape.

According to the Luxembourg Income Study Report, published by a nonprofit group based in Luxembourg that looked at income differentials in eighteen industrialized nations, poor children in the U.S. are worse off than poor children in all but two of the other countries — Ireland and Israel. A family of four that is in the bottom 10 percent in America has an average after-tax income of $10,923, including benefits from food stamps and earned income tax credits. The counterpart families in all seventeen other countries have incomes over $15,000, with the leaders — Switzerland and Sweden — all the way up to $18,829.

On the other hand, no other country comes close to the $65,536 annual income average for the wealthiest 10 percent of U.S. households with children. And no other country has such a wide gap between rich and poor families with children as the U.S. does — nearly $55,000. The closest is Switzerland, with $43,000. In Finland, Denmark, Norway, Sweden, the Netherlands, Austria, and Italy, the gap between top and bottom is less than $30,000.

And the situation just keeps on getting worse. Even though poverty levels in the U.S. declined between 1993 and 1994, the first such drop in five years, the chasm between the rich and poor kept growing. The 20 percent of Americans at the top of the economic ladder now receive as much income as *the rest of the population combined.*

"It tells a sorry story about the maldistribution of economic progress," said Henry Aaron, an economist at the Brooking Institution in Washington, D.C. "The rewards paid to people who have skills in the economy have been skyrocketing, while those who bring simply hard work and maybe muscle to the job have enjoyed no improvement in their living standards for a quarter of a century, and many have suffered."

The American Welfare Association reported that the AFDC caseload rose from 3,746,100 in July 1989 to 5,011,600 in November 1993, a leap of 33.8 percent in just over four years. This great jump reflected population increases and the fall of more children and households into poverty. The share of Americans receiving welfare has stayed around 4.5 to 5 percent for decades, rising to 5.3 percent in 1993. The fact that the number of people receiving AFDC rose from 7.4 million in 1970 to 14.2 million in 1994 is largely due to a surge in population.

So we have the following facts, provided by our government, about the level of poverty and the scope of "welfare" assistance in our country:

We now have 15.3 million American children under age eighteen living in poverty. Nearly 9.4 million of these children are white, 4.9 million are black, 4.1 million are of Hispanic origin (Hispanics can be of any race, which explains why the breakdown adds up to more than the overall total), and growing numbers of the impoverished are Asians, the fastest growing segment of the American population.

We have 12,220,000 households headed by women, these on average the poorest in the land, with a median annual income of $19,872, compared with the national average of $32,264.

At last count (1994) the AFDC program supported about 4.6 million adults (overwhelmingly mothers) and their 9.6 million children. Benefits range from an average of $120 a month per family in Mississippi to $735 a month in Alaska, with a national average of $376. Clearly, no mother, no child, lives comfortably, let alone sumptuously, on welfare. Not even when you add in the fact that AFDC recipients are automatically eligible to receive food stamps and health care under Medicaid.

But the divisions between rich and poor are getting worse, and more dangerous, and our leaders cannot agree on what to do about them. And so, our social safety net, especially welfare, is likely to become the "Willie Horton" of the 1996 elections, that lightning-rod issue of fear and passion that overrides all fact and logic. Just as no honest politician could override the stereotype of every black man being a likely rapist or murderer, so most politicians were unable to override the stereotype of a fat black woman who refuses to work riding up in a Mercedes-Benz to collect her welfare check.

Combine AFDC payments and food stamps and the total given to AFDC recipients in all states and the District of Columbia is below the poverty line — or less than $8,700 a year for a family of three.


Why Punish the Mothers?

The poor women of America have been abused more by mean-spirited members of Congress and cruel columnists than they ever were by the men who impregnated and then deserted them. I reemphasize the fact that women on welfare have become the subjects of countless myths in which they are depicted as dumb, lazy, semi-whores who are having babies like rabbits so as to get payments so large that they are bankrupting the Treasury.

Let's look at who the welfare mothers are. According to the Department of Health and Human Services, they are among the least-educated females in America, with 43.5 percent never having graduated from high school. Some 59 percent of them were age nineteen or younger when they first gave birth, and 49.6 percent were not married to the father of their baby. Many could not say for sure who the father was. Only 8 percent of AFDC recipients had earned income.

More than half of welfare mothers (53.1 percent) are just "keeping house," which presumably means looking after their children.

There was a time when a woman's "place" was in the home,

caring for the children, cooking for the male breadwinner, and awaiting the joy of producing another baby. But only Phyllis Schlafly and a few rockbound conservatives now think women were meant to stay aloof from the labor force. Some 61 million women are now in the U.S. workforce, because two salaries are essential if a family is to have a nice home with modern appliances, the ability to take vacations, and most of all the wherewithal to give their children college educations.

It is understandable that many working women detest welfare mothers, especially if the employed women swallow the myths about the "comforts" they are providing for immoral litter-bearers who refuse to work. America's social bloodstream is poisoned by a host of myths that are driving us to fight each other. For example:

Myth 1. Most welfare mothers are able-bodied people who don't want to work as long as others will give them food, booze, and shelter.

The pitiful truth is that most welfare women find it extremely difficult to find any job, let alone one that would provide them and their children a level of life better than what welfare affords. Since the stereotypical welfare mother is black, let's look at the overall statistics on black female unemployment in America. In November 1995 there were 558,000 adult black females actively looking for jobs but unable to find them, and another half million or so who wanted jobs but had given up hope of finding one.

Work was unavailable partly because of the state of the U.S. economy, and partly because of historic discrimination against black female job seekers. But the most embarrassing truth was that millions of black women had not been educated for worthwhile work in the U.S. labor force. From kindergarten onward, millions of black females have faced brutal Jim Crow, or urban isolation from job markets, with the result that they are not trained to compete. Powerful forces still think black women ought to be cooks, maids, charwomen, and nannies.

Myth 2. Poor women use their bodies the way minks produce minks, breeding babies to get larger welfare payments. Cut off welfare money and you cut off the production of illegitimate babies.

After arguing in his book *The Bell Curve* that America's social problems arise from the inherent inferiority of some of our citizens, Charles Murray wrote an equally controversial article in the *Wall Street Journal* in which he called for an end to all government economic support for single mothers to halt the rise in illegitimate births.

The idea appealed to lawmakers in Washington and state capitals who were looking for ways to cut welfare costs, and to "new eugenicists" writing in magazines and on op-ed pages, in effect, "Just let the inferior children die out and America will wind up with a superstock of high-IQ human beings."

William Bennett, former U.S. education secretary and drug czar and now a codirector of Empower America, suggested (with coauthor Peter Wehner) that Republicans should support legislation to end all forms of economic support for single mothers who have new children — including AFDC, subsidized housing, food stamps — along with an end to visitation rights for illegitimate fathers.

"These proposed policy changes are based on an important moral principal," huffed Bennett. "Having children out of wedlock is wrong — not simply economically unwise for the individuals involved or a financial burden on society, but morally wrong."

Other social Darwinists have advocated the implantation of Norplant or other medical devices to prevent pregnancy. Some suggest forced sterilization of women (minority ones, of course) who have two or three babies out of wedlock.

If Americans look past the emotional rhetoric, they'll see that data and common sense do not support these assumptions that welfare is the primary cause of "illegitimate" births.

A panel of seventy-six prominent researchers from all disciplines and political views reported late in 1994 that most studies have found that welfare benefits have little or no significant effect on whether women bear children outside of marriage. They cited several indicators to back up this conclusion:

— If welfare were to blame, you'd expect that out-of-wedlock births would be rising mainly among low-income, less-educated women. In fact, the trend has occurred among high school graduates and those with college educations. Two-thirds of all women who give birth outside of marriage are *not* poor.

— If welfare were the major cause of out-of-wedlock births,

the rate of such births should fall, or at least rise more slowly, when welfare benefits decline. This hasn't happened.

— States with higher welfare benefits do not typically have higher rates of birth to unmarried women or higher proportions of children living in single-parent families. For example, New Jersey provides more than half again as much in AFDC and food stamp benefits to a family of three as does Mississippi; but the proportion of children born outside of marriage is virtually the same in those two states, for both blacks and whites.

So why did the birthrate among unwed women rise 70 percent between 1983 and 1993? The research team cited changing sexual mores, decreased economic opportunities for low-skilled workers, more women in the labor market, and deteriorating neighborhood conditions. Focusing on welfare as the main cause of out-of-wedlock births, concluded the researchers, "vastly oversimplifies this complex phenomenon."

Someone else who wasn't buying the welfare/illegitimacy connection was Herbert Stein, who had been chairman of President Nixon's Council of Economic Advisers. Stein wrote in the *Wall Street Journal*, "People say that if we cut the welfare benefits given to young unmarried mothers, young unmarried women will have fewer children. QED, cutting the benefits will cure, or at least ameliorate, the problem. But if cutting the benefits, by, say 50 percent, reduces the number of children newly born to young unmarried women by, say, 5 percent, the problem is not reduced but is aggravated. There will be more misery among children — that is, somewhat fewer children but each in a much more miserable condition."

You don't need the research and opinions of others to see the folly of those welfare myths. Common sense tells us that it will take a lot more than cutting off aid to families with dependent children to stop women — especially teenagers — from having "illegitimate" babies.

Today's social milieu imposes precious few restraints on the hormonal and glandular eruptions of teenagers. It is cruelly hypocritical to curse youngsters who are overwhelmed by sex-based ads, TV shows, movies, and song lyrics, as the ones who are debasing and disgracing this society.

The folly of this argument is manifest in the fact that we have become a society in which sex and the exploitation of it dominates American mores. Premarital and extramarital sex are now commonplace. The stigma of bearing a baby without the convenience — or inconvenience — of marriage has virtually vanished. An abundance of beautiful white wedding gowns are now made with pouches to accommodate stomachs swollen by six or seven months of pregnancy. Do you remember how talk of "trial marriages" used to horrify Americans? Nowadays, millions of parents accept the idea of their kid living with someone of the opposite sex long enough "to be sure they're a good match." Mothers explain at bridge tables that they let their college daughter and her male guest for the holidays share the same bed because "they're engaged." Some don't even bother making an excuse.

These youngsters are victimized by a society in which sex is used to sell almost everything. Is Madonna less an attraction or moneymaker because she has a cleverly nurtured reputation for being sexually promiscuous or because she was impregnated by her Cuban-American physical trainer?

Is actor Hugh Grant sinking into oblivion because police caught him sinking into a car with a Hollywood hooker?

If you can bear to watch an evening of the current pathetic TV fare, you'll see a string of "sitcoms" where every other line is not just a sexual double entendre, but borders on the "blue" and pornographic. For the really lewd and lascivious stuff, you need only turn to a cable channel like HBO.

And Hollywood? Any Sharon Stone role will make any fourteen-year-old believe that having sexual intercourse is the moral equivalent of drag racing. Whoopi Goldberg may portray a nun on screen, but she changes bed mates faster than you can lock up a convent. Whoopi does usually get a new marriage license.

Then, there's adultery. It's still a *crime* in twenty-seven states, including Connecticut and New York. When last did you hear of cops hauling adulterers to the hoosegow? Is Diana, the Princess of Wales, less to "Di for" since she revealed on television that she has committed adultery? No. People the world over said, "Ho, hum," knowing that her estranged husband, Charles, the Prince of Wales, had committed adultery long before they were separated.

Sociologists and sex researchers claim that perhaps 40 percent of married women and 65 percent of married men have committed adultery at some point.

It is lunacy to believe that withdrawing a pittance of money to support teenagers and their babies will counteract all the sexual forces that are at work in America, causing young women to stop having sex — and babies — before marriage. Yes, lunacy. Plain, unadulterated lunacy.

It is also mean-spirited selfishness and greed that is competing against Americans' better instincts, with the outcome still in doubt. That was the point I wanted to make in a column on June 9, 1995:

> I'm sure that if I were to let the selfish, meanest part of me run wild, I could write a column demanding the immediate end of all welfare programs.
>
> Like most people, I don't like deadbeats. I do look down on those who won't carry their share of the load. I can be convinced that I am graced with great get-up-and-go, while the destitute and down-and-out are that way "because they want to be." I do pay a lot of taxes, and I can sizzle if convinced that I'm working my butt off to buy T-bone steaks for some lazy bum.
>
> But the saner me sees one child, one human being, at a time, and knows that neither I nor this society can ever benefit from draconian denials of food, shelter, education and hope for that child. The saner me knows that even the most flint-hearted congressman would not deny bread, milk or medicine to a real in-his-face child. They pass cruel, short-sighted legislative denials only because their minds and rhetoric can turn real people into a faceless mass of blobs that they can call a national "burden."
>
> How else could this Congress fashion a "welfare reform" scheme under which the "burden" is shifted to states that will be $10 billion short of the resources needed to meet it? And even shorter on compassion?
>
> The compassionate me knows that this attitude is societal suicide. But something keeps saying "compassion is for suckers."
>
> Which side of me, Mr. America, is going to prevail in this dreadful process some call "welfare reform"?

There was no question which side of Newt Gingrich would prevail. He and his cohorts kept the pressure on President Clinton with other outrageous proposals. If cutting off welfare wouldn't stop illegitimacy, Gingrich said, then how about taking the babies from their homes and putting them in orphanages?

When Hillary Rodham Clinton called that idea "unbelievable and absurd," and objected to the suggestion that children should be put in orphanages solely because they were born out of wedlock and their parents were poor, Gingrich suggested that the First Lady rent the 1938 movie *Boys Town* in which Spencer Tracy and Mickey Rooney made Father Flanagan's home for wayward boys in Nebraska look like a bit of paradise. (This brought more than a few countersuggestions that Gingrich in turn ought to watch Dickens's *Oliver Twist* for a far different view of orphanages in Victorian England.)

Movies aside, Gingrich complained, "I don't understand liberals who live in enclaves of safety who say, 'Oh, this would be a terrible thing. Look at the Norman Rockwell family that would break up.' The fact is we are allowing brutalization and a degradation of children in this country, a destructiveness."

Invited by *Newsweek* magazine to respond, the First Lady offered these arguments in rebuttal:

— Children are almost always best off with their families, unless there is convincing evidence that their well-being is threatened by abuse or neglect.

— Just because a family is poor does not mean that the parents are not good. "Poor parents struggle every day to give their children the most with the least. And often they are among the best parents. They know children need a secure home, strong values, consistency, and love."

— It is decent, as well as cost-effective, for our society to support families with special problems, including poverty, and do all we can to avoid family breakup.

The cost-effectiveness was backed up by figures from the Welfare League of America, which said that providing room and board to a child in an institutional setting costs an average of $36,500 a year, versus about $2,700 to give AFDC and food stamps to a family with one child. If the GOP welfare reform plan were to go into effect, an estimated one million children might need some form of institutional care. Gingrich suggested that private philanthropy could cover the costs. But while it's true that churches and other charitable organizations generally run orphanages, most of their operating funds come from the state and federal governments.

By the time of his State of the Union address in January 1995, President Clinton had become aware that one of his dumbest campaign promises was to "end welfare as we have known it." It had seemed so simple to vow to force poor mothers to find jobs in two years or be cut off welfare. But where were the jobs? The cost of training welfare women seemed unafford- able in a time when Republicans clamored for a balanced bud- get. Who would care for the children? The cost of adequate day-care facilities seemed prohibitive. All the severe remedies that came easily to campaign rhetoric seemed dangerously coun- terproductive in the face of real-world problems.

Under intense pressures from advocates of children, including his wife, Hillary, "new Democrat" Clinton backed away from his absurd campaign mouthings about welfare. During his State of the Union speech, the joint session of Congress gave him loud, sustained applause when he said:

"Our goal must be to liberate people and lift them up from de- pendence to independence, from welfare to work. . . . Our goal should not be to punish them because they happen to be poor. . . . We shouldn't just put [young mothers] and their chil- dren out on the street."

The applause told me that America isn't ready for a mean, nation-destroying move to simply abolish all welfare, or pound into the dirt and abandon young women who bear babies with- out benefit of marriage. Americans haven't yet bought the line of pseudoscientists like Murray that the existence of welfare en- courages millions of young women to have babies. And that the IQ level of a future America is imperiled if government subsi- dizes the low-IQ babies of "dumb" women.

Standing like a great moral roadblock in front of those rush- ing toward the drastic reform, or abolition, of "welfare" is the fact that children — deprived and often desperate *children* — still make up two-thirds of AFDC recipients. Nobody has fig- ured out how to punish the often-despised mothers or the "dead- beat dads" without being cruel to the children.

The Gingrich-Dole solution to our most compelling social and racial problems is to mandate that the states solve them, and then give the states 90 percent or less of the funds the federal government was spending while failing to solve the same problems. Most governors gleefully take the 90 percent grant knowing that they and their cronies can rip off a good chunk of it and never have to explain why the nuisance problems are still unsolved.

I know personally that "states' rights" is really a cover for egregious states' wrongs. For thirty years of my life, from 1935 to 1965, the phrase was a frightening symbol of injustice. It symbolized the right of Tennessee to segregate me in an inferior public school, to deny me the right to read a book in my town's only public library, to declare me unfit to get a drink of water in a "white" drugstore, or to sit in the city park, or to enter the town's hotels except as a bellhop.

States' rights meant that I had no rights beyond the command of any white man, including the most abusive cops. The state had rights to get surplus foods, school lunch, and other federal largess, but I as a poor black child had no right to any of it. So there were no hospitals or clinics for black people in McMinnville when I grew up, and I never saw a dentist until I went into the navy at age seventeen! Crueler denials are inevitable for poor people now because of cuts in Medicaid and "states' rights" to dole out medical care and medicine.

But thanks to Bob Dole and Newt Gingrich and their new federal budget, "states' rights" are about to reign again in America, and millions of Americans are going to be hurt by them even more than I was.

The Republicans wanted to cut $182 billion from the Medicaid program and 20 percent from antipoverty programs — and then hand them over to the states, which would cut some more and eventually decide who would not benefit from the dwindling funds. As the *Wall Street Journal* noted, "More important than any programs is the fundamental end to entitlement: states will have the right to cut people off."

I remember how those "states' rights" to cut people off were used in the 1960s when America was awakening to the reality of deep and widespread hunger that crippled the legs, hearts, and brains of countless children trapped in unconscionable poverty in wretched regions of South Carolina, Mississippi, Texas, Appalachia, and beyond. Some state officials refused to accept or distribute food given by the federal government through school lunches or in any other way.

Why are state officials likely to be more cruel than federal authorities have been? Because they would have to use a nickel of their money to supplement what Uncle Sam provides. Officials in some states would rather cut unfavored people off life-and-death programs and divert federal funds to their cronies and self-enriching projects.

They will get away with abuse of the poor because, sadly, state and local officials do not get the media scrutiny that federal officials endure. State and local pols may be "closer to the people," but usually only to the people of their color, their mindset, their party, their social class.

"States' rights" propel us backward toward the rickets, scurvy, hunger-based mental retardation — and worst of all, the racial resentments and class hatreds — of the 1950s and 1960s. That's why I was relieved when President Clinton, although forced to endorse the GOP calls for a balanced budget in seven years, decided to go to war with Gingrich, Dole, Armey, Kasich, and the fearsome seventy-three GOP freshmen in Congress over the funding of education, cuts in Medicare and Medicaid, sustaining environmental protections, the size of a tax cut for the rich, and, incredibly, federal support for welfare programs.

Here, I knew, was an issue that would be used to fan new flames of racial warfare. It struck me as ironic that I might have to fight someone over a program that I wished was not needed and did not exist. I wanted the nation to understand this, so I said in a column of December 29, 1995:

President Clinton fired up the chronic anti-poor outrage by making a campaign promise to "abolish welfare as we have known it." He lit the passions of the greedy, the ignoramuses, who blindly assail "welfare queens" and "deadbeat dads" and pretend that the poor are the villains who bring great economic woes to more privileged Americans.

Mr. Clinton learned, slowly, that it is easy to tell a welfare mother to get a job; it is harder to show her an available job for which she is trained. It is simplistic to say to a woman, "You've got three children; now get off your derriere and work to feed them." But it becomes very complicated when the mother asks who will care for her three young children while she works at a wage that won't come close to lifting her family out of poverty.

Mr. Clinton abandoned his foot-in-mouth approach to welfare. He could not stomach throwing millions of children to the wolves, knowing they would someday come back as half-wolves to devour those of us who live in great comfort.

But the Congress is controlled now by Republicans like House Speaker Newt Gingrich, whose great blind passion is to wipe out "the welfare state," no matter how cruel the impact on poor kids.

The Republicans want to cut welfare costs by [$60 billion over six years] while making inadequate grants to the states, which will decide whether and how to fund welfare schemes. History tells us to beware not just of 31 Republican governors, but also of the Democratic politicians whose top priority, truth be told, is not to use scarce money on poor, hungry, ill-sheltered, medically neglected Americans who carry no clout at the polls.

What kind of conscience allows politicians of any stripe to be so mean to the most-abused children in the land? The consciences of people who rationalize with phony "studies" that purportedly prove that welfare programs are intrinsically destructive of poor children. You've heard it all: welfare stunts IQs, destroys character, encourages out-of-wedlock teenage pregnancies. . . .

President Clinton has rejected these specious defenses of governmental child abuse. He refuses to believe that giving an impoverished child a school lunch, rudimentary shelter, some food stamps and a doctor's occasional care is "crippling" that child.

This war of philosophies about "welfare" is a large part of what the budget crisis and the recent shutdowns of government are all about. This is a war for the heart, mind and soul of this nation.

In July 1996, it became clear that the welfare system in America had been demonized to the point that none of the facts cited above, no concept of economic justice, no plea for compassion or morality, could stop the Republicans' drive to wipe out the program that most symbolized "the welfare state" that was so hated by Newt Gingrich and others. Bill Clinton, the "new Democrat," had given the Republicans a great opportunity in 1992

when he pledged to wipe out "welfare as we know it." Clinton
had promised to produce jobs, the training of people in the underclass, the child care that would make it feasible to say to welfare mothers, "Get a job." He had backed off his campaign
promise when he found out that to create the jobs, produce the
training, and provide child care carried price tags far beyond
anything even he is willing to spend.

In the heat of the presidential campaign the Republicans produced their own version of welfare reform, one of the most myopic and mean-spirited pieces of legislation that I have seen
during thirty-five years in the nation's capital. Senator Daniel
Patrick Moynihan, the New York Democrat who was the party's
expert on family life for two generations, called the Republican
measure the worst since the post–Civil War reconstruction period, when the goal was to virtually reenslave black people. He
warned that it would add another million children to the 15 million already living in poverty in America. He said that the Republican bill was so cruel that if enacted it might provoke a
million young Americans to take to the streets in violence.

What the Republicans proposed quite simply was to wipe out
the sixty-year federal guarantee of basic assistance to the poorest of Americans. The GOP wanted to take the federal welfare
money, reduce it by about $60 billion over six years, and give the
balance to the states with a mandate that they in their ways
should look out for the needy. But there would be stringent lim-
itations on how states could spend the money — virtually nothing, especially in cash, for teenage mothers of illegitimate babies
or for legal immigrants, even though their sons or husbands
might be serving in the U.S. military in Bosnia.

President Clinton could have stopped this bill by announcing
that he would veto it, even after its passage by a huge majority
in the House of Representatives. His cabinet objected strenu-
ously to his signing such legislation but his pollsters told him
that most voters consider "welfare" one of the dirtiest of words.
His guru Dick Morris told him that going against welfare would
virtually guarantee his reelection. So Clinton did what no
Democratic President of character, or with real moral moorings,
would ever have done: he announced that he would sign the bill.

He thus released many Democrats to play their own game of
craven politics and vote for it. So at the end of July, all fifty-

three Republicans and twenty-five of forty-six Democrats voted for passage of a measure that Georgia's representative, John Lewis, the civil rights movement hero, called "mean . . . base . . . downright low down." The Roman Catholic bishops said, "This legislation may meet the needs of politicians but fails too many children." Hugh Price, president of the National Urban League, said, "It's almost as if Washington has decided to end the war on poverty and begin a war on poor children."

Clinton himself told the nation that the bill was seriously flawed in that it cut too much — at least $24 billion — out of programs that give nutrition assistance to working families with children, and that it was grossly unfair to legal immigrants. But he was signing it, he said, to get rid of a system that trapped poor Americans in "dependency."

New York officials noted that the state constitution required the expenditure of funds adequate to care for the needy — funds that the state would not have when the federal government dumped on it the problems, but not enough money to meet them. One Republican representative, John Kasich of Wisconsin, told New Yorkers that they should simply change their constitution. Los Angeles faced the expenditure of $100 million a year — money it didn't have — to care for the legal immigrants that Uncle Sam was abandoning.

This welfare reform bill is certain to increase class strife and racial warfare in America when millions of people discover that the privileged in the White House and Congress have said, "Let them eat cake."

# Chapter 7

# Crime — More Than a Double Curse

Former Atlanta police chief Eldrin Bell once posed a disturbing question: "I wonder if because it is blacks getting shot down, because it is blacks who are going to jail in massive numbers, whether we — the total we, black and white — care as much? If we started to put white America in jail at the same rate that we're putting black America in jail, I wonder whether our collective feelings would be the same or would we be putting pressure on the President and our elected officials not to lock up America, but to save America."

Utter the phrase "black teenager" or "black man" to most white Americans and their first image is not of bright young students scratching their way across handicaps and over deprivations in order to get to great universities where they can distinguish themselves. For too many whites those phrases provoke images of "animals" who mug and steal, rape and kill. This shotgun stereotyping fosters the most mindless, dangerous hostility in the land.

Speaker after speaker at the Million Man March dwelt on that theme. "Why are there so many blacks in jail? Is it behavior or is it the rules?" asked Jesse Jackson, who then answered his own query, "It's racist, it's ungodly, it must change."

I see the crisis up close and personal whenever I receive letters like those I got after a column I'd written about racism in law enforcement agencies:

"Until we go back to harsh penalties for crimes committed, this senseless violence will continue to occur," wrote one reader. "These 'rotten cops' affect [sic] on society is highly exaggerated by you, so there can be more excuses for the minorities to commit more crimes and blame someone else. I guess it is time to go back to 'cruel and unusual' punishments such as flogging, the taking of a finger and frankly the Death Penalty to put an end to societies' rocketing crime and murder rate."

Another letter writer accused me of "injecting your racism into the crime problem." He went on to tell me that "blacks are executed most because they commit the most animalistic crimes."

I started to write that man asking if he had ever heard of John Wayne Gacy, Jeffrey Dahmer, Richard Speck, Joel Rifkin, Ted Bundy, or David Berkowitz, but I knew that I would be wasting my time. It is a sad fact that taken together, the acts of all these white murderers, rapists, dismemberers, and cannibalizers do not put as mean a scar on the psyche of white America as one atrocious crime by one black man.

While polls can give a sense of the public's feelings, it is difficult to measure the actual extent of racism in the criminal justice system. But you get an indication from a report entitled "Equal Justice" which was issued in 1994 by a blue-ribbon commission set up in Massachusetts to study racial and ethnic bias in that state's court system.

The final report confirmed the "existence of considerable racial and ethnic bias, both direct and subtle, in the Massachusetts court system." For example, racial minorities are underrepresented on juries and in the legal profession, the panel said, and as a result, "blacks have lost respect for the law and those who enforce it."

This, mind you, came from Massachusetts, a cradle of American democracy and the first state to have blacks in its state police force. Imagine what similar studies might find in Alabama or Mississippi, the cradles of the Ku Klux Klan, and where until a few decades ago the state police were lily-white.

The American Civil Liberties Union echoed the Massachusetts findings in a 1994 report that said, "Racial bias in the criminal justice system is increasingly recognized as one of the most important civil rights issues of the day. Race-based disparities span the judicial process. . . . Although such bias can usually be rationalized in non-discriminatory terms, the cumulative effect of the institutionalization of racism is overwhelming."

Complicating the situation is a Catch 22–like vicious circle. When whites read stories of black robbers and rapists, or see black youths on TV, handcuffed and being pushed into a paddy wagon, this increases their expectations of more black crime. That in turn leads to harsher police tactics, sentencing, and other policies that cause blacks to lose respect for the legal system and for authority — which produces more scenes that provide fodder for bigots and pseudoscientists to declare: "Sure, there are more blacks in jail, but it's not bias, it's because they commit more crimes."

Blacks *do* commit a disproportionate number of the violent crimes in America. Most of the crimes committed *by blacks* are committed *against blacks*. But that doesn't justify the fallacious notion that blacks don't give a damn about reducing crime. Blacks can't afford *not* to give a damn — not when every day they watch their children killed in street-corner drug fights and see more and more of their young men going to jail. Not when a terrified eleven-year-old girl in a crime-ridden Washington, D.C., neighborhood plans her own funeral, all the way down to choosing the dress she wants to be buried in. And not when the Department of Justice tells us that one out of every twenty-one black men can expect to be murdered, a death rate that is double that of American servicemen in World War II.

America has reached the point where building prisons is this country's newest growth industry. Over the last ten years, the U.S. has doubled the number of people locked up, and over the last twenty years, it has quadrupled the number — to the point that we have the highest rate of incarceration in the world.

I'm not really surprised at this, or at the cries I hear for mandatory sentences for everything from jaywalking to killing your mother-in-law. They are based on a notion that seems to make sense — a notion expressed in its most simplistic, succinct form by Ben Wattenberg, a fellow at the American Enterprise Institute: "A thug in prison cannot shoot your sister."

But does it really make sense? Do we want to, can we imprison 40 or 50 million "thugs"? Adam Walinsky cautions, "The police need not function as the intake valve of a criminal justice system devoted to the production of more prison inmates, of whom we already have more than is healthy."

The use of sentencing laws and prisons to control crime can never have more than a marginal effect. In a 1993 study "Understanding and Preventing Violence," the National Research Council noted that the amount of prison time served per violent crime in the U.S. tripled between 1975 and 1989, and then it asked, "What effect has increasing the prison population had on levels of violent crime?" Its answer: "Apparently very little."

The problem is that for most whites, who control police departments, the courts, the jails and prisons, black criminal behavior justifies the brutal discriminations that engender black rage and criminality. Few lawmakers or other Americans want to talk about why there is so much crime and violence, why minorities are so disproportionately, and often unfairly, involved — and how society can change this nation-threatening situation.

On October 20, 1995, Alonzo Jackson and Rasheed Plummer, both sixteen, went shopping at an Eddie Bauer warehouse outlet store in Fort Washington, Maryland, a middle-class, predominantly black suburb of Washington, D.C.

The boys were on their way out of the store when they were stopped by two uniformed off-duty Prince Georges County policemen moonlighting as security guards, who demanded that Jackson prove that he owned the shirt he was wearing. According to the boys' account, not disputed by the store, Jackson told the officers he had bought the shirt the day before and did not have the receipt with him. The security guards reportedly told him to take off the shirt, leave it at the store, and go get the receipt.

Jackson went home and found the receipt, returned to the store, and got his shirt back — but not his dignity. Since then, Eddie Bauer's has publicly apologized and tried to smooth things over, but the two teens have filed an $85 million lawsuit against the retailer, alleging, among other things, false imprisonment, defamation, and violation of civil rights.

Incidents like this happen because a large number of white people think race is a critical factor in crime. In a 1993 poll, one out of every three Americans agreed with the premise that African Americans "were more likely to commit crime and violence." Many black men are in prisons, or have come close to being in prison, because of mere racist expectations of criminal behavior.

Remember Susan V. Smith, the Union City, South Carolina, mother who told police that a "black man" had hijacked her 1990 burgundy Mazda and driven off with her two young sons? A nationwide search was launched, as South Carolina authorities flooded the country with fearsome drawings of the alleged black hijacker — until the truth finally came out that Susan Smith had buried her young boys at the bottom of a lake in her car.

These kinds of incidents add to racial polarization and hatred and are bitter reminders of the stereotyping of all black males as potential kidnappers, rapists, and killers — stereotyping that warps the minds of many white people — and some blacks — and bolsters the stupid notion that race is the root cause of crime.

Sure, there are plenty of examples of white crime. Jeffrey Dahmer may kill and eat people. The Menendez brothers may slay their parents. Lorena Bobbitt may cut off her husband's penis. But no white TV viewer personally sees himself or herself inside these white criminals. No white person sits in front of the TV, thinking, "Charles Manson, the Unabomber, the people who blew up that building in Oklahoma City — all us white people are murderers by nature."

But that absurd generalization about blacks flashes through the minds of millions of people during every TV news show. I have chastised myself many times when a horrible new crime is promo-ed on television and I say, "God, don't let the killer be black!"

When the newsperson says, "Police say the suspect is a black man," I know that a whole race of people will once more be indicted and convicted in the minds of white viewers.

The idea that blacks are genetically prone to crime received a "scientific" boost when Murray and Herrnstein wrote in *The Bell Curve* that "taking the scientific literature as a whole, criminal offenders have average IQs of about 92, eight points below the mean. . . . The relationship of IQ to criminality is especially pronounced in the small fraction of the population, primarily young men, who constitute the chronic criminals that account for a disproportionate amount of crime."

This belief that blacks are inclined to crime is a powerful force. To the shock and dismay of some blacks, the Reverend Jesse Jackson seemed to give more comfort and ammunition to the "blacks are animals" crowd a few years ago when he told a Chicago group of African Americans this about his own neighborhood in Washington:

"There is nothing more painful to me at this stage in my life than to walk down the street and hear footsteps and start thinking about robbery — then to look around and see somebody white and feel relieved."

Not only white racists but "moderate" white columnists loved that remark, because it seemed to relieve white people, the American establishment, and political and economic systems of any guilt for associating blackness with crime. "Even Jesse fears black men!" they can say. Jackson surely must have been embarrassed by his statement, part of his "campaign to stop black-on-black crime." But carried away in his new high-hype campaign against an admittedly serious problem, Jackson told that Chicago audience: "This killing is not based on poverty; it is based upon greed and violence and guns."

I don't dismiss the effects of poverty as easily as he does, but Jackson certainly pinpointed a couple of the root causes of violence in America and a reason why blacks do commit more crimes than whites. Poor teenagers do fight greedily over drug-peddling turf and the riches that are at issue. They do covet that pair of $150 sneakers they see Michael Jordan advertising on TV or the $400 boom box that the neighborhood drug courier carries around. But hell, when they lack any honorable recourse, who's surprised that blacks maim and murder for big bucks?

And Lord knows, Jackson was on target when he fingered guns as part of the story of American violence. The U.S. is a loose-cannon arsenal. In 1993 more than 570,000 gun felonies were reported to police. Seven out of ten homicides that year were committed by the use of guns (four-fifths of them by handguns), and guns were used in 42 percent of all robberies and one-fourth of aggravated assaults. A 1994 U.S. Justice Department study concluded that "greater gun availability increases the rates of murder and felony."

Throughout the 1980s and 1990s, at least 4 million new guns were manufactured or imported annually — there are now an estimated 211 million guns in private hands in this country, enough to arm every adult and more than half our children. Nothing seems likely to halt the firearms explosion; in fact, pressured by the National Rifle Association, more and more states are making it legal and easier for citizens to carry weapons, even *concealed* weapons. In the last two years, ten more states have passed laws that allow citizens to carry concealed weapons, bringing to twenty-eight the total number of states that permit this dangerous practice, with several more considering the change. An outrageous number of concealed knives and guns are showing up in schools — even elementary schools!

Who totes the most guns? someone asks, as if there is a statistical way to apportion blame.

It seems commonsense clear to me that a disproportionate number of black youngsters tote guns and knives because they live and go to school in areas where their lives are in greater peril than those of white youngsters. This factor is diminished, however, by the fact that guns are costly, thus more whites — especially white women — can afford to purchase a handgun. Thousands of white preteens and teens have been found toting around their mothers' weapons. Blacks think they have double the need of whites to arm to the teeth, while whites have double the economic capacity to buy guns. Still, many whites think they fear guns more than blacks do, despite the fact that blacks are the primary victims of black criminals. And far more whites than blacks join the National Rifle Association and lobby furiously against gun control.

We are all victims of gun madness.

Another factor in the crime rate is demographics. Criminologists have known for a long time that males between the ages of fifteen and twenty-four commit a disproportionate amount of crime. Although the upper end of that age group has been declining in numbers, a new wave of young teens is moving in, bringing with it a scourge of youth violence — gang wars, drive-by shootings, drug dealing, schoolyard violence. Between 1990 and 1994, the murder rate for fourteen- to seventeen-year-olds jumped 16 percent. Homicide is the second leading cause of death for fifteen- to twenty-four-year-olds.

And then there are the politicians, pointing fingers and scrambling to outdo one another with ill-conceived quick fixes, designed to win support from frightened voters by showing that they are "tougher on crime" than the next office seeker.

While greed and guns, demography and demagogues, all play roles in spurring violence in America, the number one factor is social conditions. I have written and argued for years that there is a direct correlation between a community's rate of violent crimes and its level of racism — reflected in poverty, dearth of jobs and good schools, level of family breakdown, drug trafficking, sexual exposure and abuse, and general hopelessness and despair.

Crime is a result of deeper social trends. A child is born to a mother who has no job, no hope, no future. That child grows up in a crowded, dilapidated home, with a parent who's rarely around (too often one who's in prison), in a neighborhood with no green space, no recreational facilities. Is there any doubt that crime and violence will flourish in those circumstances?

A study published in the June 1995 *Journal of the American Medical Association* argued that poverty, not race, accounts for the sharply higher incidence of domestic homicide among blacks. The crime difference between races — blacks have a domestic homicide rate six times that of whites — virtually disappeared when crowded living conditions were used as a measure of socioeconomic status.

"New Orleans blacks were no more likely to murder a relative or acquaintance than were whites in similar socio-economic circumstances," said the author, Brandon S. Centerwell, an epidemiologist at the University of Washington in Seattle. "When blacks and whites were matched for the ability to purchase uncrowded housing, the risk of intraracial domestic homicide in New Orleans's black population was not significantly different from that in white populations."

In a similar study he conducted in Atlanta, Dr. Centerwell found that the major difference between black and white homicide rates is attributable to poverty, not to issues of black culture or black value systems.

Enraged, dehumanized people strike out at whoever is closest to them. In a society that is racially segregated, blacks have almost no one else to attack other than other blacks during the "social" hours in bars and clubs, or black relatives at home. That seems to be changing somewhat, but not necessarily for the better. In 1995 we saw numerous stories of black men filled with fury over their humiliating joblessness going to a former workplace to kill their former bosses, black or white, and fellow workers.

Is this genetic? Are blacks just emulating the behavior of whites who think their "manhood" has been destroyed?

Most experts also pooh-pooh the idea of a link between crime and genes. At a 1995 conference in Maryland, reported in the *Baltimore Sun,* one hundred scientists and other scholars agreed that there is no direct evidence that specific genetic mutations can make someone more likely to commit a violent crime, and such mutations may never be found.

In fact, the genetic "explanations" can be counterproductive in efforts to combat crime, because they encourage passive attitudes toward social justice and a neglect of social problems, warned Dorothy Nelkin, a New York University sociologist.

It is these social conditions that we should really be looking at. The Alternative Schools Network, a private organization that supports a coalition of schools and learning centers in Chicago, reported in 1994 that statistics from 1990 show a link between high school dropouts "who are poor and have limited job opportunities" and violent crime. The group noted that 72 percent of the men jailed in Illinois are high school dropouts — with the figure rising to 80 percent in the city of Chicago. These men have a hard time getting work, their income declines, and there's not much they can do to earn an honest living.

The record is clear that crime is not rooted in racial passions alone. If it were, black mayors and police chiefs would have curtailed it. What also bedevils America is a related, furious class conflict.

The poor are likely to be painfully aware that they can't buy those expensive Michael Jordan sneakers for their kids; can't always put a full, let alone healthy, meal on the table; can't go to college or get medical care when it's needed. Little wonder that disproportionate numbers feel alienated and turn to crime. People who are outsiders, who feel they don't belong, war in almost kamikaze recklessness against all who are in the privileged and protected "establishment."

The FBI crime report issued in December 1995 was a stunner. It showed that crime rates had dropped sharply in the first half of 1995, with murders down 12 percent nationally and serious crimes of all kinds off by 1 to 2 percent.

But the general public is definitely not out celebrating V-C (Victory over Crime) Day. Bombarded with media accounts of crimes and politicians suggesting that crime has become pandemic in the United States, most people still say crime is the nation's most urgent problem and their greatest personal concern. There's no indication they feel much, if any, safer, no matter what one year of FBI statistics may say.

A *Wall Street Journal*/NBC News poll found that two out of five Americans had changed their routines recently because of their fear of crime. Many no longer shop after dark; they try to go with friends, and they avoid potential danger spots like convenience stores.

Fearful people may be reacting to past experiences. The effects of crime are cumulative. Rates may be down from three years ago, but Americans have a sixth sense that they are three times more likely to be murdered, mugged, or robbed than they were thirty years ago. In New York City, for example, while the 1,182 murders in 1995 are only about half the 1990 high of 2,245, they are four times the pre-1960 average of three hundred a year. And it is hard to forget that a total of twenty thousand New Yorkers have been murdered over the past decade.

Crime has also become less predictable, more random, and therefore more frightening. For the first time ever, Americans are now more likely to be killed by a stranger than by a family member or a friend, the FBI reports. And the violence is occurring in what once were considered "safe" havens. We *expect* violence, thus a race war is well within our thinking.

Get in an argument on the school playground, and you may be stabbed or shot by a classmate. Cut in front of a car on the freeway, and the driver may pull alongside and fire shots at you. Walk out of the shopping mall, and you may find a carjacker waiting in the parking lot. Sit at your desk, and a disgruntled ex-coworker may burst in and start shooting.

Americans are especially vulnerable to hysteria about crime

today because they don't know how to restore the tranquillity of yesterday — a time when a family put a milk bottle on the porch with money in it, certain that only the milkman would take it; and when you could go to bed on a hot night with your windows open, protected only by a little latch on the screen door.

What Americans forget when they glorify yesterday is that when we put our money in the milk bottle, we didn't have millions of youngsters who were largely bereft of parental supervision, and whose "churches" were street gangs. It was a time when families were a bulwark against crime, not a cause of it, and the streets of America — even the meanest streets — didn't bristle with handguns and automatic weapons, protected by a powerful lobby like the National Rifle Association. We were just learning about the Mafia and organized crime, and most people had never heard of heroin, cocaine, or LSD.

Besides the memories of more tranquil days, Americans' fear and hysteria about crime are being fanned by politicians and the media. Congressional debates over crime bills in 1994 and 1995 produced endless political posturing. Republicans shouted that Democrats were "soft on crime" and President Clinton felt compelled to endorse crazy, counterproductive proposals in order to prove he wasn't a coddler of murderers and rapists.

And what has this baseless racial fear, this phony get-tough attitude gotten us? The distinction of being the world's number one jailer.

We have a federal prison system that is running 25 percent over capacity and state prisons that are 17 to 29 percent over. Financially strapped states are housing inmates in tents, trailers, hallways, gymnasiums, or releasing them early. And this is costing us $31 billion a year for the construction of prisons and the maintenance of inmates, many of whom are the victims of endemic white racism.

More significant than the numbers are the people behind them. Blacks now comprise 50.8 percent of the inmates in our prisons and jails. One out of every eleven black adults is in prison or jail, or on probation or parole; at any one time, 6 to 7 percent of black males twenty-five to thirty-four years old are in state or federal prisons. While blacks comprise 12.5 percent of the U.S. population, they make up 55 percent of the new incarcerations. According to the Bureau of Justice statistics, the proportion of black male adults behind bars in 1994 was almost eight times higher than the proportion of white males. If present trends continue, an absolute majority of black males aged eighteen to forty will be in prison and camps by the year 2010.

The war on drugs has been responsible for much of the increase in the U.S. prison population. Nearly half of all new commitments since 1980 are a result of drug offenses, while 16 percent are for violent offenses. This has brought the proportion of inmates convicted of drug offenses in federal prisons up to nearly 60 percent and in state prisons to 25 percent, compared with just 6 percent in 1983. According to the Justice Department, more than one in five federal prisoners is a low-level drug offender with no previous arrests and no involvement in sophisticated criminal activity. About half of all inmates held by states are not in for violent crimes.

This country was torn for a few months of 1995 by black anger and white guilt over an appalling racial and class disparity in punishment for the possession and use of two types of cocaine.

If you are caught with 5 grams of crack cocaine (about two pennies in weight, $500 in street value), even though there is no intent to sell it, a judge must impose a mandatory minimum sentence of five years. But you have to have 500 grams of powdered cocaine (more than a pound, worth about $50,000) before you draw the same five-year mandatory minimum that the 5-gram crack user faces.

On the face of it, this seems unfair. It takes on darker overtones when you know more about who uses crack and who uses powder. Because it is cheap, crack is the drug of choice in the ghetto — which is to say, the drug of choice for young blacks. The more expensive powder is the favorite of well-to-do whites. Actually, a study by the U.S. Sentencing Commission indicated that 46 percent of crack users are white and 38 percent are black, but 90 percent of all crack defendants in federal courts are black. Police tend to ignore white crack users, but focus venally on black users and peddlers.

Most of the blacks caught or arrested on narcotics charges are not hard-core dealers. Criminologist John Hagedorn of the University of Wisconsin at Milwaukee says two-thirds or more of participants in drug-sales rings "also work straight jobs and would like to settle down with their families in homes with white picket fences."

The situation is so unfair, so stupid, that you'd think every member of Congress would have recognized it immediately and gone along with a request by the Sentencing Commission to wipe out the discrepancy by increasing the punishment for powder use to the same level as that imposed on crack users.

But the House of Representatives said no, and incredibly, President Clinton swallowed some bogus advice and refused to strike down an injustice that will contribute to war-like explosions in the teeming prisons and deadly streets of America.

The premise behind the vastly different sentences was that crack is highly addictive and that there's a lot more violence associated with its use. Representative E. Clay Shaw (R-Fla.), the original sponsor of the mandated sentence, defended it, declaring during the debate in the House that minority neighborhoods have been devastated by crack and residents are pleading, 'Come in and arrest the traffickers.'"

That brought an angry response from Representative Maxine Waters, a black Democrat from California, who told Shaw, "I don't want you to ever believe that you care more about my community than I do or think that somehow your policies and your beliefs are right for my community. . . . No black leader has said to you, 'Lock up our kids.'"

Waters pointed out that crack is the only drug with a mandated minimum sentence for possession and that young men were likely to become career criminals while serving time in jail for a minor drug charge. Still, the courts have upheld the crack-powder distinctions.

Although it has been documented that Caucasians sell most of the nation's cocaine and account for 80 percent of its customers, there have been proposals in Congress to make selling drugs in public housing more severely punishable than selling drugs in affluent neighborhoods.

That kind of bias is not new. In 1991, the U.S. Sentencing Commission conducted a study that found evidence of racial disparity in the imposition of mandatory minimum sentences. The bias, it charged, reflects the very kind of discrimination that the Sentencing Reform Act was designed to reduce. A year later, the Federal Judicial Center reported that in cases where a manda-

tory minimum could apply, African American offenders were 21
percent more likely and Hispanics 28 percent more likely to receive at least the mandatory minimum prison time.

The most controversial aspect of sentencing, racially or otherwise, remains capital punishment. In February 1990 the General
Accounting Office — the investigative arm of Congress — reported "a pattern of evidence indicating racial disparities in
charging, sentencing, and imposition of the death penalty."

According to the GAO, persons who murdered whites were
more likely to be sentenced to death than those who killed
blacks. Blacks, said the GAO, are executed for killing blacks *and*
whites, but whites are rarely executed for killing blacks.

Historically and currently, says the ACLU, it is race, not the
severity of the criminal offense itself, that is the overriding factor in death penalty sentences. In federal courts, 90 percent of
defendants selected for capital punishment under the "drug
kingpin" provisions of the 1988 Anti-Drug Abuse Act are minorities, even though three-fourths of those eligible for such
prosecution are white. Half of the three thousand–plus death-
row inmates around the country are from minority populations,
including 40 percent who are black, according to the Death
Penalty Information Center.

White Americans don't seem to want to know the extent to
which crooked cops abuse the fundamental rights of nonwhites,
and why abusive cops may become key figures in triggering a
race war.

The problems run all the way from local cops right up to the
agency that once was virtually above reproach — the FBI. Abuse,
brutality, even criminality, are rife in every big city police force,
and in rural areas, too. Many innocent people sit in our bulging
prisons because political cries of "Take the advantage away from
criminals" have provoked this society to give the likes of Detective Mark Fuhrman of O. J. Simpson trial fame carte blanche to
go after people, especially minorities, on flimsy or false charges.
So while they're supposed to be wiping out crime, too many of
our law enforcers are contributing to the great racial divide.

— Near Pittsburgh, Jonny E. Gammage, a thirty-one-year-
old black businessman, was pulled over on a traffic stop on October 12, 1995. Officers at the scene said Gammage attacked
them and they had to defend themselves. Gammage was pinned

to the ground, his face pressed to the pavement, as one of the five officers stood on his neck and pressed down with a metal club. Gammage died of suffocation. His case might have died, too, except that Gammage's cousin is Pittsburgh Steelers lineman Ray Seals. Two officers were charged with third-degree murder, but critics say it was too little, too late.

— Thousands of law enforcement people from members of local police forces to agents of the FBI and Bureau of Alcohol, Tobacco and Firearms (BATF) participated in "good ol' country boys" roundups in the hills of Tennessee. According to reports, these annual get-togethers featured T-shirts showing Dr. Martin Luther King's face behind a target and O. J. in a hangman's noose. "Nigger hunting licenses" were sold, along with other items that degraded African Americans.

— In July 1994, after a two-year investigation, the New York City Police Department issued a report saying it had found "willful blindness" to corruption throughout the ranks of the NYPD that had allowed a network of rogue officers to deal in drugs and prey on black and Hispanic neighborhoods. Predatory cops ran wild in the city's poorest neighborhoods and the brass was deliberately blind to them. A ring of officers assigned to take guns and drugs off the streets broke down doors of apartments in northwest Harlem in order to steal drugs, guns, and cash, investigators said. Most of the fake raids were on Dominicans they thought were unlikely to report their operations to higher police authorities.

This litany is not meant as an indictment of all law enforcement officers. I know lots of "good" cops — honest, brave men and women who respect the Constitution and love the law. They risk their lives to uphold the law and protect citizens of all races. These officers are a laudable, underappreciated part of this violence-ridden society, and I have no doubt that the vast majority of America's law enforcement force are appalled, embarrassed, and ashamed by the actions of a few who reflect negatively on them, too.

Still, these actions are an all-too-common déjà vu for blacks. They bring back memories — not all that ancient — of fire hoses and police dogs and truncheons, and of white police officers who were the enemy, not the protector.

Gilbert Branche, who was a Philadelphia policeman for

twenty-seven years, and is now assistant executive director of the National Organization of Black Law Enforcement Executives, told the *Washington Post* that the belief that police are brutal "is almost institutionalized within the minority community."

One of the ironies of the loss of esteem for law enforcement agencies is that it is conservatives who now are complaining the loudest about corruption in the FBI, the BATF, the IRS, and among other federal lawmen. These are the same critics for whom, just a couple of years ago, nothing was too un-American if it was anticrime and locked up criminals. These politicians sowed the wind with a torrent of demands for reinterpretations of the Constitution and passage of punitive legislation to give more power to police and "take the advantage away from the criminals." Now we are all reaping the violent whirlwind.

The social tornadoes are blowing through our courtrooms, too.

No one is soft on crime. But many are stupid about it. Consumed by racism and hatred of two-bit drug peddlers, conservatives and others who are almost paranoid about crime believe almost exclusively in punishment as an antidote to lawlessness. They cheer when an eighteen-year-old American gets caned in public in Singapore for vandalizing cars. They want to build walls around the inner cities and ban from their communities anyone free on parole after serving time for a serious crime. They would waive the Constitution so the apartments of public housing residents can be searched without a warrant, and deprive prison inmates of aid to pay for classes behind bars. And they would like to impose the death penalty for just about every serious crime.

One of the most promising movements in law enforcement is community policing, which gets cops out of their squad cars and puts them on foot (or sometimes on bicycles) and in storefront police stations, right in neighborhoods. They can spot troublemakers before they mug or rape or sell dope, and trouble spots like abandoned housing, vacant lots, and broken street lights.

Perhaps most important of all, this approach gets officers engaged with their communities, not estranged from them. And in return, the police get an invaluable weapon — information and cooperation from people in the neighborhood who might otherwise shun them.

As one officer in a community policing center in Kansas City, Missouri, explained to *Washington Post* reporter Pierre Thomas, "The people of this community are our eyes and ears, the people who put these [bad] guys behind bars. We are trying to build more trust. We go door to door a lot. Initially, people would only crack their door; eventually, they started to let us in."

President Clinton summed it up this way: "We know what works in fighting crime also happens to improve relations between the races. What works . . . is community policing. The crime rate is down, the murder rate is down where people relate to each other across the lines of police and community in an open, honest, respectful, supportive way. We can lower crime and raise the state of race relations in America if we will remember this simple truth."

**Chapter 8**

# Double Murder, Double Tragedy

During my adulthood I have seen a dozen developments that truly strained American race relations to the point of possible warfare. Half a century ago black Americans — and much of the world — were outraged when a black lad in Mississippi, Emmett Till, was lynched for merely whistling at a white woman. In 1944 there was a furious reaction to the imprisonment of fifty black men who had staged the Port Chicago "mutiny" outside San Francisco by refusing to load ammunition after two ships blew up, killing 320 men. I shall never forget the nationwide tensions when the late, great Paul Robeson defied and outraged both McCarthyites and liberal whites by visiting the Soviet Union, saying nice things about it, and in many other ways tweaking the goatee of Uncle Sam. And anyone doubting the possibility of a nationwide race war need only recall 1968 and the violence that followed the assassination of Dr. Martin Luther King, Jr.

As destructive as those events were, not all of them together equaled one event of 1995 in its power to rend the fabric of societal relations. None of these other volatile events came close to producing more belligerent racism than the O. J. Simpson trial. This double-murder case involved all the passions and principles and factors that make race the overarching problem of this society. Every imaginable aspect of courtroom justice, the validity of the jury system, the powers of judges, the ugly specter of men beating their wives, the factor of drug abuse, the ability of the rich to "buy" a verdict, the role of a defendant's fame, the custom of juries "nullifying" evidence, the modern habit of lawyers stacking juries with members of one race, the constitutional issue of illegal searches and seizures, the curse of policemen lying and planting evidence, the legitimacy of lawyers "playing the race card" — all this and more made this trial as explosive as any in the nation's history.

The land mines of that historic legal struggle are still lightly buried across the American landscape, and that is why I must discuss them at length, with details you readers probably missed, to explain the imminence of a race war.

The moment I heard the news that Nicole Brown Simpson, the white former wife of football hero O. J. Simpson, and a Caucasian male friend had been found murdered in Los Angeles, I knew that the ultimate American social tragedy was about to unfold. I knew that this nation was about to see sordid, riveting elements of a human drama that would engross, entertain, titillate, in ways that no novel, no soap opera, no sleazy TV talk show ever could — and that at the end there would be a tragic widening of the already gaping racial divide in America.

I knew that the stories of these two murders would immediately grab the glands of millions of American white men, prejudicing them in ways they would never admit to publicly. More than eight decades had passed since boxer Jack Johnson roiled white America by flaunting his white bride, and half a century since Till was lynched. Interracial marriages had become so commonplace in all parts of America that the surface assumption was that when a Caucasian woman gave her body, even her love, to a black man, the matter no longer stirred jealous fury in the hearts of white men. But I knew better.

The huge headlines, and the long television stories about the California murders would enliven the insecurities of millions of white male psyches. The old college girl's chant, "Once you go black, you never go back!" surely would take on feverish new meaning.

A black friend of morbid wit said to me, "Doesn't O. J. know that we can fuck 'em now, but we still can't kill 'em?"

But I knew that the societal repercussions would go beyond any white-man fears of black men and the age-old stories and myths of their sexual prowess. There were the fears and resentments of black women who have recently complained loudly about "white women taking our men." With the nation's jails and prisons overcrowded with virile young black men of marriageable age, and with a large percentage of black households headed by single women, O. J. would for many become a symbol of black men who "betray" black women. He had, after all, left a black wife and his black children to marry a teenager whom some called "white trash."

And on a more general level, a million blacks and whites would gossip about how "O. J. lived white" and was never "part of black America." Simpson worked *among* white people, ran through airports *for* white people, partied *with* white people, lived *amidst* white people on an estate few blacks could afford. He was not running through Selma or Birmingham, risking his life in any civil rights endeavor, involving himself in any causes to lift black youngsters out of the poverty and illness that almost destroyed him as a boy.

Cocaine came before caring for Simpson — or so millions of black Americans believed. Some would say initially that if O. J. Simpson got the electric chair, it was what he deserved.

But I knew immediately that there was more that was tragic about this case than a resurgence of splenetic passions over interracial fornication and marriage. Here was a case certain to strain every fiber of America's criminal justice system, including white people's assumptions about the inherent criminality of black people, especially black males, and black people's distrust of prosecutors and police witnesses. *Everything* would be challenged, even the rights of the media. Television in the courtroom would become the focus of national debate as never before.

This case produced a great racial schism primarily because most Americans, of whatever race or background, started out in this case with preconceived notions of Simpson's innocence or guilt, and even though the televised trial was one of the most-watched events in American history, most Americans did not — could not — follow it closely enough to let any evidence alter their early judgments.

I watched all but a few hours of this gripping TV extravaganza. At the end, for my personal benefit, I wrote a chronology of the major events and pieces of testimony that I thought had to be considered before anyone could make any fair judgment as to Simpson's guilt or innocence. I still believe that no one has a personal right to "convict" Simpson, or declare him innocent, who has not pondered such a chronology.

Most Americans know some of the details of the very beginning of this tragedy. At 11:40 P.M. the night of June 12, 1994, Sukru Boztepe arrived at his Brentwood home to find his neighbor, Steven Schwab, sitting by the pool of their apartment complex with a large, white Akita dog that had four bloody paws. The Akita had followed Schwab and his own dog home less than an hour earlier. At about midnight, Boztepe and his wife, Bettina Rasmussen, took the Akita for a walk, hoping to find its owner, after the dog kept running to their window and scratching at their door. The dog led them to Nicole Simpson's home where Boztepe and Rasmussen spotted a woman lying on the ground. Rasmussen noted that "an ocean of blood" covered the scene on Bundy Drive.

The Akita was Nicole's dog. The butchered body near Nicole's was Ron Goldman, a friend of hers who was a waiter at the Mezzaluna restaurant, where she had dined earlier that evening.

Detective Mark Fuhrman of the Los Angeles Police Department was dispatched to the murder scene, where, moving about the crime scene alone, he said, he found one bloody glove. When two veteran LAPD detectives, Tom Lange and Philip Vannatter, arrived at Bundy, Fuhrman was "taken off the case." Fuhrman, who had once confronted Simpson while investigating a dispute between O. J. and Nicole when they were married and living together on North Rockingham Road, just "hung around" the murder scene, witnesses said.

The stories of the first week or so, which were based mostly on Los Angeles Police Department (LAPD) and prosecutor leaks, led me to an early conclusion that Simpson was "as guilty as sin." I had learned as a reporter many years earlier that it was dangerous folly to pretend to know what was going on in the marriage of any other couple. But the media stories about Simpson's past, and about the alleged evidence against him, led me to fear that he was beyond any defense lawyer's salvation.

I, like almost every homicide detective, say, "Look for the ex-husband," anytime a separated or divorced woman is murdered — especially when there is evidence that the woman was sexually active. Whispers swept across America like the wind that O. J. had "stalked" Nicole and had seen her having intercourse with other men. That seemed a clear motive of passion.

Meanwhile, the press was aflame with leaks and rumors, most of them spread by the LAPD, that blood at the Bundy murder scene matched that of Simpson, that "Negroid hair" was found on a blue knit cap found at Bundy, that blood was found on the driver-side door of Simpson's Ford Bronco; that there was "a trail of blood" from the Bronco to Simpson's house, and inside his foyer; that O. J. had bought a fifteen-inch knife at a Los Angeles cutlery store on May 3, just weeks before Nicole's and Ron Goldman's throats were slit almost to the spine.

It was hard for me or anyone else to reject Los Angeles District Attorney Gil Garcetti's public declaration that he had a "solid" case against Simpson.

I became perhaps 80 percent "sure" that Simpson was the killer after that gripping drama of June 17, just four days after the murders were discovered, when I and 95 million other Americans watched the freeway police "chase" O. J. fifty miles, with O. J. holding a gun at his head, in a Bronco driven by his lifetime buddy, Al Cowlings. The impression the world got was that O. J. was fleeing to somewhere, going to Nicole's grave, or heading to where only God and Cowlings might ever know. What we did learn was that Simpson had broken a promise to turn himself in to the police, and that in that Bronco were $10,000 in cash, O. J.'s passport, a fake mustache, and other items with which to hide Simpson's identity.

Who can forget the stark drama that began at 6:46 P.M., Pacific Daylight Time (the heart of prime time on the East Coast), when Cowling's Bronco cruised along Interstate 5, provoking him to have the following exchange with a 911 dispatcher:

OFFICER: "911. What are you reporting?"
COWLINGS: "This is A. C. I have O. J. in the car."
OFFICER: "O.K., where are you?"
COWLINGS: "Please, I'm coming up the Five freeway."
OFFICER: "O.K."
COWLINGS: "Right now we all, we're O.K., but you got to tell

the police to just back off. He's still alive. He's got a gun to his head."

OFFICER: "O.K., hold on a minute . . . Monica."

COWLINGS: "He just wants to see his mother. Let me get him to the house."

OFFICER: "Hold on a moment. O.K. Where are you? Is everything else O.K.?"

COWLINGS: "Everything right now is O.K., Officer. Everything is O.K. He wants me to get him to his mom. He wants me to get him to his house."

OFFICER: "O.K."

COWLINGS: "All I — That's all we ask. He's got a gun to his head."

OFFICER: "O.K., and sir, what's your name?"

COWLINGS: "My name is A.C. You know who I am, Goddamn it!"

OFFICER: "O.K. All-righty, sir, hold on just a moment."

ANOTHER OFFICER: "Hi, what's your name?"

COWLINGS: "Aw . . ." (hangs up.)

This freeway chase was a mind-boggling addition to the letter that O. J.'s close friend Robert Kardashian had read to the media only hours earlier. It said in part:

To whom it may concern:

First, everyone understand, I have nothing to do with Nicole's murder. I loved her, always have and always will. If we had a problem, it's because I loved her so much.

Recently we came to the understanding that for now we were not right for each other, at least for now. Despite our love, we were different, and that's why we mutually agreed to go our separate ways.

It was tough splitting for a second time, but we both knew it was for the best. Inside, I had no doubt that in the future we would be close friends or more. Unlike what has been written in the press, Nicole and I had a great relationship for most of our lives together. Like all long-term relationships, we had a few downs and ups.

I took the heat New Year's 1989 because that's what I was supposed to do. I did not plead "no contest" for any other reason but to protect our privacy and was advised it would end the press hype. . . .

Paula, what can I say? You are special. I'm sorry, I'm not going to have, we're not going to have, our chance. God brought you to me, I now see. As I leave, you'll be in my thoughts.

I think of my life and feel I've done most of the right things. So why do I end up like this? I can't go on. No matter what the outcome, people will look and point. I can't take that. I can't subject my children to that. This way, they can move on and go on with their lives.

Please, if I've done anything worthwhile in my life, let my kids live in peace from you, the press.

I've had a good life. I'm proud of how I lived. My mama taught me to do unto others. I treated people the way I wanted to be treated. I've always tried to be up and helpful, so why is this happening?

I'm sorry for the Goldman family. I know how much it hurts.

Nicole and I had a good life together. All this press talk about a rocky relationship was no more than what every long-term relationship experiences. All her friends will confirm that I have been totally loving and understanding of what she's been going through.

At times I have felt like a battered husband or boyfriend, but I loved her — make that clear to everyone. And I would take whatever it took to make it work.

Don't feel sorry for me. I've had a great life, great friends. Please think of the real O. J. and not this lost person.

Thanks for making my life special. I hope I helped yours.

Peace and love, O. J.


O. J.'s behavior aroused all the questions imputing guilt that I had ever heard in any grade B movie about any fugitive: "If he's not guilty, why is he running?" "What guy takes his passport, ten thousand bucks, and a face change to his dead ex-wife's grave?" "Was that chase staged to gain sympathy from a public that has already found him guilty?"

But that bizarre "flight from justice," with dozens of LAPD patrol cars and helicopters, and news helicopters, following him, provided plenty of evidence that millions of Americans regarded Simpson as an icon. Blacks, Hispanics, and whites lined the freeways shouting, "Go O. J., Go! A crude sign said "Cut Loose the Juice!" Admirers had festooned the gate at Simpson's home with placards saying, "WE SUPPORT YOU O. J.!" and "WE LOVE YOU O. J. MAY GOD BE WITH YOU."

Eventually, Cowlings drove Simpson to the latter's Rockingham Park home, where he was arrested amidst a frenzy of newsmen, all of them dealing with rumors that Simpson would plead guilty and use insanity as his defense.

"There is an utterly macabre nature to all this," said ABC's Peter Jennings.

"This is one of the most amazing stories of all time," said Michael Kinsley, then a host of CNN's program "Crossfire."

Amazing? Yes, and more. Because that dramatic "chase" drowned out the report that on that same Friday, June 17, 1994, Simpson had been indicted on two counts of premeditated murder, charges that required his detention without bail and left the superstar subject to possible execution if convicted.

O. J. got less than he bargained for in "the chase." Columnist Frank Rich of the *New York Times* would write:

> It was not until Mr. Simpson ended his Bronco ride in surrender that he surrendered the illusion of invulnerability fame had bestowed on him. Then Americans turned on him — not only because of the dawning realization that he might have killed others but because he failed to defy his own destruction.
>
> Whatever fate awaits him in court, O. J. is already being cannibalized for this betrayal. We don't look kindly on celebrity gods who fail, forcing us to crash-land from fantasy back into the mire of our own mortality. By Monday a *Time* magazine cover signaled the change in mood by blackening O. J.'s skin to send him back to the ghetto he long ago escaped. Now the media sprint is on to prove that O. J.'s entire image, pristine only yesterday, was a fraud.

Americans turned on Simpson, sure enough, but the Bronco chase was far from the most important reason. He was formally convicted in the court of public opinion on June 15, just two days after the bodies were found, when chilling headlines declared that Simpson had a long history of beating and battering Nicole.

The LAPD had released records showing that on at least eight occasions Nicole Simpson had called the police for protection from violence by her husband. The stories of June 16 were devastating to Simpson. The *Washington Post* story said:

> While police remained silent about their investigation into the murders of the former wife of O. J. Simpson and an acquaintance, court and city records here [in Los Angeles] reveal a violent side of the former football superstar.
>
> In 1989 police reports and court documents, Nicole Brown Simpson indicated she feared her husband and had called police a number of times for help because of her physical arguments with the former Heisman Trophy winner. In one case, she suffered a split lip and a black eye, said a city official who reviewed the files.

This article, like others across America and the world, revealed that sports icon Simpson had pleaded "no contest," meaning guilty, to this charge of battering his wife.

Los Angeles city attorneys had tried to jail Simpson for thirty days, but higher authorities had decided to give the great NFL star an easier punishment of two years probation, 120 hours of community service, and a gift of $500 to a Santa Monica shelter for battered women. Simpson also would have to undergo counseling twice a week for three months, and then once a week for another three months.

The police tape that terrible morning of New Year's Day 1989 portrayed an eerie scene of the worst of battered wives — Nicole running out of the bushes in just her bra and some sweatpants, shouting, "He's going to kill me!" She supposedly had fallen into the arms of a policeman, who noted cuts, a swollen lip, the blackened left eye, swelling and bruises on her neck and face, and the reddened imprints of hands across her neck as if someone had tried to strangle her.

God, this seemed more than enough to establish a motive, an emotional predisposition, for Simpson to kill his wife. But there was more. And Garcetti and the LAPD would make sure that America knew about it.

On June 23 newspapers blared forth headlines about a Nicole Simpson 911 call to police on October 25, 1993, that suggested

Simpson was more violent, far more inclined to kill, than the Hertz ad hero who just ran through airports to his waiting rental car. On October 25 Simpson had broken down the French doors at Nicole's rented house on Gretna Green Way in Brentwood.

By this time O. J. and Nicole had been divorced for more than a year. You could say that he was a menace, a "stalker" who had no business anywhere near her home — except for the fact that Nicole and O. J. had been dating for the previous six months, trying to determine how to restore their marriage.

But why, then, this wild scene of Simpson at Gretna Green, so furiously angry that he causes Nicole to dial the 911 dispatcher and engage in this dialogue:

NICOLE: "My husband . . . my ex-husband just broke into my house and he's ranting and raving."

DISPATCHER: "Has he been drinking, is he on drugs, is he armed?"

NICOLE: "No, no, no."

DISPATCHER: "Is the fight resulting from something you have done?"

NICOLE: "Oh, a long time ago. It always comes back."

The conviction of Simpson in the minds of the public might have been delayed if the press had told the public the truth about that piece of the 911 tape.

The media reported that Simpson had gone ballistic when he saw a picture of one of Nicole's old boyfriends in her apartment. The truth was that Nicole's "a long time ago" referred to O. J. looking through her window and seeing her having oral sex with a man later identified in court testimony as Keith Zlomsowitch. Had the public known the reason for Simpson's rage, it would not have leaped to the conclusion that he was a maniac naturally inclined to murder. The rest of that 911 tape revealed the following:

Nicole asks O. J. to calm down, to remember that their kids are upstairs.

"Who cares about the kids . . . I don't give a fuck about the kids," O. J. says.

"O. J., the kids are sleeping," Nicole pleads.

Simpson responds angrily, "You didn't give a shit about the kids when you were fucking in the living room. They were here. Who cared about the kids then? . . . Oh, it was different then."

What the public also didn't know was that the *National Enquirer* had run an article full of information that O. J. knew only Nicole could have given them about their personal relationship. So part of that October 1993 blowup involved O. J. shouting, "I've been reading all this fucking shit in the *National Enquirer*, and you fed 'em this shit. . . ."

An overlooked part of that 911 record was also Nicole's statement that O. J. had driven up in a white Bronco, yelling at her and her "roommate." The "roommate" apparently was a ne'er-do-well would-be actor whom Simpson had befriended, who was "rooming" at Nicole's Gretna Green place, and who O. J. suspected was fucking Nicole throughout the six months when Simpson and Nicole were supposedly trying to arrange a reconciliation. Brian "Kato" Kaelin was his name, and he would become a major figure in future court proceedings.

When the cops arrived at Gretna Green, Simpson told them that, yes, he had broken down the French doors and that he would take full responsibility for replacing them.

The public had heard so much that was shocking about Simpson that only a few read closely a *USA Today* article of August 1, 1994, about the release of a 460-page grand jury transcript that included testimony by Keith Zlomsowitch, who had been Nicole's lover in 1992.

Zlomsowitch — who, ironically, was operations director for the Mezzaluna restaurant where Nicole and her family ate just hours before her murder — testified that Simpson was a jealous, obsessive stalker of Nicole during this period of their separation. "Keith" told the grand jury that he and Nicole had sex on the couch of a candlelit living room one spring evening of 1992. He said Simpson showed up at the Gretna Green house while he was giving Nicole a neck massage in her bedroom by the swimming pool.

According to Zlomsowitch, Simpson was enraged, saying to him and Nicole: "Look what you are doing . . . the kids are right here by the pool. Look what you guys are doing . . . I watched you last night. I can't believe you would do that in the house . . . I watched you . . . I saw everything you did."

Garcetti's office took the position that this proved Simpson to be so obsessive about Nicole that when he couldn't win her back, he killed her.

Simpson's lawyer Robert Shapiro argued, "If any man by chance came upon this type of behavior in the proximity of children and all that was done was caution them, this shows great control and great restraint."

*USA Today* quoted jury consultant Robert Hirschhorn as predicting that the defense would argue before the Simpson jury that "if watching your [separated] wife have sex with another man doesn't send him into a murderous rage, then nothing will."

Simpson's legal team went further and said that O. J.'s best friend, football star Marcus Allen, had confessed to Simpson that he had had a sexual affair with Nicole, and that Simpson had forgiven Allen and allowed him to have his wedding at O. J.'s house. This, lawyer Johnnie Cochran argued, was evidence that Simpson was no jealous maniac bent on killing anyone over Nicole. A court ruling thwarted Cochran's efforts to force Allen to testify at Simpson's trial.

Simpson's defense suffered from more than the unassailable evidence of his obsession with his wife. The thousands of reporters and television commentators and talk-show hosts were a monolith of condemnation. "No man ever strikes a woman," they said. "Wife-beaters are always potential killers," others said. "Just because a wife is unfaithful is no excuse to beat or kill her," was another cry.

As if all this were not enough to poison any potential jury, or the public, the media rushed into an orgy of stories about how this "naive," tender white girl got wooed into a death web by the older, already-married football hero.

The biggest and best newspapers told us how Nicole was born in West Germany, her mother's homeland, and grew up in Monarch Bay, south of Los Angeles. She was a homecoming princess at Dana Hills High School just a year after her sister Denise had been crowned queen. Two pretty girls. Both well stacked. The kind to catch the eye of any lecherous man, especially one who might think his fame entitled him to pluck the juiciest plums from the closest tree.

Nicole, full of dreams about what her good looks and sexy body might draw, went to Hollywood just after turning eighteen. She struck up a brief romance with a record producer named Val Garay who described her as "a sweetheart, a very sweet girl."

Then, at a Hollywood club, Nicole met O. J. Although he was married, and she knew it, she went to bed with him. O. J. fell so far in love that he divorced his black wife within a year. Nicole fell to the point that she lived with O. J. as just a lover for five years. In 1985 they were married, eight months before the birth of Sydney, their first child. A son, Justin, was born in August 1988.

This bit of history would explain partly why black Americans and white Americans would view the double murders so differently, whatever the evidence that Simpson was the killer. Whites would see Simpson as a predator, as someone as bad as any movie pimp, as an immoral black guy who seduced a nice teenage white girl into his wicked web, and then beat and abused and finally killed her.

Black people would in private say that Nicole was "white trash," using her blond hair, her big breasts, her teenage pussy to woo a famous, rich, middle-aged black man away from the black woman who had sustained and nurtured him through the toughest years of his life.

Was there any chance that courtroom proceedings would wipe out this emotional reaction? Could any jury surmount these racial and sexual factors and measure the evidence presented dispassionately? I doubted it. I said at the outset that there wasn't a chance that any Los Angeles jury would convict Simpson.

Throughout all the days of the revelations about the sometimes violent love-hate relationship between O. J. and Nicole, I thought that the prosecution had skillfully (and venally) played the ace of hearts. The spousal-abuse "card" would be almost impossible for Simpson's lawyers to trump, especially after the tabloids reported breathlessly that O. J. had also beaten and abused his first wife, a black woman.

Yet, on June 20, it was a confident Simpson, showing no emotion, who appeared briefly for arraignment before Judge Patti Jo McKay to plead not guilty to murder charges.

The prosecution was playing to the public with extraordinary brazenness. Simpson had his actual life at stake, but the top prosecutor, Garcetti, had his public and political life on trial. Garcetti was elected to this powerful job primarily because his predecessor, Ira Reiner, had failed in the case of Rodney King, a black ne'er-do-well who had been beaten mercilessly by white L.A. cops while a citizen was videotaping their abuses. Garcetti took office and lost the world-watched case of Erik and Lyle Menendez, two brothers who shot their parents to death and then claimed that the parents had so abused them sexually and psychologically that they had been driven temporarily insane with fear. Their first trials ended in hung juries.

Garcetti felt that he simply could not lose the Simpson case and remain politically viable in Los Angeles County. So in the days following the gruesome murders he was trying to convict Simpson in every media outlet he could reach.

I could not believe it when I read in the *Washington Post* of June 20: "District Attorney Gil Garcetti said today that he expects a temporary insanity defense in the first-degree murder trial of O. J. Simpson and that because of widespread sympathy for the football superstar it will be a 'profound challenge' to find a jury that will unanimously reject such a defense."

The truth was that neither Simpson nor any of his lawyers was thinking remotely of pleading insanity. Simpson was saying over and over, privately and publicly, "I did not murder Nicole."

Garcetti was so outrageous in his efforts to poison the public, and in his efforts to hide from defense lawyers the evidence he claimed showed Simpson's guilt, that on June 24 Superior Court judge Cecil J. Mills aborted the grand jury investigation on grounds that the jury might have been influenced unduly by the storm of publicity.

Garcetti cried some public crocodile tears over the leak of the 911 tapes that revealed Simpson's abuses of Nicole. He said he strongly condemned the LAPD for giving the media the tapes that were broadcast on every radio and TV station in the area from which a jury would be selected. The *Los Angeles Times* had already received a report of a 1985 quarrel between O. J. and Nicole when the gridiron gladiator smashed the window of her car with a baseball bat. When the cops, including Fuhrman, showed up, Simpson told them: "It's my car. I'll handle it. There is no problem here."

The campaign of leaks intended to demonize Simpson had gone so far that Garcetti, Los Angeles police chief Willie L. Williams, and City Attorney James Hahn met secretly and agreed on an "information ban" — a blackout that was never honored.

Garcetti continued to say, publicly and often, that Simpson was the only suspect, and that he was sure he was the murderer.

But now, with the grand jury dismissed, there would have to be a preliminary hearing at which Garcetti and his prosecutors would outline before a judge their case against Simpson.


Illegal Searches and Seizures

I first began to think that O. J. might be innocent on June 30, when, in the preliminary hearings, LAPD detectives told how and why they seized thirty-four pieces of evidence from Simpson's Rockingham estate *without a warrant*.

June 30, 1994, was to be a watershed day in this murder case that gripped the world as probably none ever had. The prosecutors, Marcia Clark, a smart, quick-tongued brunette, and William Hodgman, a businesslike man with no noticeable flair, were supposed to tell Judge Kathleen Kennedy-Powell why O. J. Simpson ought to be put on trial for two ghastly murders. They were supposed to answer the questions the world was asking: Did they "rush to judgment" in charging O. J. with the murders?

Why did Hodgman and Clark reject out of hand the defense's suggestion that the murders were committed by more than one person, perhaps ordered by a drug lord who had long failed to collect money due from Nicole or her druggie friends?

Had the Los Angeles Police Department collected blood, physical and other evidence that was so overwhelming that it compelled a judge to rule that one of the nation's greatest celebrities, and a black celebrity at that, should be tried on charges that put his life, or his freedom forever, at risk?

Or was this a case where the entire prosecutorial combine was so driven to "win a big one," that they unwittingly or rapaciously committed a conspiracy to do whatever was necessary to convince twelve jurors that Simpson had murdered a less-than-faithful wife, and a restaurant waiter who had been at a ghastly place at the wrong time?

I began to have some "reasonable doubts" that Simpson was the murderer in the early days of those preliminary hearings.

It was noteworthy, I thought, that the police had no murder weapon, no witness to the murders, no bloody clothing of Simpson's. But they did have blood droplets from the Bundy murder scene. And one bloody glove. And a knit cap. And another glove, and a blood spot on Simpson's Bronco, and spots of blood — all found, allegedly, at O. J.'s home by that detective who was off the case, Mark Fuhrman.

Why, I asked myself, did this Fuhrman hang around the Bundy crime scene after he was officially removed from the case?

Fuhrman's earlier testimony had revealed that he had previously been to the Simpson's Rockingham home to answer one of those domestic-abuse calls. He had seen the white woman, Nicole, in fear and humiliation, then the black superstar in macho defiance of the investigating police. In these preliminary hearings, Mark Fuhrman gave Judge Kennedy-Powell no clue that the interracial sex taboo that poisoned the psyches of so many men had also poisoned him.

But, at that time, the biggest issue was not Fuhrman, or his views of African Americans, or his opinions of interracial sex. The judge wanted real evidence that Simpson had murdered Nicole and Ron Goldman.

Most of all, Judge Kennedy-Powell wanted evidence against Simpson that would survive the test of constitutional scrutiny. She, probably more than any judge on earth, was aware that Shapiro and his new lawyers, Gerald Uelmen, a national expert on evidentiary matters and constitutional protections, F. Lee Bailey, famous for courtroom dramatics, and the noted constitutional scholar Alan Dershowitz would challenge the use of thirty-four pieces of evidence gathered during the warrantless search of Simpson's estate. They would claim that this evidence was gained in violation of the Constitution's Fourth Amendment protections against illegal searches and seizures.

The exclusion of evidence because of constitutional violations by police officers had become an issue of violent rhetoric in America. The presidents and cabinet officers of the Nixon, Ford, Reagan, and Bush administrations had always played "the crime card," campaigning on themes that Democrats were "soft on crime," and had enacted laws that gave criminals an advantage over law enforcers.

Fuhrman, Vannatter, and their associates offered to Judge

Kennedy-Powell explanations of their behavior at Simpson's estate that no ordinary person would accept, let alone a skeptical judge who must have heard cops lie in court time after time after time.

I count as friends and confidantes judges at every level of America's criminal justice system. Almost to a man or woman, these judges have told me that they are troubled most by police lying in their courtroom. But the judges don't know what to do about the "thin blue line" of police perjury that is invoked against all defendants, but in the most vile and pernicious ways against the poorest or the most vulnerable of minority defendants.

"I hear these cops week after week, lying through their teeth I am sure, but I just don't know what I can do about it," one great judge told me. "Can I, on my hunch that a cop is perjuring himself, wipe out the case of prosecutors — often against someone I feel is not guilty in the case at hand, but is a social abomination overall?"

The preliminary hearings produced a fascinating — and dismaying — show of police behavior, and of deferential treatment of the police by judges.

Why would the top detectives on this double murder case leave the Bundy scene immediately, driven by detective Fuhrman, who supposedly was "off the case," and rush to Simpson's home? Was Simpson their immediate suspect? Oh, no! they testified. Had Fuhrman told detectives Vannatter and Lange and/or Phillips of his visit to the Rockingham estate when O. J. was accused of beating Nicole? No, no. Vannatter testified that they were simply on a mission of mercy to inform Simpson of the death of his ex-wife and to get him to make arrangements for the care of his children.

Shapiro scoffed at this expression of a noble motive, this insistence that the cops had not "rushed to judgment" that O. J. was the double murderer.

Vannatter testified that he and the other detectives arrived at the Rockingham estate about 5:30 A.M., and that they rang the bell at the gate of Simpson's walled-in property for fifteen or twenty minutes, but got no response. They telephoned, but no one in Simpson's home answered. They called the security company that looked after the football star's home, but got no information as to where Simpson was.

What to do? What to do?

Fuhrman provided the answer. He had wandered off alone, just as he had done at the Bundy scene, and lo and behold, in the early morning darkness he had spotted a drop of blood about one-eighth to one-fourth inch in size near the chrome on the door of a Ford Bronco he said was "haphazardly parked."

I looked at the photographs on TV and saw nothing "haphazard" about the way the Bronco was parked.

Then Fuhrman's claim to have seen evidence of blood on the door of the Bronco became critical.

Vannatter seized upon this as an excuse to invade Simpson's property without a warrant. He told Judge Kennedy-Powell, "I made a decision that we should go in there and check and see if everything was OK. . . . We were within five minutes of a very, very brutal murder scene. I was concerned that this could be a second murder scene, whether someone was stalking Mr. Simpson and his wife. I didn't really know at that point what I had or what I was looking for."

What Vannatter had was a lame excuse for violating the Constitution. What he didn't have was a search warrant. So he gave Fuhrman the go-ahead to scale Simpson's wall and open Simpson's gate so the three other detectives could enter. I thought at the time how extraordinary it was that Vannatter purportedly feared they were entering "another crime scene," but he called for no police backup. None of the detectives wore a bulletproof vest or drew a gun.

Shapiro argued doggedly that "improper procedures were used from the beginning of this investigation." Lead prosecutor Marcia Clark said, "They had to do something to assure themselves that any people inside were safe. . . . Had they not gone in, we would justifiably have accused them of being derelict in their duty."

Once on the Simpson grounds, the detectives awakened a strange hanger-on, Brian "Kato" Kaelin. O. J. had given him a place to stay to get him out of Nicole's home. Kaelin told a weird story of hearing three thumps in the night behind the O. J. guest house in which he was living. The police also awakened Simpson's daughter, Arnelle, who testified she never gave them permission to search her father's house, or the grounds.

While Vannatter and Lange and Phillips were collecting

Simpson's shoes, socks, and other pieces of evidence, who again wandered off alone? Fuhrman. With a tiny flashlight, his gun tucked away, he goes behind the guest house and, amidst cobwebs and leaves with no blood on them, "discovers" a bloody left-hand men's glove that matched the right-hand glove at the Bundy crime scene.

I recall saying to myself, "This Fuhrman is just too much. He keeps discovering evidence to link O. J. to the murders."

I did not know at the time that Fuhrman had arrived at the Bundy crime scene first and was alone amidst the evidence. He had arrived at the crime scene wearing a jacket which, at some point, when he was unobserved, he put in his car. What was in that jacket, which was never seen again? I did not know that at about 4:30 A.M. Fuhrman had a police photographer take a picture of him pointing at the lone glove at Bundy, as if to say, "This matches the glove at Rockingham." Trouble was that Fuhrman had not yet gone to Rockingham. The photo was passed off by the LAPD as one taken at 7:30 A.M., but lighting experts showed in the trial that it was taken in full darkness — a suggestion that Fuhrman was indicating a glove match even before he made his "discovery" at Rockingham.

I repeat that I didn't know these facts when I watched Fuhrman and Vannatter testify, but my instincts told me that something was rotten in L.A., and I said so in my column on July 7, 1994.

> The prosecution and its detectives tried to lead us to believe that O. J. murdered Nicole and Goldman, returned to his estate, climbed the back fence just where he would make loud bumps on the back of quarters occupied by a dubious friend, "Kato" Kaelin, and leave a bloody glove there — with "Kato" almost pleading later with one of the detectives to walk where he would find the glove.

But, just as every journalist and legal expert expected, Judge Kennedy-Powell refused to suppress the evidence on Fourth Amendment grounds. Municipal judges rarely make decisions on such high-falutin' constitutional issues. They leave that to the higher courts. And the top courts have already carved out

exceptions to the Fourth Amendment prohibition of unreason-
able searches and seizures. The California Supreme Court had
said in 1972 that police officers could proceed without a warrant
when they perceived an "imminent and substantial threat to
life, health or property."

Beyond that, the climate in Los Angeles and across America
was such, in the wake of the double murders, that any judge
who threw out the evidence gained in the search of O. J.'s property would have been tarred, feathered, and skinned alive in the
media, and probably right outside the courthouse.

Then up popped the *New Yorker* and *Newsweek* magazines
with reports that Fuhrman had a history of bigotry. On July 22,
1994, I wrote:

> In the last few days a media drumbeat has intensified the factor
> of race in this case, but the men I've talked to say that holes in
> the prosecution's case, including doubts about police honesty
> and skepticism about the validity of some blood tests, are what
> will prevent some jurors from finding Simpson guilty of first-
> degree murder.

Judge Kennedy-Powell had made it clear that Simpson, forty-
six, would not again soon enjoy anew the luxury of his Brentwood home. He would go back to a 7- by 9-foot cell (63 square
feet compared with his 5,752-square-foot home) in the Men's
Central Jail in downtown Los Angeles, where he would remain
one of the most watched prisoners on earth.

## The Jury System

Everyone knew that the selection of a jury would be critical. In
this case the jury system was on trial along with O. J. Simpson.

In my column of June 20, I had said:

> The evidence leaked to the media by the police, capped with
> Simpson playing the role of fugitive, does seem to bar any belief
> other than that the celebrated former athlete committed one of
> the most grisly crimes of the century.

Yet, I am not convinced that prosecutors can get a jury to agree that Simpson committed two premeditated murders for which he should be put to death.

Remember the bystanders shouting "Go, Juice, Go!" and the signs saying "Save the Juice!" during that Friday evening drama? Put one person like that on the jury and there will be no conviction that carries the death penalty. And possibly no conviction at all. . . .

Thus the venue of the trial was of overarching importance. Technically, Simpson should have been tried in Santa Monica, but that community did not have the facilities to accommodate the worldwide mob of media that was certain to show up. Downtown L.A. was the only practical venue. This troubled the prosecutors and all who believed Simpson guilty, because a jury in Santa Monica would most likely be predominantly Caucasian, while a jury in L.A. would be predominantly black. A trial in Los Angeles before a mostly-black jury would have the issue of "jury nullification" hanging over it. Meaning that black jurors might "nullify" whatever evidence the prosecution produced and out of a passion for "black solidarity" declare the black superstar "not guilty."

In every law school and courtroom in America, but mostly in Garcetti's offices, the point was made over and over that one black juror could block Simpson's conviction.

Garcetti knew that it would be impossible to get a jury devoid of blacks, and that some blacks surely would recoil at the thought of voting guilty and sending Simpson to the gas chamber. So he announced early that he would not ask for the death penalty. Many experts saw this as something more than simple pandering to potential black jurors. They said it showed Garcetti was not so sure that DNA evidence of the blood and hair samples that he possessed would place Simpson at the Bundy crime scene beyond reasonable doubt.

I wrote on August 29, 1995:

Defense charges that Fuhrman is a racist with psychological problems who "planted" the glove on Simpson's property may create serious doubts within some jurors.

Then there is the evidence that police investigators and forensic experts were sloppy, even bungling, in handling the blood samples used for DNA testing. Many experts in science and math still consider DNA testing as "witchcraft," which is why it is not acceptable in all courts, even some within California. Add evidence of mishandling blood samples and the DNA tests will be of diminished acceptability to the courts.

We Americans have always had trouble with the jury system. In his First Inaugural Address Thomas Jefferson related "equal and exact justice to all men, of whatever state or persuasion" to "protection of the Habeas corpus, and trial by juries impartially selected." We talk high-mindedly of a jury of one's peers. What does all this mean? Would a jury of Simpson's peers have been twelve Heisman Trophy winners? Or twelve NFL running backs of any race? Or just twelve black athletes? Or twelve renters of Hertz cars? Or twelve of his neighbors in Brentwood?

For most of this country's history, a black man was nobody's peer. In certain parts of the United States he could not serve on any jury, regardless of whether the defendant was black or white. Jefferson's impartially selected jury did not exist.

And just as there was no agreement as to who of what race or background should sit on juries, there was no common understanding of the independence, the power, the overall roles of juries. Blacks had been lynched hundreds of times in the South, but all-white juries almost always nullified the evidence and acquitted the white alleged killers.

During the period before the U.S. Civil War, northerners white and black blinked at the fact that southerners *legally* owned black slaves, and they helped blacks along the Underground Railroad to escape to freedom. Many whites were prosecuted for their acts, but white juries usually acquitted them.

No matter the history, it was obvious early on to both the prosecution and the defense that the racial makeup of the jury could be critical to the final outcome of Simpson's trial. The selection of Lance Ito as the trial judge was important — and especially interesting, given the fact that Ito's wife was a senior officer in the LAPD. Since the defense did not object to Ito, almost everyone assumed that the makeup of the jury meant everything.

That's why Simpson personally decided that he needed a high-powered black lawyer to lead his defense. Shapiro had shown flashes of passion in the preliminary hearings, but he clearly lacked an understanding of the role that race would play. Shapiro was making stupid public statements about how he would not "play the race card." O. J. knew intuitively that if Shapiro controlled his defense, he would go to prison for the rest of his life.

That is why Simpson told Shapiro to hire Johnnie L. Cochran, a celebrated black lawyer who had been a prosecutor before becoming a great defense attorney. The prosecution countered by adding practically unknown black Republican lawyer, Christopher Darden, to its team. These would become two of the most fateful decisions of "the trial of the century." On July 22 Cochran had Simpson plead "absolutely, 100 percent not guilty," and so began the legal and verbal wars that would mesmerize America and the world for more than a year.

Both sides then hired experts to "read" the voir dire answers of prospective jurors, to study their body language, to try to discern who had already convicted Simpson on the basis of leaks, and who might so distrust the cops that they would never vote to convict O. J.

On September 26 I wrote some unsolicited advice to the Simpson team:

> O. J. Simpson is paying millions of dollars to a defense team that is larger than his old Buffalo Bills football squad. Yet, I have the gall to offer him free advice about how to pick a jury.
>
> Multiple forces of racism — some deeply covert, others open and virulent — will be absolutely critical to any jury decision . . . So a reasonably "race neutral" jury is important to both the defense and the prosecution.
>
> That is why one of the critical questions to potential jurors is whether they are usually inclined to believe the police rather than the defendant, or whether they think policemen often lie to gain a conviction. The verdict could hang on jury trust or distrust of the police.

I gave my unsolicited advice knowing that Cochran, Shapiro, Bailey, Dershowitz, blood expert Barry Scheck, and the rest of Simpson's incredibly costly "dream team" were way ahead of me.

They had focused in on just the things that troubled me, and surely would trouble some jurors, whatever their race.

Simpson had rushed home from Chicago that morning of June 13 and been handcuffed as soon as he arrived at his estate. The implications of assumed guilt were so obvious that Vannatter quickly had the cuffs removed. But Simpson volunteered to go to police headquarters and, without his lawyers present, give a long statement in which he declared his innocence. I noted that the prosecution decided not to let either the public or the jury know what Simpson said — obviously because his statement made a persuasive case for his innocence.

More important, the defense kept highlighting the fact that on June 13, the day the bodies were found, Simpson gave police a sample of his blood upon returning from Chicago. Police nurse Thano Peratis testified that he drew 8 cc of blood from Simpson's arm. The defense said only 6.5 cc could be accounted for. Testimony established that Vannatter had personally taken the vial of blood from the police department to Simpson's Rockingham home.

The jury immediately saw the possibility that 1.5 cc of Simpson's freely-given blood could have been on his socks, his foyer floor, in the Bronco, and on a gate at the Bundy crime scene. The prosecutors tried in many ways, some transparently absurd, to establish that Peratis never took 8 cc of Simpson's blood, but I never believed this and knew the jury wouldn't. I could not escape the belief that Simpson's blood was used by the police to convict him — not in any "plot" to frame him, but in a desperate effort to ensure that they won "a big one."

Scientist Robin Cotton had told the jury of blood matches indicating that the odds were 57 billion to 1 that some of the blood at Bundy was Simpson's. Since there weren't 57 billion people in the whole wide world, her impressive testimony solidified the beliefs of millions of Americans that the murderer had to be O. J.

But those in the court of public opinion who had long before "convicted" Simpson had forgotten, if they ever heard, the May 11, 1995, exchange when defense lawyer Peter Neufeld asked Cotton if those awesome statistical figures about blood matches indicated the probability of Simpson's guilt.

"Of course it doesn't," she replied.

What did this mean for a juror? Only that after the most elaborate and costly DNA tests imaginable, and charts full of bewildering numbers, this scientist said the numbers didn't really say what the odds were that Simpson was the murderer.

Then on June 26 the noted geneticist Bruce Weir admitted in court that his numbers, his calculations of genetic frequencies in the blood stains, were "consistently wrong." Any juror wanting to dismiss the DNA evidence as "witchcraft" or numerical mumbo jumbo now had reasons to do so.

Still, Scheck and Neufeld continued to punch holes in the prosecution's blood case. On August 3 they got the esteemed microbiologist John Gerdes to say that bloodstains on Simpson's Bronco appeared contaminated, and that he would not trust the LAPD's lab work. Dr. Henry Lee said of the blood evidence, "Something's wrong." Forensic pathologist Michael Baden gave devastating testimony about the L.A. coroner's errors of commission and omission. And if "doubt" on the part of jurors was of primary interest in this case, what were those passing judgment on O. J. to make of the August 17 testimony of fingerprint expert Gilbert Aguilar that seventeen prints were removed from the Bundy crime scene that didn't match Simpson's — or the fingerprints of any of the officers or others known to be at the place of that murder. Baden had said a week earlier that "the medical examiner . . . cannot tell how many assailants there were," thus giving credence to defense claims that two or more "professionals" had slain Nicole and Ron.

The revelations about Vannatter toting around Simpson's blood, the wrenching testimony of police criminalist Dennis Fung about flaws in the collection of evidence, the incredible testimony about lapses in the coroner's procedures, all were hammered on by the defense. The question in every juror's mind was in my mind: Would I send anyone, celebrity or not, to prison for life on the basis of testimony by these detectives, or evidence collected by the LAPD's bunch of incompetents?

I knew that my answer was no when I watched and heard the testimony of Dr. Henry Lee, the world's foremost forensic scientist. Lee made a believable case that two people might have committed the murders, adding to my doubts that Simpson could have prevailed in what even the prosecutors called a brutal struggle with Ron Goldman and come out with no scars, bruises, or other signs of such a struggle on his body. Dr. Lee, who clearly had no axe to grind, was persuasive in trashing the LAPD lab, and in talking about how the evidence against Simpson was contaminated.

I think that with four words he convinced the jury not to convict when he said: "Something is wrong here."

But June 15, 1995, a day that would expose Garcetti's mistake in adding Darden to the prosecution team, may have been the most fateful of all. Most of white America had declared Darden a hero simply because he, a black man, dared to accuse a celebrated black man, Simpson. Whites, who so often are automatic suckers for blacks who proclaim themselves to be "Republican," or highly moral advocates of "family values," never saw that Darden was often inarticulate. His displays of emotion about spousal abuse were maudlin. He became a joke in black America when he whined about use of the word "nigger" (even when it was used in testimony to quote Fuhrman or someone else), claiming he had never used the word. Other blacks watched knowing that there probably is no black man anywhere who has not used the word "nigger." Some of us blacks use it as a shield, a way of saying to whites, "Words will never hurt me." Some of us use it as an expression of bond — "Hey, brother, what are us niggers going to do to stop the latest assault by Newt Gingrich?" We use it as a way of describing a black man who won't sacrifice to help his fellow blacks — "That nigger's got twenty million, but he gave just five hundred dollars for the rebuilding of the NAACP." But in using the "N word" all blacks know that they are different from a white man who uses it in bigotry and hatred. Some jurors quickly decided that Darden was of the ilk of Supreme Court justice Clarence Thomas — a sellout.

Other black jurors saw early on that Darden was not among the most competent lawyers in this trial:

June 15 brought Darden's Waterloo, and probably the end of any chance that the jury would find Simpson guilty. Darden was going to spring the steel trap, deliver the courtroom coup de grâce, by forcing Simpson to try on, before the world, the glove found at the murder scene and matching the one Fuhrman had said he found at Rockingham.

Darden had been told by his boss, Gil Garcetti, and others not to go through with the glove demonstration. But this unheralded black lawyer wanted to "get" his celebrated black foe,

Cochran. Darden felt sure he could blow the case open with his dramatic action. Here, as was often the case during the trial, he forgot a fundamental rule: lawyers shouldn't ask questions when the unknown answer might wound them. Darden's strange display of macho ego helped the defense as much as any single courtroom event except the unmasking of the bigot Fuhrman.

Simpson, wearing latex gloves to protect this precious evidence, tugged and pulled at the gloves just a few feet from the jurors, then pronounced them "too small." Darden had taken a colossal gamble and lost. He, Marcia Clark, and others tried in many ways to recover from this shocking day, but they never produced anything to wipe out most jurors' observation that the murder gloves were too small to fit O. J.'s hands.

Yet, there was a drumbeat of apologias in the conservative media for Darden's goof. Latex gloves impeded the other gloves from sliding on. Blood had shrunk the gloves. O. J. had been photographed at football games wearing precisely the same gloves, or the same kind of gloves, found at the murder scene. O. J. was faking when he tried to pull on the gloves. Watching on TV, I concluded that the gloves simply didn't fit O. J. So did most jurors.

## TV in Courtrooms

"God, how lucky we are that all Americans can see this trial on television. The potential for a racial explosion is muted by the fact that John Doe can see the gloves incident and hear the critical testimony," I said often, in different ways. It was hard for people who saw the glove demonstration to second-guess the jury's reaction.

In the wake of that trial, legal and public opinion has been skewered in a way that makes it unlikely we shall see, in the next generation, TV cameras in federal courtrooms. This is a pity. I repeat what I wrote on October 6, when Judge Ito was threatening to throw the cameras out:

Every American will learn something important about the role that racial passion will play in this case. We need to hear the lawyers and scientists battle over whether DNA is still part witchcraft, or so reliable that a decision regarding guilt in a murder case can be based on it. Only by seeing the proceedings for ourselves, on television, can we make a reasonably informed decision as to whether the jury system has been hopelessly corrupted in America.

## Summation

By the end of November 1995, it was obvious to me that the Simpson trial had poisoned the social bloodstream of America. It was like a jet of venom that contaminated everyone who touched it. O. J. had been permanently damaged, no matter what the jury verdict, by leaks about his marital violence. Nicole had been slandered with stories of her sexual activities. Judge Ito had had his legal reputation impugned; and his wife, Captain Margaret York, had known the sorrow of having Fuhrman claim that she "slept her way to the top" of the LAPD; Cochran had been charged with spousal abuse and of producing a child by a white lover while he was still married to a black woman; Marcia Clark had been sued by her estranged husband, who argued she was an unfit mother of their children, neglecting them to spend all her waking moments on the Simpson trial; some jurors had had their reputations ruined by claims of misbehavior and dismissal from the panel; several news agencies had been accused of and apologized for unprofessional conduct; Nicole's sister, Denise Brown, was wounded by stories suggesting she was having an affair with a Mafioso, who gave testimony alleging that Vannatter had boasted privately that he and the other detectives were not on a "mercy mission" when they entered Simpson's property, but were out to get the guy who secretly was their suspect. So Vannatter was damaged seriously, and the entire LAPD, including its black chief, Willie Williams, were besmirched almost beyond repair.

While I was marveling at how this trial had polluted the stream of political and social discourse in America, I had no idea that the hero of the piece might be a simple investigator.

Americans were arguing fitfully about the unfairness of a system that allowed O. J. Simpson to "buy an acquittal." It was outrageous, they said, that he could hire lawyers who were far beyond the pocketbooks of any average citizen. They missed the point: the discrepancy in financial resources was what consigned so many blacks, Hispanics, and other poor people to jails and prisons. Here was a major reason why a third of young black men were caught up in the negative side of the criminal justice system. Money was the reason you could visit death row in all the states of America and not find anyone who was rich and white.

But those Americans, not all of them white, who deplored Simpson's ability to buy a higher level of justice, were the ones condoning cuts in government-paid legal services for the poor.

Simpson's ability to hire a who's who of lawyers was obviously crucial, but so was his ability to hire "investigators," especially those who went doggedly after facts about detective Fuhrman.

The courts had frustrated the defense's efforts to get Fuhrman's military and police department personnel records. F. Lee Bailey had set Fuhrman up by asking in court if the detective had, in the previous ten years, used the word "nigger" to describe African Americans. Fuhrman, in great arrogance and greater stupidity, swore that he had not. The defense already had two women, Natalie Singer and Kathleen Bell, ready to testify that Fuhrman had used "nigger" and other racial epithets in their presence. But Cochran knew that he needed more.

In one of the most fateful developments imaginable in any great trial, Simpson's investigators learned of a North Carolina screenwriter named Laura Hart McKinny, who over ten years had taped interviews with Fuhrman in which he said "nigger" often, and also described how he as a policemen dealt with "niggers." Cochran had to go to North Carolina and get the courts to pry loose the tapes from a reluctant McKinny, who naturally did not want to lose a property that might be worth a lot of money.

The media went wild with the Fuhrman tapes, running provocative excerpts, such as the following, reprinted from *U. S. News & World Report.*

POLICE FORCE: "We've got females and dumb niggers and all your Mexicans that can't even write the name of the car they drive."

HIS HOMETOWN: "People there [in Washington state, where Fuhrman was born] don't want niggers in their town. People there don't want Mexicans in their town. They don't want anybody but good people in their town. Any way you can do to get them out of there, that's fine with them. We have no niggers where I grew up."

CHOKEHOLD: "We have to eliminate a chokehold because a bunch of niggers down in the south end of L.A. said this is bad."

WHITE AREAS: "In all of southern California. Think about that. Westwood is gone. The niggers have discovered it. When they start moving in to Redondo and Torrance — that's considered — Torrance is considered the last middle-class white society. When that falls. . . ."

LOADING UP: "There is going to be a massacre in the future and they know that. There is the Rolling '60s nigger group. They went into a sporting goods store and stole 50 Uzis, 3,000 rounds [of ammunition]. . . .

RAPE CALL: "What if I've just been raped by two buck niggers and some female [officer] shows up? What is she going to do?"

ALWAYS STOP: "Niggers drivin' a Porsche that doesn't look like he's got a $300 suit on, you always stop him."

BODY SHOTS: "We just handcuffed him and went the scenic route to the station. We searched him again and found the gun. Went over to the baseball diamond and talked to him. When I left, Dana goes, 'No blood, Mark.' No problem, not even any marks, Dana. Just body shots. Did you ever try to find a bruise on a nigger?"

SIMPSON CASE: "I'm the key witness in the biggest case of the century. And if I go down, they lose the case. The glove is everything. Without the glove — bye-bye."

Many whites express shock that a police officer would be so explicit in his hatred for people of another race or his derision of women. Yet, these same whites clearly were ready to suspend the Constitution to combat "black lawlessness," which many believed to be genetic in origin. Those who had long ago decided that Simpson was the killer began to protest loudly that the defense had "put Mark Fuhrman on trial."

Blacks wanted an example made of Fuhrman so as to warn other cops to stop going into courtrooms lying, or planting evidence, so as to send innocent blacks to prison.

Legal scholars across America said the word "nigger" from Fuhrman's mouth would translate to "acquittal" from the jury.

Fuhrman's lawyer, Robert Tourtelot, who had defended him unyieldingly against charges that he was a racist, resigned when he learned what Fuhrman had said on the tapes. But Fuhrman quickly found another lawyer to give protective advice after he was called for more cross examination — *without the jury present.* That advice was that Fuhrman invoke Fifth Amendment protections and answer nothing. Asked by the defense, Judge Ito, following California law, refused to force Fuhrman to invoke "the Fifth" with the jury present. Ito had limited stringently what the jurors could hear from the McKinny tape recordings, barring especially the playing of Fuhrman's boasts about how he had participated in coverups of police misconduct, including the fabrication of evidence to create probable cause for arrests, and in the beatings of black suspects.

Christopher Darden committed one of the worst of his many errors when, again posturing about how much the "N word" hurt him, he asked McKinny why she had not asked Fuhrman to stop using racial slurs during the interviews.

"For the same reason I didn't tell him to stop when he told me of police procedures, coverup. . . . I was in a journalistic mode."

Some jurors' ears stood up like those of a Doberman pinscher with a burglar approaching. "What coverups?" It was the first they had heard about Fuhrman boasting of police misconduct. Well, the first hearing except for what some jurors surely learned during conjugal visits.

Race — and racism in the criminal justice system — was now openly at the heart of the Simpson trial.

Those who wanted Simpson convicted assailed, not Fuhrman, but the defense lawyers for "playing the race card" and "changing the trial to a prosecution of Fuhrman." It was clear to them that, barring some remarkable closing arguments by Clark and Darden, Simpson would "walk." So the prosecution moved desperately to get Judge Ito thrown off the case at the last hour. But they soon thought better of that ploy.

Clark was brilliant in her closing arguments, and Darden did his best work of the trial. The prosecutors knew that Fuhrman was a monstrous burden, so they used extraordinary words to try to shuck him off.

"Do I wish there had never been a Mark Fuhrman?" Clark asked rhetorically. That answer could be read in the bags under Marcia Clark's eyes, and in the body language of a woman bent under the weight of two months of terribly adverse developments. She had to know that every lawyer and judge, every journalist, and most citizens were watching to see with what, if any, skill she conducted herself.

On September 26 she met her problem head-on:

"Did [Fuhrman] lie when he testified here in this courtroom saying that he did not use racial epithets in the last ten years? Yes.

"Is he a racist? Yes.

"Is he the worst LAPD has to offer? Yes.

"Do we wish that this person was never hired by LAPD? Yes.

"Should LAPD have ever hired him? No.

"Should such a person be a police officer? No.

"In fact, do we wish there were no such person on the planet? Yes."

It was a scene unlike any ever seen in any American courtroom. A scene made excruciatingly fateful because the trial was in Los Angeles, which had become notorious for grotesque abuses carried out by its policemen in earlier times. It was an especially poignant scene because Clark was pleading with nine black jurors and a Hispanic to wipe out their life histories of fearing and hating policemen like Fuhrman. She wanted them to hear even louder than her disavowal of Fuhrman her next words:

But the fact that Mark Fuhrman is a racist and lied about it on the witness stand does not mean that we haven't proven the defendant guilty beyond a reasonable doubt. And it would be a tragedy if, with such overwhelming evidence, ladies and gentlemen, as we have presented to you, you found the defendant not guilty in spite of all that because of the racist attitudes of one police officer.

Just "one police officer"? Marcia Clark knew better than any juror that Fuhrman was a lot more than that. She had the challenge of her legal life crowding in on her. On September 27, David Margolick wrote in the *New York Times:*

Exhaustively and, at times, exhaustedly, Ms. Clark sought to show that Mr. Simpson had 78 unaccounted-for minutes on June 12, 1994, and that he used them to drive to Nicole Brown Simpson's condominium at 875 South Bundy, where he brutally murdered her, then stabbed to death a star-crossed good Samaritan named Ronald L. Goldman.

Ms. Clark said that math, science and physical evidence pointed ineluctably to Mr. Simpson: everything from blood at the crime scene so rare that one would have to search billions of people to find a match, to expensive shoes sold in only 40 stores, and which were coincidentally in Mr. Simpson's size to rare leather gloves — only 200 pairs of which were sold in the year that Mrs. Simpson bought them for her spouse — that Mr. Simpson could be seen wearing at football games. Then there were bloody shoe prints reaching into Mr. Simpson's Ford Bronco and the twin evidentiary Rosetta stones that are keys to the prosecution case: the bloody glove found behind his house and bloody sock in his bedroom.

I watched Clark's closing argument and was impressed by the ways in which she tried to make the DNA evidence stand up, and to wipe out the catastrophic Darden "experiment" when the gloves didn't seem to fit Simpson. She said of the blood:

Now, first of all, I want to hear Mr. Cochran actually stand up in front of you and tell you he believes the blood was planted. I want to hear that because that is incredible. That is absolutely incredible.

When you think about that, think what evidence have you been given to show you how that blood was planted. To show you when that blood was planted. To show you who planted that blood. . . .

But the reason that they have to say this, defying logic, defying common sense, is because, ladies and gentlemen, his blood on the rear gate, with that match, that makes him 1 in 57 billion people that could have left that blood — I mean, there's what? There's 5 billion people on the planet? That means you'd have to go through 57 billion people to find the DNA profile that matches Mr. Simpson's. There's only 5 billion people on the planet.

Ladies and gentlemen, that's an identification. O.K.? That proves it's his blood. Nobody else's on the planet. No one.

But Clark's every thrust was parried by Cochran or his bull-dog associate Barry Scheck.

"There is a cancer at the heart of this case," Scheck said in those hours just before Ito would give the case to the jury. He hammered on the "contamination and corruption" of evidence in the LAPD crime laboratory, characterizing it as "a black hole" through which blood, fibers, hair, and other evidence were pushed before being presented in court as "evidence."

"If it is contaminated and corrupted there, it doesn't matter how many times it is tested," Scheck shouted, "you get the same result."

The jurors would say later that Scheck really impressed them.

Clark was obviously weary. But not as weary as any of the jurors who had been sequestered precisely a year to the day before she began her closing argument. The panel had been locked up longer than any in the history of American criminal trials. The actual jury had changed dramatically over the year, with ten members having begged successfully to be released, or having been dismissed for alleged misconduct.

But there was just no way that a white woman could trump the "race card" that Fuhrman represented. Garcetti and his colleague had to hope that their black man, Darden, could do it. With everything against him, Darden would, in the prosecution's sad September, give his best performance of the trial.

He was dramatic and quite believable in his portrait of Simpson as a celebrity used to getting what he wanted, but who on June 12, 1994, was rejected by both his obsession, Nicole, and his new lover, Paula Barbieri.

"Rejection," Darden argued, lit Simpson's "short fuse."

Darden professed to have no doubt that O. J. was the double murderer.

"This is a rage killing and it is up front and it is personal," he said to a colossal worldwide audience. "And that is why you see all the brutality that you see. . . . Common sense tells us that. I mean, we know that just from life experience and from living in L.A., we know what kind of killing this is. This is a rage killing.

"And he's using a knife because he is there to settle a personal score, a personal vendetta that he has.

"He stabs this woman, all right, in the neck. And he's right there. I mean, it's one on one. And the rage that he has, the anger, the hate that he has for her that night at that time, it's like it flows out of him and into — into the knife and from the knife into her.

"With each thrust of that knife into her body and into Ron's body there is a release, you know, a small release," he continued. "It's like a tiny time capsule, you know, like Contac. There was a release, a gradual release, of that anger and that rage."

Millions of TV watchers' skins crawled as they listened to Darden's graphic portrayal of a man with "a short fuse" who, having been cuckolded by assorted men, finally exploded into death-dealing anger the night of June 12, 1994.

But in his summation, Cochran kept driving the jurors' minds back to Darden's try-on-the-gloves disaster with his preachered rhyme, "If it doesn't fit, you must acquit."


## Shocking September

Much of the nation watched with heart-pounding intensity in September when Fuhrman returned to the witness stand, after a zillion newspaper articles and radio and TV accounts about how he had perjured himself in denying under oath that he had used the word "nigger" in ten years.

But jurors didn't hear him again! What were jurors to make of the fact that on March 15 they had heard Fuhrman deny that he had used the word "nigger" in ten years, that in September they had heard him disparage niggers on tape, but they never again saw in court the man who supposedly had found the blood spot on Simpson's Bronco, had scaled Simpson's wall without a warrant, and had found the crucial bloody glove on Simpson's property?

Judge Ito knew the commonsense requirements for a fair trial. He fashioned a compromise under which he would tell the jurors that Fuhrman had become "unavailable" to testify further, and that they could consider this in weighing his credibility.

Clark and Darden objected. They became heat-seeking human missiles, appealing angrily to the court of appeals. The appeals court told Ito that he must not give any such instruction to the jury. Cochran, Scheck, and other defense lawyers responded apoplectically, but futilely.

On September 27, Cochran began an assault on prosecutors who he said "rushed to judgment" in their "win at all costs" desperation. He spoke of a "massive police conspiracy" to convict Simpson, placing at the center of that conspiracy Mark Fuhrman, whom he called "a lying, perjuring, genocidal" cop.

Only insensitive fools could doubt that for this jury at this time Cochran was masterful. Clarence Darrow never grabbed so completely the brains, the hearts, the other organs of a jury in so nation-wrenching a case.

Cochran hammered on the issue of police misconduct, firing the nerve endings of most jurors. He sought to undermine the prosecution's time line, disputing Clark's assertion that Simpson had seventy-eight "unaccounted-for minutes" in which to commit the murders, get home, shower, and get dressed for a flight to Chicago. This contesting of the time line may, if we can believe some jurors, have done more to win acquittal than any playing of "the race card."

Whatever the reality, Cochran never let up on his criticisms of bumbling, ineptitude, racism, and brutality within the LAPD.

Cochran feared that Darden might have scored critically when he said of Simpson: "He's a murderer. He was also one hell of a great football player. But he's still a murderer."

Cochran had said, trying to diminish anger over the 911 calls to the police by Nicole about O. J.'s abuse of her:

"He [Simpson] is a human being; he's not perfect. He's not proud of some things he did, but they don't add up to murder." Then Cochran repeated O. J.'s assertion before the jury that he "could not, would not, and did not" kill Nicole.

At this stage, I saw clearly what this trial meant in terms of the 1996 presidential campaign, and of the kinds of legislation that would emerge from the Congress. I saw its impact upon the mood of people in the state legislatures, and of ordinary citizens of America. The Simpson trial had provoked a torrent of mail that reflected a great rise in race hatred in America. I had become accustomed over thirty years as a nationally syndicated columnist to receiving some really mean letters, including threats on my life, but I had never seen anything like the mail about the O. J. Simpson case.

"All you niggers really know how to do is rape, murder, and produce monkey babies for us white folks to feed and shelter," was the message on one tearsheet.

But the Simpson case provoked a lot of letters from doctors, lawyers, college professors, and housewives, who said in many ways that the great threat to America was not institutionalized white racism, but "jungle level black racism." A Michigan woman asked me to explain why "black men are raping white women all over the place, but you almost never hear of a white man raping a black woman." She said it frightened her that "the worse the black crime, the less likely a black jury is to convict the black criminal."

I knew as I read my mail that the Simpson case would not inspire white America to open its tennis courts and tea parties, because whites had new "evidence" that blacks in the country clubs would assimilate socially to the point where there would be more interracial sex and marriage. Nicole Brown was not by any means the only pretty white girl eager to leap into the bed of a moneyed, well-connected, and presumably well-hung black man.

"This interracial sex can lead to nothing good," I heard from a woman caller who said she was "eighty-eight years old and never let my body cross the racial boundaries."

So, with phone calls like that, and piles of skull-denting letters beating up my psyche, I braced for the verdict of the Simpson jury.

By the time of the closing arguments, even white conservatives like my TV colleague Charles Krauthammer were predicting not a hung jury, but acquittal. I was sure that intellectually they knew that Clark and Darden had failed to prove O. J. guilty even beyond their doubts, but they persisted in arguing publicly that O. J. would "walk" only because of black racism and "jury nullification."

On September 29, the *Washington Post* headline said "Simpson Defense Stresses Race; Jury Deliberations Could Begin Monday."

Even the best newspapers in America would not reject the canard that Cochran had "played the race card" to gain some end-of-trial advantage. Even enlightened white editors would not accept the truth that *race* had been, start to finish, the dominant force in this case.

On September 28, Cochran did stress race. He should have been disbarred had he not done so. The media line of coverage made it clear that racial attitudes and passions controlled this case even more than it controls most everything else in America.

The Verdict

Some white Americans pretended to believe that "the race card" became dominant only when the McKinny tapes were revealed and Cochran and the defense "put Fuhrman on trial." But way back when the murders were revealed, I saw the role of race and, on April 12, 1995, deplored the fixation on race, saying, "The media are virtually guaranteeing that the O. J. Simpson trial will become an American social tragedy by focusing too constantly on its racial aspects."

While I was moving far away from my early assumption that Simpson was "guilty as sin," I saw white America digging in, on racial passions alone, with the belief that Simpson was a double murderer, and that ignorant black jurors were going to let him go free because of *their* racism. The great American principle that a person is "innocent until proven guilty" had vanished in the Simpson case. The only thing remotely positive about the white public attitude was that no demagogues were in the streets exhorting a mob to string Simpson up. There was no danger of "frontier justice" or an "Emmett Till solution." No, he would not be physically lynched.

Notice that I never, ever said I believed Simpson was innocent. I said that Clark and Darden had not proved that he was guilty. I wrote that the behavior of some in the LAPD and on the prosecution team struck me as unconstitutional, criminal, and grossly un-American.

Most of all, I said that this trial more than anything in our history had lifted the cover off a problem of arrogant, venal, unlawful law enforcement in America. I said that this problem was setting American against American, and it went far beyond normal white-against-black animosities. But would white America see what I saw?

What agonies the Simpson jurors had to endure! The evidence of Simpson's physical abuse of Nicole was powerful. The pictures of her beaten face, of O. J.'s note of apology, and her warning that if she were found dead, we should believe that O. J. did it were next to impossible to dismiss. And what juror could ignore Darden's final argument that the public hero, O. J. Simpson, was in private "a bomb with a short fuse," a man "full of anger, full of rage, full of jealousy" who finally exploded murderously the night of June 12, 1994?

But each juror knew the weaknesses of the prosecution case — of the inability of Clark and Darden to answer such critical questions as:

- If Simpson committed the gruesome murders, and drove the Ford Bronco home, why wasn't there more blood in the Bronco?
- If Simpson had slashed Nicole and Ron Goldman, with blood flying everywhere, how did he get rid of his bloody clothes? How did Simpson enter his house, go up stairways with white carpeting, and into his white-carpeted bedroom without dropping any blood?
- With so much made of evidence that the murderer wore Bruno Magli shoes of Simpson's size, what happened to those shoes?
- How could Simpson make the shoes, the murder knife, and all other physical evidence disappear so efficiently?
- How could Simpson have gotten out of the murder-bloody clothes, cleanse himself, and get dressed for a trip to Chicago in what even prosecutors admit was just a few minutes?

Jurors would say that they believed these things were impossible, so they found Simpson "not guilty."

The jurors never were told that the prosecutors also were baffled by the missing links, and some prosecutors secretly concluded that O. J. had help in committing the murders. They used every tactic they could to find evidence that O. J.'s son Jason, and/or his lifetime best friend, A. C. Cowlings, participated in the murders, disposed of the murder weapon and O. J.'s bloody clothes, and transported him back to Rockingham — but not in O. J.'s Ford Bronco. But the LAPD never found a single piece of evidence with which to charge Jason or Cowlings with murder, or even accessory to murder. Some jurors revealed later that they believed that Simpson *knew* who committed the murders because he ordered the killings, but the jury was never asked to vote on any such surmise. In truth, a tangential tragedy of this case is the fact that the disgraced, demoralized LAPD, in foolish pride, took and still takes, the position that Simpson is their only suspect, and they will not look elsewhere.

Twelve honest jurors — do not forget that two were Caucasian and one Hispanic — could not resolve all the questions that give rise to more than "reasonable doubt." So the jurors took the case from Judge Ito after those highly emotional closing arguments. Most of us pundits had predicted that they would deliberate a long time and announce that they were hung, hopelessly. I thought they would vote 10 to 2 for Simpson's acquittal.

What a shock that after only four hours of deliberation the jurors informed Judge Ito that they had reached a verdict. Ito made the world wait overnight to learn the jury's decision, for he had an agreement with the LAPD that he would give it time to deploy forces so as to prevent the kind of rioting that occurred in the Rodney King case. Furthermore, Cochran was in Chicago and other principals had gone far and wide, expecting the jury to deliberate for at least a day.

So it was the morning of October 3, 1995, when most of America and the world stopped to learn the jury's verdict. Almost no one was working at 10 A.M. Pacific time, when the jury foreman was to deliver the verdict that was awaited more anxiously than any jury decision at any time in America's history. At 10:09 the world heard "We, the jury in the above entitled action, find the defendant, Orenthal James Simpson, not guilty of the crime of murder. . . ."

Sighs, gasps, cheers erupted across the land.

The courtroom TV cameras showed Ron Goldman's sister weeping uncontrollably.

TV network cameras showed black law students at Howard University cheering raucously. That brought white anger to fever pitch.

Within hours, a thousand writers tried to describe what had happened. I was particularly impressed by *Time* magazine's assertion that:

> To many whites, O. J. entered the trial as a fellow white man and grew darker as the proceedings went on. He was the perfectly assimilated minority hero until he was associated with terrible crimes. Then he became just another black male under arrest, presumed to be guilty of everything. In their imagination he was transformed in the course of a year from one of their own to Bigger Thomas [Richard Wright's tragic character in *Black Boy*].
>
> It could not have gone unnoticed by black Americans, who looked around them for the past year, that a great many whites seemed a bit overeager to hang another black man in spite of a prosecution case that was proved, in the very least, to be friable.

How interesting that *Time* had seen O. J. as blacker the moment he was accused of murder.

But how dismaying to see the number of American journalists who viewed the "not guilty" verdict as much more wrong and sinister than *Time* did. The phone calls to my office and home provoked me to write another column on the subject:

> In a stunning verdict after just less than four hours of deliberation, twelve weary jurors have told America — and the Los Angeles Police Department — that O. J. Simpson is not the murderer of his ex-wife Nicole and of her friend Ronald Goldman.
>
> And that roils a nation in which a majority long ago decided that the black former football hero was indeed a raging killer. . . .
>
> We hear charges that the tired, homesick jurors simply

"rushed to judgment," depriving their verdict of the moral and legal authority that longer deliberation might have provided. That argument overlooks the likelihood that the moment that jury heard detective Mark Fuhrman denouncing "niggers" on tape recordings, proving himself a perjurer, and saw that he never returned to testify, every juror was filled with reasonable doubt about the prosecution's case. . . .

Yes, "race cards" were played in this high-stakes game. Detective Mark Fuhrman was the ace of spades, casting a dark shadow over the desperate efforts of the prosecution. That "race card" was not introduced by Simpson's lawyers. It was played, with disastrous consequences, when the LAPD sent Fuhrman to the crime scene.

Gut feelings aside, what fair person would not have doubts about Simpson's guilt when it was clear that the police, and perhaps some prosecutors, violated Simpson's constitutional rights and manipulated, even manufactured, evidence against him?

There was another card in this mind-searing game: the ace of hearts, representing public revulsion over the testimony that Simpson had beaten and abused Nicole in shameful ways. But the ace of spades, Fuhrman, overwhelmed the ace of hearts. . . .

This jury has sent a message to every police department in America — a message that, tragically, most will reject.

The Simpson verdict's repercussions were powerful, adding greatly to white stereotypes about black men and their alleged propensity to commit violent crimes, especially when white women are the victims. A national lynch mentality followed the verdict, and in many quarters blacks who never knew O. J. Simpson became co-victims of a racist reaction.

"There's no way in hell he could be innocent," a white woman screamed to a *New York Times* reporter.

"Even if he did kill her, a lot of us are glad he got off," said an African American telecommunications salesman to two *Washington Post* reporters. "That can't begin to balance out all the black men who have been lynched, jailed, beaten for things they didn't do. It's a glorious day."

Could anyone look seriously at the reaction to the Simpson verdict, and its relationship to blatant injustices in our criminal justice system, without concluding that a race war explosion is inevitable?

The fallout from this incredibly destructive trial must have Alfred Hitchcock spinning in his grave in disgust that he never imagined anything as bizarre, with so many lingering suspicions and mysteries.

The man the jury found not guilty, O. J. Simpson, is a pariah, punished almost as much by a mob psychology based on early suspicions and assumptions as if he had been found guilty. He has become a pathetic character, talking too much to a white America that will never listen, because of his need to plead for a chance to make a living to support his children.

Christopher Darden, the goat of the trial, has become a millionaire, because he could re-try the case in a book, and on television programs where he was welcomed as the brave black lawyer who dared to try to imprison a black sports icon. In his media retrials, of course, Darden won every time. It didn't hurt that this black man who, in mid-trial, accused Simpson of having "a fetish for white blondes," titillated the public with suggestions that he and Marcia Clark engaged in torrid sex during the trial. Whites and a few blacks rushed to buy his book, seemingly never caring whether Darden had a fetish for white brunettes.

Clark hasn't denied a Darden connection, because she has a book coming that she hopes will outsell Darden's and make her a multimillionaire.

Cochran has become a towering figure in black America, but still the butt of jokes on the talk shows whose hosts decided long ago that the court verdict doesn't matter. They regard Cochran as a glib racist lawyer who let a black double-murderer go free. Cochran bested Darden in the courtroom, but can he outdo him on the bestseller lists?

Judge Ito continues to take a beating in many circles, and, insofar as I know, is not writing a book in which he can retry the case.

No one takes polls anymore, but the differences of opinion are deeper than ever. Blacks disagree with blacks, whites with whites, but most notable is the smoldering separation of whites and blacks on the verdict and the reaction to it. Whites persist in assailing the mostly-black jurors who they think rendered an outrageous "not guilty" verdict, even without deliberating a decent amount of time. Blacks think whites have thrown away the cherished American presumption of innocence and, after the verdict, arrogantly superimposed their personal prejudices.

These conflicting views lie on America's psyches like a thousand tons of fertilizer, ignitable by a trigger of hatred here or a spark of violence there. We will not soon escape this peril.

# Chapter 9

# The "Nice" Black Man of Hope

I would not have bothered to write this book if I had not believed, two years ago, that the United States is hopelessly doomed to implode in an Armageddon of racial strife. During a long, many-faceted career I have known many white Americans of great wisdom and fairness, and I have benefited magnificently from my associations with them. Over five decades I have seen a lot of white guilt — as during the 1963 March on Washington — and I know that many white ministers, housewives, corporate heads, would still take any reasonable remedial actions to cast the yoke of racism off this country. I have looked and listened eagerly for these white Americans to rise up and be heard.

I do remember a better time when Americans of all races were unafraid to say that our destinies are intertwined, and that it is suicidal for us to let blind political ambition or naked economic greed provoke us into violent orgies of racism. I have looked, day after day after day, for signs of a wisdom wake-up, when we all invest our energies and cast our votes for what best lifts the level of life of all who live upon these blessed shores.

During many depressing years it appeared that no wake-up call would ever be heard by our mostly-white power structure.

Then early in 1996, one remarkable sign arose that alerted even the most race-conscious Americans that we needed to abandon a race-shrouded approach to the future. That sign was something called "Powellmania," the incredibly powerful cry from *within the Republican party* calling for retired African American General Colin Powell to be drafted to lead the nation into the twentieth century.

The cry for Powell's leadership turned out to be greater among American intellectuals than among the politicians who controlled the GOP, but it was sufficient for me to believe that enough Americans might heed my alarm, and that they would do the things needed to prevent this society from sinking into an abyss of hatred and venality.

It is, I think, important for us to look at the Colin Powell phenomenon, and at the crushing burst of that bubble, to get a clue as to whether this nation has already sunk hopelessly deep into the morass of racism.

I don't know where the Powell-for-President clamor began, or who started it, but I do know why. A lot of powerful Americans of all political leanings looked at the crop of Republicans vying to unseat President Clinton and almost vomited. Bob Dole, who would be the oldest and most hot-tempered man ever to assume the presidency? Phil Gramm, that drawling advocate of a return to seventeenth-century policies and values? Lamar Alexander, that Tennessee and Washington pol who was masquerading as "an outsider" free of blame for any of the messes that he deplored? Pat Buchanan, that hate-filled sometime journalist who oozed the fiery bigotry that would set America aflame? Responsible, caring Americans wanted a better choice than Clinton or any of the Republican candidates. Even more than was the case during the gloomy days after World War II, Americans wanted a heroic leader like Dwight D. Eisenhower who could inspire a new sense of national unity, optimism, sense of purpose. Some decided that Colin Powell, the black general who had fought bravely in Vietnam, who as chairman of the Joint Chiefs of Staff led the war to rein in Iraq's Saddam Hussein, and who had given wise counsel about America's role in the post–Cold War era, was precisely the overall leader the times required.

On August 21, 1995, *U.S. News & World Report* gave us a cover story calling Powell THE MAN TO WATCH.

"As Americans grow more disenchanted with their leaders and with both political parties, Colin Powell is seriously considering an independent run for president," the magazine said. It revealed its poll showing that Powell had a favorable rating of 57 percent among black voters and a whopping 73 percent among white voters. His unfavorable rating was the same — a mere 5 percent — among blacks and whites.

I laughed as I read the article, knowing that Powell was getting up to $60,000 per speech on the lecture circuit. He had a $6 million advance to write a book, and then faced a long, grueling book tour. I said to my wife, "Colin's not running for anything but the bank."

As I got into the *U.S. News* article, I realized that it was a "thumbsucker" — nothing more than the suppositions and speculations of a writer who knew nothing other than what he could suck from beneath his fingernail. I was certain of this because I saw my picture in a group of politicians and journalists who supposedly made up THE POWELL NETWORK. Me? Hell, I had never talked to Powell at any time about his possible involvement in elective politics.

Yet, the writer who gave this phony information about me would write authoritatively: "Flirting with a run for the presidency is a good way to sell books, of course. But after two years of touring the country giving speeches . . . and working on his book, Powell has grown more serious about politics — and about running for president. During the past year, he also has grown more intrigued by whether he might be able to defy both history and conventional wisdom and win the presidency as an independent."

I laughed aloud, certain that Powell was too smart to lurch toward the dead end that is an independent run for the presidency. But wait a minute! Some powerful white politicians were wooing Powell. I noted this in a column of August 23:

Bill Bradley, the widely respected sports hero and political-social leader announced that he will not run for a fourth term in the U.S. Senate. But the New Jersey Democrat hinted he might make an independent challenge for the presidency. He immediately telephoned the war hero, retired Gen. Colin Powell. And that has set off some wild speculation that a Bradley-Powell blitz could finally smash the Democratic-Republican lock on American politics.

The despotism of custom has ruled our presidential politics for generations, with state rules and money-raising laws tilted to ensure survival of the two-party system. Ross Perot saw that with his personal bankroll of billions of dollars, and his ability to generate incredible publicity for his candidacy, he could get only 19 percent of the vote in 1992.

But now, disgusted, some 62 percent of Americans express a desire for a third party. Bradley echoes them in suggesting that our current political system is visionless, bankrupt, out of touch with the American people. . . .

Both Bradley and Powell obviously are very concerned about the deepening racial polarization in America, and the extent to which racial passion and violence influence the most critical political and economic decisions. A ticket of these two men could be a great healing force.

But who should head the ticket? Some say, "Powell is the one people in both parties are clamoring for. It would be the same old racism if Powell were forced to play second fiddle." Others say, "No, the country isn't emotionally ready for a black president, just all of a sudden. Many would say they'd vote for a ticket headed by Powell, but most would be lying. Electing Powell or some other black as vice-president would get the country ready for a black president. . . ."

The odds still are that no third party offers a panacea for the "despotism of custom" that enshrines our Republicans-or-Democrats system, however woeful it may be.


American journalists, from publishers to editors to columnists and reporters, are like a bunch of lemmings or jungle vultures. They dive into the political seas as one, or they leap upon some political carcass in thoughtless unison. But rarely in our history had they abandoned thought, reason, political possibility, to the extent they did in creating Powellmania.

On August 2, under the headline POWELL'S APPEAL TRANSCENDS RACE, *USA Today* said, "Poll after poll shows that the USA's best-known military figure, retired Army general Colin Powell, could win the presidency — if he'd choose to run." A sample of views on Powell:

Richard L. Berke in a column in the *New York Times:*
One of Gen. Powell's most powerful attractions is that while race
relations have been strained by harsh debates over issues like affirmative action and redistricting, his appeal transcends race in
more ways than one. He can inspire pride in other blacks. Yet, he
can also relieve guilt among whites, some of whom may be de-
lighted with the notion that there's a black, clearly no flaming
liberal, who just might get away with being tough on blacks in
ways that no white could be.

Clarence Page, syndicated columnist:
   History tells me conservatives will be making a big mistake if
they throw away the need to broaden the party's appeal to mainstream voters of all colors. Positive feelings about Gen. Powell
are so high that Stanford University political science professor
Paul Sniderman says his national polling on racial attitudes indicates General Powell's race actually "magnifies his political
strength." When whites of all ideological stripes encounter a
black individual whose character refutes negative racial stereotypes, "their response is to respond even more positively to him."
Either party would be nuts, in my view, to ignore the wellspring
of good feeling.

The media drumbeat had barely begun. The three most talked
about black men in America were Powell, O. J. Simpson, and
Louis Farrakhan, and I found it remarkable that so many whites
could profess to hate and fear Farrakhan, loathe Simpson, but
love and admire Powell.

It was extraordinary that almost no one wanted to deal head-
on with the issue of Powell's blackness. A noted Jew, long active
in the civil rights movement, called me at home to say, "Carl, I
could never say this publicly. But the country isn't ready to elect
a black president." A white fellow board member of the Freedom Forum said, "The country won't elect him as President directly. He'll have to become Bob Dole's vice president and
prepare the country for him taking over the top job."

There was hardly a home in America where people weren't
talking about the race factor, but the media kept ducking the issue by pretending that Powell had an appeal that transcended
race.

White intellectuals, both Democrat and Republican, sought to purge themselves of guilt about the fact that blatant racism once again was popular in the United States, by citing with glee polls and statistics showing that Powell had more white than black support. Then, as Powell began his book tour and tens of thousands of whites smothered him with adulation, white pundits said with certainty that he could get the Republican nomination if he wanted it.

I said on Washington's top-rated TV talk show, "Inside Washington," "When Bob Dole and Newt Gingrich and Pat Robertson and Pat Buchanan allow Colin Powell to get the Republican nomination, I'll sit on top of this WUSA building for a week — in a dunce cap."

I got a quick reply from Dole saying, "Dear Carl, I'll buy the dunce cap. And it'll be a perfect fit!"

That was a reminder that once upon a time there was a Bob Dole of charming and wicked wit, a really likable guy until he Dr. Jekylled into a mean, snarling politician.

I tried to cut through two fantasies, one about whether whites would elect Powell, the other about what the ultimate response of black voters would be:

> In the current mania over Powell, a lot of people in and out of the press are acting as though he is just a war hero who can invade the White House from any of three fronts. They see Powell as just a nice, smart patriot who can enter the Oval Office as a Republican, an independent, or even as a Democrat.
>
> It is amazing how the media and others behind the Powell boomlet ignore the fact that while he may be a brilliant, wise, charming, handsome hero, Powell is still a black man in a racially polarized society.
>
> Is it really likely that in a time of great division over affirmative action, of mindless fear of crime when many whites see most black men as threats, of demagoguery over immigrants, the American white majority would elect the black son of Jamaican immigrants to the presidency?
>
> Prominent black politicians David Dinkins of New York, Tom Bradley of California and Doug Wilder of Virginia are among many who have discovered that at least 10 percent of white people lie when they tell pollsters they'll vote for a black candidate.

Muscle spasms, then rigor mortis, take over when they try to pull the lever for the black candidate.

For months, and even now in the bookstores, it seems that Powell is different. He apparently is truly appealing to voters of every race who have become dismayed by their political choices. Not only is he of a personal quality equal to or above anyone in the presidential race so far, but he has appeared not to be a threat to white people (as some perceive the Rev. Jesse Jackson to be) or to any major part of the electorate.

But in these recent days, as he has edged toward becoming a real presidential contender, Powell has become a "threat" to some powerful forces.

He has now declared that government has no right to control a woman's choice regarding an abortion — and is suddenly being picketed by rabid anti-abortionists. He has written off any possible support from the National Rifle Association, or from the rightwing Christian Coalition that will play a powerful role at the Republican convention in San Diego next August. In delivering some devastating criticism of California Gov. Pete Wilson and his anti-affirmative action stance, Powell has made himself an enemy of so-called "angry white men."

It took only a couple of days for Powell to shed the label of "the nice black man that whites can vote for." He spelled out sane policies that outrage the politically insane, who seem in such great supply.

However much Powell, you and I may wish that America truly has crossed a racial Rubicon, allowing a black man to become president, to be a saving unifier, the reality is that if he runs, Colin Powell will face an uphill battle. Yes, because of racial passions.

Powell had by this time made it clear that he wouldn't run as an independent. He also indicated that he would not run as a Democrat. If he ran it would be as a Republican. But he still did not erase the mystery about his personal politics. What did he really stand for?

Powell began to give hints and clues. In an interview with the *New Yorker* magazine he said that his Republican mentors, Ronald Reagan and George Bush, had not experienced racism, were not sensitive to it, and failed to truly understand it. He said that Bush and Reagan were "two of the closest people in my life," but racism "was the area where I found them wanting."

Powell said he "almost went crazy" when he read a Republican newsletter saying affirmative action programs were no longer needed to combat "vague and ancient wrongs." He remembered shouting, "Vague? Vague? Denny's wouldn't serve four black Secret Service agents [in Annapolis] guarding the President of the United States. Vague?"

That interview made it clear to Republican conservatives that Powell was no Clarence Thomas, no black traitor, no black suck-up to black-hating members of the GOP.

On September 14, 1995, in the very conservative *Wall Street Journal,* the not very conservative bureau chief and columnist Al Hunt made one of the most thoughtful comments that I had read up till that time. Hunt said:

> The most relevant question about Colin Powell isn't whether he's moderate or conservative, or precisely where he comes down on abortion, or even whether he's more of a Democrat or a Republican. It's whether the 58-year-old former chairman of the Joint Chiefs has a capacity for boldness or whether, as authors Michael Gordon and Bernard Trainor suggest in a recent book, he's "risk averse to the point of timidity."

Powell did nothing to deter speculation that he would run. Or the creation of "Draft Powell" committees across the land. I noted that an old friend of mine, John Reagan "Tex" McCrary of the "Tex and Jinx" television talk show, was trying to coax Powell to run. I remembered how Tex had, in 1951, put on a Madison Square Garden rally where he had thirty thousand people chanting, "We want Ike." Through this and other tactics McCrary persuaded Eisenhower to run.

Now Tex, at age eighty-four, had roped Stephen Ambrose, Ike's biographer, into a scheme to draft Powell. He had gotten the old lion of Republican conservatism, Barry Goldwater, to endorse Powell. McCrary was going to hold a Thanksgiving Day rally for Powell that would make the Madison Square Garden event seem puny. Tex did everything but hornswoggle Powell, who fidgeted in unease but never said no.

There were stories that the "tailor of presidents" was outfitting Powell. And that the general had contacted New York cosmetics heir Ronald S. Lauder about raising funds for his campaign. Charles Krauthammer, my conservative colleague on the talk show "Inside Washington," wrote:

> Three weeks into America's version of tulip mania, the Powell swoon continues. By now Colin Powell, mystery man, has turned into a national Rorschach test. Everybody sees in him what he wants to see and, *mirabile dictu*, is pleased.
>
> For centrists, he, of course, is a dream come true, sound on every issue from abortion to taxes. His credo — Republican fiscal conservatism but with Democratic compassion — is so perfectly oxymoronic it makes a centrist's heart flutter. And all this in a person of color.

I never thought that Powell ever believed he could get the Republican nomination. But at one point I said publicly, "Either he's going to run, or he's the biggest tease since Mae West and Mario Cuomo."

After all, the polls did show that only he, of nine GOP candidates, could defeat President Clinton in 1996. Neither Clinton nor Dole was sleeping well knowing that Powell might become their President.

Suddenly, faced with what appeared to be a very real threat, the keepers of the Republican faith began to pop up everywhere. POWELL'S NOT ONE OF US, GOP CONSERVATIVES SAY was the headline on a Robert Novak column.

Pat Buchanan went on ABC's "This Week" to denounce Powell as "a Bill Clintonite." The right-wing firebrand said a war would erupt within the GOP if Powell were nominated. "You'd have right-to-life parties sprouting up all over the country, you'd have the Christian Coalition people breaking loose, you'd have people walking out of the convention . . . ," Buchanan said.

Powell began to see how rough the road to nomination at the San Diego convention might be. Someone had leaked stories that his wife, Alma, suffered from depression and had been on the drug Prozac.

One wag said that if Powell could get just the Prozac vote,

"he would win in a landslide." But it was no joke for Alma and Powell's children.

Powell turned this into a plus for the nation, pointing out that depression is a serious and widespread ailment for which millions of people the world over need treatment. It was no shame for anyone, including his wife, to have known depression.

But the incident was more sinister than that. Even though no one knew of any real skeletons in Powell's closets, even though he faced no ethical challenges that came close to those faced by House Speaker Gingrich, even though he hadn't financed any porn movies, as Gramm had, and had no divorce to explain away, as Dole and Gingrich had, Powell was warned that members of his family might be dragged through the mud.

Still, as Powell met again with his political strategists, his probable money-raisers, his public relations specialists, the favorable polls proliferated, and so did the ugly clouds of opposition. In mid-October Powell seemed to trim his sails, shade his views, so as not to alienate the Republicans who dared to support him, however weakly.

On October 22 I said:

In recent days, Powell has said that he supports most of House Speaker Newt Gingrich's conservative "Contract With America," without spelling out what he does not support. More startling were Powell's comments Monday on CBS. He moved from harsh criticism of the Christian Coalition to praising it for "focusing our attention again on the fact that we are a nation under God, focusing attention on the family, focusing attention on the need to love and raise children in a caring environment."

He added, "I am generally in line with the Christian right, although we disagree on some of the legislative agenda."

By Wednesday, Powell was denying that he was sucking up to the far right. He said he was merely "sharpening" his "thinking and views."

*USA Today* reported him as saying that he sees himself in sync with the Republican mainstream but at odds with the narrow edges of the party on abortion, gun control and school prayer.

It seems clear that in a couple of weeks Powell has transformed himself from war hero and book author to typical politician — a pol who is now courting all factions of the GOP.

I never thought Powell would take seriously all the press clippings and rush headlong to grab the keys to the White House. I believed even less that he would try to become the Republican standard-bearer. But the evidence is unmistakable that he is trying to convince himself and the Republican kingmakers that they can be a winning team.

The first and most fascinating question is whether they can ever be a team.

## Suddenly, the Enemies Strike

Powell should have known that there was no way he could shade his views on the controversial issues and retain the support of the mass of Republicans.

It is a rule of American political life, and of American journalism, that the press will build a man up with fervor, then bring him down like forty hyenas bringing down a sick wildebeest.

Conservative writer R. Emmett Tyrell, Jr., scolded the media for glorifying Powell, a general, when the history of generals in politics from Ulysses S. Grant to Douglas MacArthur to Charles de Gaulle to Spain's Francisco Franco had been uninspiring. Even Eisenhower, Tyrell said, "was not wholly satisfactory. He did almost nothing to build up his party. He was reluctant, as all generals are, to campaign. Doubtless Gen. Powell suffers from this shortcoming, too."

George F. Will, the acerbic columnist who is the best at cloaking demagoguery and flirtations with racism in a shell of "intellectualism," came out on October 29 with "22 Questions For Colin Powell."

Typical of Will's snide arrogance was the following:

During Nelson Rockefeller's 14 years as New York's governor, the top income tax rate more than doubled and state and local taxes more than tripled. Not surprisingly, the growth of private-sector jobs was four times faster in the nation as a whole than in New York, which experienced a 1,000 percent increase in welfare spending. The state had fewer than 400,000 welfare recipients when Rockefeller became governor but had 1.4 million when he left. You call yourself a "Rockefeller Republican." Why?

You say you are in the "sensible center." Does that mean people to the right of center are not sensible?

Your friend Bob Woodward, the reporter, writes that after you watched the Conservative Political Action Conference convention on C-SPAN you said to a friend, "Can you imagine me standing up and talking to these people?" What is it about "these people" that makes talking to them hard for you to imagine?

Which parts of the Contract With America do you consider "a little too hard, a little too harsh, a little too unkind"?

Powell surely would notice, as I had, that conservatives like Will never say directly that the people in Chicago's South Side and in south central Los Angeles are lazy, inferior, and not fundamentally the victims of anti-black racism. They purport to quote some black like conservative professor Glenn Loury, who doesn't get the privilege of saying in Will's column that generations of white racism have rendered those blacks in Chicago's and Los Angeles's ghettos so uneducated and hopeless that painting them white now would not make much of a difference.

What made a difference was that the country had responsible journalists to answer Will. Even as Will was writing, so was Colbert I. King of the *Washington Post*. King took note of the flak that Powell suddenly was catching from the media, then wrote a column whose biting logic ought to be remembered every time we dissect and redissect this political saga. King wrote:

The heavy flak Powell's catching from the inflamed right over his moderate positions on abortion, gun control, affirmative action and other social issues should give him a taste of what he'll be up against if he makes a run for the Republican nomination. In that sense, fair warning is fair play.

Now that the adulation of the book tour is behind him, the retired chairman of the Joint Chiefs must decide whether he has the stomach for what promises to be a bitter fight — or whether the whole thing is too much to swallow.

Powell has been having fun. But filing deadlines are just around the corner, so now it's time, as he says, to fish or cut bait. And the sharks are waiting.

Pat Buchanan told a conservative gathering that Powell's brand of Rockefeller Republicanism was "the ideological equivalent of Satanism." That presumably was an attempt at humor.

Buchanan is symbolic of what Powell faces on the far right. And such people would just as soon lose the White House as see the party they've hijacked fall into the hands of someone like Powell.

But don't get carried away with comparisons. Powell is no imitation Ike; neither is America anything like what it was in 1952. Eisenhower did not confront a world without a Soviet-dominated communist empire, or a nation set on edge by a civil rights revolution, various social, right-to-life and environmental movements, mind-blowing technological changes and oceans of red ink. Besides, everybody's so touchy these days.

And Ike wasn't confronted with a poll that said 16 percent of registered Republican voters had friends and neighbors who would vote against him because of his skin color. Powell scores well among voters, but as the *Weekly Standard* magazine poll showed, in his case, race still matters.

On this score, Powell says he doesn't want to run as the "poster boy for blacks." Not to worry, general. For many African Americans, unreserved racial loyalty is a thing of the past; Clarence Thomas got that out of our system.

Right in the middle of this media orgy, *Business Week* magazine held a symposium of the chief executive officers of one hundred of America's largest corporations, 63 percent of whom identified themselves as Republicans, 29 percent as independents, and only 8 percent as Democrats. They were asked whom they preferred as the President to lead America into the twenty-first century. Forty-one percent chose Powell, compared with 19 percent for Dole, 9 percent for Gingrich, 6 percent for Bill Bradley, only 4 percent for President Clinton, the same as for Phil Gramm.

That could have been an overwhelming signal to Powell that race didn't matter among the political movers and shakers, the big money men, the ones who could tell all his assailants, except for a semilunatic like Pat Buchanan, to back off.

Even *my* head was swimming. So on October 29 I typed out my first and final advice to the man some said could change

American politics forever, and could just by saying yes and getting elected wipe out the miasma of bigotry and racial fears that
kept this society from becoming a tranquil beacon to a troubled,
violent world. But what honest, useful advice could I give? This
is what I wrote:

Various polls show that the Republicans could win the White
House with Powell but not with any other of the declared GOP
candidates. Powell would defeat President Clinton by some 10
percentage points, most polls show.

That result confounds me. My mail says that this society is
more anti-black, more racist in every regard than during the tur-
bulent 1960's. In that bloody era, the enemies of a color-blind
America were the known bigots, mostly in the South. Now I see
the politicians of California, the militiamen of Michigan, the letter writers of Illinois, New York and New Jersey spouting venom
so poisonous as to suggest that no black man could possibly be
elected president.

The "racial divide" clearly is wider now in the North, West
and East than it was in the 1960s. And wider than in 1982 when
the polls said the mayor of Los Angeles, Tom Bradley, was going
to defeat George Deukmejian and become the first black governor of California.

Whites in California were not as enthralled by Bradley as
whites across America now seem to be with Powell. But so many
whites told pollsters that they would vote for Bradley that the
black mayor's triumph seemed certain. Then on Election Day a
sort of racial palsy took hold. Whites couldn't pull the Bradley
lever. Deukmejian won by less than 1 percent.

Powell has to wonder first whether he can win the Republican
nomination. If he can, that would put him far ahead of Bradley
in terms of white support. But what is likely if he becomes the
GOP nominee?

The general's 10 percent margin over Clinton would evaporate
if 5 percent of voters abandoned him for reasons of race or whatever. History shows that at least 10 percent of Americans lie
when they tell pollsters they will vote for the black candidate. A
10 percent white defection from Powell would make the election
a razor-thin contest.

It all might come down to the votes of blacks newly registered by attendees at the Million Man March, where Powell did not participate. Would Louis Farrakhan urge blacks to vote for Powell? How many Americans of whatever race might reject both Powell and President Clinton and vote for Ross Perot, or for someone else who represents a choice outside the privileged two major parties?

But Colin Powell is a certified fighter. He risked his life above all else to become America's premier military leader. He would risk only the humiliation of a surprise defeat in a run for overall leadership.

So much is at stake that I am now compelled to say, "General, go for it!"

But Powell knew that there were more worrisome statements and things that he had to factor into his decision. He prided himself on his "Thirteen rules," one of which was "Check small things." So he did check every poll. He told me he had read every column that I wrote about whether he should run, although he never discussed the matter with me. But among the "small things" was the evidence that the far right of the GOP was far more venomous in secrecy than Paul Weyrich and David Keene of the American Conservative Union had been in their November 3 press conference assailing Powell. The general had read such "small things" as the article about Pat Robertson, head of the Christian Coalition, telling talk-show host Charlie Rose that Powell was an "enemy of religion" who had "equivocated" on the question of whether a human being has "the ability to have a personal relationship with God."

Powell knew of another "small thing" — of Chris Ardizzone, the legislative director of Phyllis Schlafly's Eagle Forum, telling the anti-Powell rally that Nelson Rockefeller was "a conspicuous adulterer." This, of course, after emphasizing the fact that Powell had declared himself to be "a Rockefeller Republican." The sleazy suggestion was that Republican right-wingers and their gumshoes would do their best to smear Powell as "a conspicuous adulterer."

This straight-arrow war hero, who personified "family values," suddenly had to face the prospect that the right wing of the party he was about to adopt would try to assassinate him with concocted stories of his adultery — not to mention stories about the sexual activities of the rest of his family.

Now there was new significance in the fact that on the Thursday night before he was to tell the nation of his decision, Powell had a visit, at his home, from Newt Gingrich. Powell had expected Gingrich to dissuade him from challenging Dole, Gramm, Buchanan, and the rest of the squadron of declared GOP candidates. He may even have suspected that Gingrich wanted him to stay out of the way of a dramatic Gingrich entry into the campaign.

During a two-hour private session in Powell's library, Gingrich gave Powell the impression that he and the leaders of the conservative revolution would welcome Powell's participation. But Powell ought to be aware, Gingrich said, that while the general could wage a successful campaign, it would be "hell" in terms of the invasions of privacy and the grief his family would have to endure.

"You've got to really want this," Gingrich said.

That stirred Powell's fighting spirit, and then Powell related the conversation to Alma and to his two closest advisers, Kenneth Duberstein and Richard Armitage — "two white men," some black Democrats would later note, when questioning Powell's "blackness."

Mrs. Powell, Duberstein, and Armitage each had to wonder whether Gingrich had sneaked to Powell's house to really welcome him to the GOP race or just to scare hell out of him with a warning about attacks upon the private lives of Powell and his family members.


Day of Decision

There weren't 150 million Americans waiting to hear Powell's decision on seeking the GOP nomination, as was the case for the O. J. Simpson verdict. But millions of Americans waited, with different measures of hope.

It was a strange press corps that gathered in a dreary hotel ballroom on a cold November Wednesday to hear whether Powell would run. Some surely had read the statements by whites saying that they now could not vote for Powell because it would give "them" too much power, "them" meaning black Americans. So race did matter — still.

The cream of Washington's huge press corps should have known by using simple deduction what Powell's announcement would be. This meeting hall was the kind of place where you might come to bury someone, or a dream, but never to launch a bold and historic campaign for the presidency of the United States.

Most of my colleagues think of themselves as moderates, or part of "the mushy middle" — their way of pretending that they are fair because they have no strong ideological moorings. That's why the room held so many journalists who had openly urged Powell to run, or who, to hide their conservatism and racism, *pretended* they wanted him to run as a Republican.

That's why they had for months pumped air into the Powell boomlet until it became "Powellmania." In their delusions, they failed to see what was going on in the Powell family and what was going on in the Republican party.

Powell's wife of thirty-three years had grown up in Birmingham, Alabama, which at the time of her girlhood was surely one of the most violently racist cities on earth. Deeply imbedded in Alma Powell's subconscious were memories of German shepherd police dogs snarling at and biting black civil rights demonstrators, and of bombs exploding in a black church, killing black girls attending Sunday school. And swirling around these memories were recollections of Alabama governor George Wallace being shot during a campaign speech, and Robert Kennedy being shot to death early in his campaign for the presidency, and John F. Kennedy being shot to death after winning the presidency.

Such memories weigh heavily upon a person, and even if she never said it outright, Alma knew the dangers her husband would face in seeking the powers that millions of Americans would resent him getting.

And the elitists of the press corps would impose their values and assume that anyone, including Colin Powell, would be utterly seduced by all the newspaper articles and television statements that he was the man to save America from political self-destruction. Tim Russert of NBC and Jack Germond of the *Baltimore Sun* both said they thought any man with a chance to become the nation's first black President would find the nomination irresistible.

But Alma Powell had seen her husband achieve a lot of "firsts," and she knew the price he and his family had paid for this trail-blazing. She recalled the days of relative poverty when military pay was their only income. She and he had just discovered another "American way of life" in which he got $60,000 per speech and a $6 million advance to write a book, enabling them to buy a house in high-prestige McLean, Virginia, and to know that never again would they have to worry about how to pay any bills.

Just as important, perhaps, Alma Powell had discovered a measure of privacy — actual minutes during which there were no military aides, Pentagon policymakers, White House bureaucrats, or media people intruding into private gestures and conversations.

The press could speculate about what all this meant in Powell's decision-making process, but the press could never know. Mrs. Powell would probably never know, because Colin stated he would never ask Alma point-blank whether and why she opposed his running for the GOP nomination. In good marriages there are questions and answers that no partner ever has to put into words. Neither pleas for help nor provocations from a partner who wants the other to change his or her mind.

My suspicion — only a suspicion — is that while Colin Powell was almost seduced by the entreaties of Republicans such as William Kristol, Reagan's former education secretary William Bennett, and Barry Goldwater, Alma Powell knew that they were not really the voice of the Republican party as this party has been for at least two generations. Powell's distinguished cousin, Bruce Llewellyn, told the press that "it's hard to lead a party that doesn't want you." I think Mrs. Powell knew that, but also knew that she dare not say it.

Colin, too, probably knew that he had seen just days before his press conference the real welcome mat that the GOP would spread for him — a muddy, bloody mess with shards of glass and sharp nails reaching skyward. Paul Weyrich of the Free Congress Foundation and of National Empowerment Television was one of several far-right Republicans who had called the November press conference at which to lambast Powell. Weyrich had already declared that if Powell got the Republican nomination "it would be as if Ronald Reagan never lived and Nelson Rockefeller never died."

Not knowing the full background, many journalists in that press conference on November 7 could still hope against logic that Powell would say he was running. But even the general's body language reflected his primary military principle: you only enter a war when overwhelming force is on your side, and victory is almost certain.

This presidential campaign was no place for a cautious man who felt he could not handle the pain and humiliation of losing, nor put his family at risk.

So, in a remarkably straightforward, classy way, Powell said:

The question I faced was: Should I enter politics and seek the Presidency of the United States?

Many of you have encouraged me to do so. I have been deeply honored by the hundreds of letters I have received and by the hard work of grass-roots organizing committees. I thank all of you for the faith and confidence you had in me.

For the past few weeks, I have been consulting with friends and advisers.

I have spent long hours talking with my wife and children, the most important people in my life, about the impact an entry into political life would have on us. It would require sacrifices and changes in our lives that would be difficult for us to make at this time. The welfare of my family had to be uppermost in my mind.

Ultimately, however, I had to look deep into my own soul, standing aside from the expectations and enthusiasms of others, because I believe I have a bond of trust with the American people. And to offer myself as a candidate for President requires a commitment and a passion to run the race and to succeed in the quest; the kind of passion and the kind of commitment that I felt every day of my 35 years as a soldier. A passion and commitment that, despite my every effort, I do not yet have for political life, because such a life requires a calling that I do not yet hear. And for me to pretend otherwise would not be honest to myself, it would not be honest to the American people and I would break that bond of trust.

And therefore I cannot go forward. I will not be a candidate for President or for any other elective office in 1996.

I will continue to speak out forcefully in the future on the issues of the day, as I have been doing in recent weeks.

I will do so as a member of the Republican Party and try to assist the party in broadening its appeal. I believe I can help the party of Lincoln move, once again, close to the spirit of Lincoln.

I will give my talent and energy to charitable and educational activities. I will also try to find ways for me to help heal the racial divide that still exists within our society.

My reaction was, I think, equally straightforward:

In the gentle dream world of polls and popularity contests, retired Gen. Colin Powell came as close to the U.S. presidency as any black man ever has, or will in the next 50 years.

He showed leadership, wisdom and grace when millions of Americans of all races and classes cried out for these things.

But in the real world of dumb, dirty, dog-eat-dog politicians, this war hero never had a ghost of a chance of winning the Republican nomination. The GOP bosses were not remotely ready to name any black man the party standard bearer.

Bands of GOP character assassins were on sordid forays looking for dirt with which to attack members of Powell's family.

It was clear that Powell could invest his heart and soul, his newly gained fortune into a fight for the Republican nomination, but he would leave the GOP convention in San Diego a disillusioned man. Small wonder that the fire built in his stomach by weeks of public adulation went out fast.

I felt secure in predicting, "The only thing Powell will run for is the bank," because I knew he couldn't bank on a GOP that has been hostile to blacks for generations.

The pity is that as the GOP candidate Powell could have done much to close the dangerous racial and class divide in America. But he was absolutely right in not exposing his family and his life to a futile fight to get a Republican nomination that was too far from his grasp.

We pundits went on for weeks about how "the ultimate nightmare" of having to run against Powell had been lifted off President Clinton; how the "big winner" was Senator Dole, who now had "a clear shot" at the Republican nomination; and how Gingrich didn't have to worry about a black moderate putting roadblocks in the way of his ideological blitzkrieg; and how the nation had lost the opportunity for candidate Powell to be a healing force and close the dangerous racial divide.

Well, Clinton went on to enjoy a boom in public support, but mostly because Gingrich and Dole made the monumental mistake of forcing shutdowns of the federal government in an effort to extort Clinton's acquiescence in Gingrich's outrageous plans to balance the budget in seven years. Dole was badly injured in this budget charade, but more so by the injection of over $20 million of Steve Forbes's personal money into his own campaign to win the Republican nomination.

Incredibly, by Valentine's Day, the pundits were saying anew that none of the Republican candidates had a chance to defeat Clinton, so the salvation of the GOP and the nation (fatefully intertwined, naturally) was to have Dole, Forbes, Gramm, and Buchanan go to Powell on bended knee and beg him to accept a draft as the Republican standard-bearer.

This time, the Powell family must have laughed almost as heartily as I did, knowing that no such draft delegation would ever show up at the general's door.

Then came the polls showing that Dole could win if Powell would agree to be his running mate. Powell told me exclusively that he absolutely would not run with Dole. The senator himself showed my front-page *Chicago Sun-Times* article to his braintrust during the Illinois primary.

"The reaction could not have been worse if Dole had exploded a bag of shit," one member of the senator's inner circle told me.

All this, mind you, without the slightest public suggestion that Dole or other GOP powerbrokers really wanted Powell on the ticket.

"Powellmania" was a mirage on an American political desert that is becoming ever closer to a killing field.

Sometimes people need a reason to be better than they think they can be — a special prod to elevate their behavior beyond the popular meannesses of a cruel time. Powell seemed to be that reason, that prod, for millions of white Americans. But with him out of the political picture, the creators of Powellmania lapsed back into the animosities and fears that have driven them for years.

The campaigns of Clinton and Dole were devoid of hope, of any redeeming values. There were events and signs that the alienated within America were turning more and more to terrorism against other Americans.

A social explosion seemed inevitable.

# Chapter 10

# Education — Black Hope and Despair

The race war probably would have come to America a generation ago, led by angry disillusioned black men who had fought in World War II, Korea, and Japan, but for the flickering promise of "education."

"Education is the answer," I heard and read myriad times during my boyhood and young adulthood. The condescending meaning, of course, was that when African Americans got more education and culture and were not "just out of the trees," as Nixon put it, white people would accept them and the two races would live happily ever after.

Normal black skepticism was intensified by the fact that in all of the South and most of the rest of America, whites made it very difficult for blacks to get that "education." From drastic laws in the South forbidding whites to teach blacks to read and write to outrageous Jim Crow statutes to the gerrymandering of school districts in the North, whites ensured that precious few black people would be liberated by learning. Thus did whites protect their supremacy in business, commerce, and all other areas of American life; they limited the number of ex-slaves who might aspire to "social equality."

Still, black people clung to the cliché "Education is the answer." There was nothing else to resort to except total rebellion. Whatever else one might say about them, the ex-slaves were survivors. With education, they figured, they ultimately would outwit the most wicked of white men.

The first generation of blacks to get real education and legal acceptance opted first to widen the parameters of educational opportunity for black people. When Thurgood Marshall and his colleagues won the great *Brown v. Board of Education* decision in 1954, they really believed that education would be the answer, because they foresaw the end of tarpaper shacks and other grotesquely inferior elementary and secondary schools for black youngsters. When they won admission of blacks to the universities of Oklahoma, Texas, Alabama, and Mississippi for African Americans, they thought the road was paved for annual armies of intelligent black men and women who, by virtue of their skills and character, could not be rejected by the gatekeepers of American business, government, and life in general.

The country came close to war with terrible riots in Detroit, New York, Washington, D.C., and other places, but they were always in isolated pockets. Every education triumph by the NAACP drove war-making anger away.

But then came another generation of white subterfuge and naked lawlessness in which black Americans were denied the education that had been proclaimed "the answer." Black disillusionment came on like a tidal wave, with millions of African Americans "drowning" in it, as a metaphor for drugs and crime, while others swam free full of rage, a metaphor for the uprising that is yet to come.

Now, near the end of the century, I find white people justifying their lawlessness, denying 33 million black people of learning opportunities. People actually believe in a "Bell Curve" that shows that education is not the answer, because African Americans can never absorb enough education.

I ask myself, how can Americans become so smart scientifically as they become so much stupider socially and morally?

I first began to understand the magnitude of the damage that disillusionment had done in 1987 when I read in the *Washington Post* that at McKinley High School in Washington when the honor roll was announced, many black honorees refused to stand when their names were called. Bright black kids could not stand against the peer pressure that said those who had made the honor roll were nerds, geeks and, worst of all, "acting like Whitey." Youngsters who spoke and wrote well were treated as traitors to the black race, because their good grades exposed them as "using Whitey's language." How, I wondered, could any black kid believe that the language that had been used so beautifully by Frederick Douglass, Martin Luther King, Jr., Mary McLeod Bethune, and Whitney Young belonged to "Whitey?"

The white "intelligence" frauds had told black children, "You are dumb; God and evolution made you that way; those of you who show great intelligence are freaks, or impostors of white men and women." Those honor students at McKinley acted as if they believed this — as if they really were ashamed of their own brain power.

That newspaper story infuriated me. It meant that the know-nothings had imposed their pressures in ways that made the claims of black ignorance and failure self-fulfilling prophecies.

I first expressed my outrage in a column in which I said:

> I understand that the legacies of slavery and poverty are such that millions of young blacks still grow up in homes where there is no history of formal educational achievement, no appreciation of trained intelligence. I know that millions of teenagers have never understood or accepted the reality that ignorance is a greater enslaver than the Ku Klux Klan could ever be, and that learning has liberated more people than all the armies ever assembled by man. But I find it almost criminal that the know-nothings are successfully pressuring youngsters of great promise to hang back at their level.
>
> This is one of those problems that cannot be solved by a civil rights law or a government grant. It requires that black people devise programs to counter destructive peer pressures. This means building up incentives and rewards that make it more than worthwhile for high schoolers to reject anti-achievement pressures.
>
> Praise and recognition by respected professionals could become as intoxicating as getting along with the gang.

Then it occurred to me that a journalistic expression of anger cost me nothing and would do nothing to change the attitudes of black underachievers. We black people were too much inclined to deplore negative things about our children and their environment, and too little inclined to do anything to change them. That is when I decided that this society was obligated to put on positive pressures to wipe out the overweening influence of the "know-everything" social scientists and the know-nothing high school peers. The nation needed incentives so powerful that they would inspire black high school youngsters to place their scholastic achievement above the social approval of their peers.

I had no idea of the efficacy or stupidity of my actions when I put up $16,000 of my money for a scholarship program I called Project Excellence. I simply hoped that my friends would donate in total another $16,000 so I could give eight $4,000 scholarships to black college-bound youngsters who had busted their academic butts to show that they were not doomed by inferior genes.

My friends, and many strangers, responded in ways that made me believe that this country would never let the professors of hate lead them to national doom. That first year, Project Excellence had $208,000 and gave $4,000 grants to fifty-two youngsters.

In the years since, black high school seniors in Washington, D.C., and the contiguous counties in Maryland and Virginia have fought doggedly to win nominations from their high schools for a Project Excellence scholarship. The Cafritz Foundation, the Freedom Forum, and an incredible array of individuals, foundations, and corporations responded so generously that by 1996 we had made more than $29 million available to just over sixteen hundred black students.

These youngsters have shown me, as no professorial treatise ever could, the correctness of those who say that IQ is a minor and often meaningless factor in deciding the potential or the worth of human beings. Let me tell you the stories of a few of those sixteen hundred youngsters who resisted negative peer pressures and embraced excellence.


Jeremi Duru

Jeremi Duru is a young black student who overcame tremendous obstacles and burdens. He finished in the upper 10 percent of his class at Montgomery Blair High School, a tough science and math magnet school in suburban Washington, and went on to Brown University, from which he graduated in the spring of 1995.

But Duru had many friends who were not as fortunate. At the Project Excellence Dinner when he received his scholarship, he spoke eloquently and emotionally about what happens when society gives up on an individual or an entire group:

"Without hesitation I can rattle off the names of several elementary school friends who have evolved into academically underachieving drug dealers. Something is happening to divert the African American male from the less traveled path of intellectual achievement onto the more traveled path of illegality and nonsense, and that has made all the difference. That is the absurd notion that it is somehow *bad* for black men to achieve academically. That is the reason that we have far more brothers in jail than in college. That is what convinced a thirteen-year-old straight-A student named Malcolm X that he should become a manual laborer instead of a lawyer, and it took him a trip to jail to sort things out.

"This notion is what accounts for the all-too-often-uttered phrase "You're just trying to act white" toward a brother who seeks knowledge. We've got to do something about this idiocy so that young black males can grow up with the self-confidence in their intellectual capacity that every human being deserves. I've heard many people say that the African American male is an endangered species. That may be true, but I haven't seen all those people scrambling to set up sanctuaries for them.

"I say to you, please don't count them out; just help them out. Intelligent black males, many of them, do exist. I see them every day, hanging on the walls at school doing nothing. In the friend whom I referred to earlier, I see a man who could discover a cure for cancer. But instead of anatomy and biology, he's taking remedial English, two gym classes, a study hall, and home economics.

"So as we celebrate the wonderful students we have here, let's imagine how we would feel if our celebration of achievement was four- or five-fold. Let's not think about what we've done for the community, let's ponder what else we can do for the community. I'm telling you that if given a chance, these guys can change the world. All we have to do is change their mind-set."

## John Morcos, Dorian Baucum, and Taryn Richardson

John Morcos dreamed all his life of becoming a cardiologist — a challenging goal for a youngster from poverty and a broken family. The prospects looked even bleaker after he managed only a B-minus average in his first two years at Crossland High School in Temple Hills, Maryland.

Then, a combination of events combined to turn his life around. A chemistry teacher recognized the curiosity, insight, and enthusiasm that had never been tapped in Morcos; he challenged the youngster as no one had before and Morcos responded. At the same time, Morcos realized that he had to work much harder in school if he wanted to get to medical school and become a doctor. Finally, says Morcos, "I did a lot of praying."

The result was a decision at the beginning of his junior year "to get my act together." By his senior year in high school he got all A's in courses so difficult that where 4.0 is supposed to be perfect, he had a grade point average of 4.5. That won him a five-year $90,000 Project Excellence scholarship to the Massachusetts College of Pharmacy and Allied Health Sciences in Boston.

Now in his fourth year at the Boston school, Morcos has never received a grade below B-plus in any class, and compiled a scintillating 3.86 grade point average for his first three years. He was elected president of the freshman class and captain of the wrestling team, and he has tutored fellow students in biology and chemistry. In his "spare time" Morcos earns a little extra money cutting hair in his dorm.

"John is one of the most outstanding students I've seen in eighteen years here," says chemistry professor Fred Garafalo. "It's not just that he gets all A's [which he did his entire sophomore year]; he's phenomenal at thinking critically and creatively and tossing ideas around."

An advocate of experimenting with "new ways" of teaching that get students more involved, Garafalo insists that "you can't tell everything about a student by grades and SAT scores. Some kids come with great test scores but that doesn't mean that they're good at interaction and conceptual ideas. Others, like John, have a whole lot more on the ball than they're given credit for. In their souls, they really want to know what's happening. They love learning."

Two other Project Excellence scholarship winners who followed Morcos to the Massachusetts College of Pharmacy and Allied Health Sciences have also proved how difficult it is to predict academic achievement.

Dorian Baucum, a graduate of the much-maligned Washington, D.C., public schools, matched Morcos A for A in his freshman year at college and has demonstrated the same burning desire to learn and ability to shine in classroom give and take.

In addition, Baucum "is giving so much back to the community," says Nancy Fee, associate director of admissions. He lives in a special dormitory with English-as-a-second-language students. He volunteered to talk to a sixth-grade inner-city class that Fee had "adopted." His message to the kids: "You need to work hard to realize your dreams." This February, he went to Honduras with a faculty member to help distribute medication to the needy.

Taryn Richardson almost didn't make it to the Massachusetts college. Despite getting excellent grades in high school, her SAT scores were below 900 and she was choosing from among several small predominantly black colleges. Massachusetts College of Pharmacy stretched its admission requirements and found a place — and scholarship money — for Richardson last fall. She responded with a 3.1 average in her first semester.

Forget about grades and test scores. Don't give up on youngsters who come from worlds of poverty and broken families. Like John and Dorian and Taryn, these are kids who, observes Fee, "can change the world."


Lower Education

I wish I could leave readers believing that America's future of greatness and tranquillity is secure because there are millions of youngsters getting fair chances at all the learning and educational opportunities that they can absorb. I wish I could say that in every great city in America there is a Project Excellence, or something like it, that helps send to college at-risk youngsters of potential greatness.

I wish I could leave readers believing that a race war is impossible because we are giving minority and poor teenagers a stake in America, guaranteeing that their despair, their rage, will never rise to the point of their participating in, or even condoning, violent warfare.

But I would be a deceptive fraud if I did that. Especially when I know that millions of American kids — black, brown, yellow, white — are entrapped in bitter urban despair, rural hopelessness, and most of all in the imprisoning belief by some politicians that this society can't afford, and need not try, to educate everyone who wants a college education.

We have seen the federal government shut down, and some politicians wiped out, during torrid debates over what should be Washington's role in our lives — our health care, our need for clean water and a healthy environment, and surely the education of our children. The conservatives, especially in Gingrich's House of Representatives, made it a primary goal of their "revolution" against "the welfare state" to get Uncle Sam out of the business of funding education. President Clinton drew a line at almost every schoolhouse door, and we wound up with a historic crisis of government.

This crisis of federal government gridlock will continue. It will be fueled by soaring passions over race and class, and by naked greed and the mindsets of our little kings. And it will be dangerous.

Legislation enacted in 1996 indicates that the know-nothings are gaining power on Capitol Hill and in the statehouses of America. Respect for the empowering and protective values of education is waning throughout much of the United States, largely because the leaders of the so-called Republican revolution have been successful in associating government-sponsored schooling with what Gingrich et al. call the "discredited, failed" philosophies of Roosevelt's New Deal, John F. Kennedy's New Frontier, and, especially, Lyndon B. Johnson's Great Society.

The slick, modern Republicans do not openly demean the children from lower- and middle-class families who struggle desperately to get the learning symbolized by a college degree; they just move to deny them the assistance they need to gain higher education.

To understand the extent to which the Republican-controlled Congress seeks to turn back the clocks of learning, and what that portends for America's future, you must consider some facts about higher education in America in the early 1960s, when LBJ decided to provoke a revolution on the nation's campuses.

I have shown in my memoir, *Breaking Barriers,* that there were several Lyndon Johnsons: the abuser of power, who used it to gain sexual favors from dependent women, or to amass wealth that he did not earn or deserve; the ruthless LBJ, who would abuse his staff verbally and otherwise, or cut an opponent off at his knees, or control a vote count to ensure that he won by one or a few votes; the insecure Lyndon, who would drink whisky to excess and become nasty and irrational, or who made Vietnam War decisions on the assumption that he had to prove he was tougher than "that goddamn cigar-smoking General Curtis LeMay"; the Johnson whose proffered solution to every international problem was to "bomb out of existence" the Japanese, or the North Vietnamese, or the Soviets, or whoever was at a given time a threat to the United States; and the Johnson who was secretly pained that he had no degrees from Harvard or any other prestigious university, but was looked down on by the media and the Kennedys because he had only attended Southwest Texas State College in San Marcos, Texas, where a mere 1,357 students were enrolled.

The greatest, most likable Lyndon Johnson of them all was the one who gained vision about the value of education and the responsibility of government to provide it during his tough days at Southwest Texas State. There were times when he, as vice president, and I, as a State Department official, would trade "poor boy" stories. He would tell how, at Southwest Texas State, he lived in a tiny room above the garage of then president Dr. C. E. Evans, showering and shaving in a gymnasium down the road. He boasted that he lived in that room for three years before the college business manager caught on and sent him a bill.

Johnson's soliloquy, repeated to me over many glasses of Cuttysark, included tales of his sweeping floors, selling socks, doing a dozen more jobs, but still finding one hardship worse than that of the day before. Then along came William T. Donaho, the superintendent of schools of Cotulla, Texas, who offered him the princely sum of $125 a month to teach boys and girls in the little Welhausen Mexican School.

Johnson would recall that he could "never forget the faces of the [Mexican children] and the pain of realizing and knowing then that college was closed to practically every one of those children because they were too poor. . . . I made up my mind that this nation could never rest while the door to knowledge remained closed to any American."

It was this compassionate Johnson, who often cried during his own soliloquies, who was determined as President to mold the 89th Congress into the greatest force for mass education that America had ever known. With the help of congressional leaders such as Carl Perkins of Kentucky, John McCormack of Massachusetts, Adam Clayton Powell of New York, and Carl Albert of Oklahoma, he prodded Congress to enact the Elementary and Secondary Education Act of 1965, which he signed in the spring of that year. Johnson set out immediately to throw the weight and money of the federal government behind the broadening of access to college education. He was a man obsessed with this goal. On August 26, 1965, after the House passed the Higher Education Act, Johnson said:

> More than a million students can benefit in the next year by guaranteed low interest loans — a program I urged for the past 15 years. More than a quarter million needy students can get part-time jobs to help them continue their college studies. More than one hundred thousand students of exceptional promise and great financial need can receive opportunity grants.
>
> The bill passed by the House also strengthens our colleges by providing books and trained personnel to enrich college libraries and funds to assist our less developed institutions of learning.
>
> Finally, the House has challenged our universities to face the problems of the city through community service programs.
>
> This bill not only strengthens higher education; it adds to the mental might of the Nation.

On September 2, after the Senate passed this bill, Johnson was almost rapturous in talking about its impact upon America's future:

> The Senate's passage of the Higher Education Act is a triumph for Congress and for millions of students and teachers upon whose achievements our destiny largely depends.

This legislation is the most comprehensive program for higher education in our history. It will provide opportunity grants for 140,000 talented young Americans who want — and should — go to college but cannot afford it. It will assure loans for more than a million students to ease the burden on their families.

This legislation offers grants for less developed colleges to improve their faculties and teaching programs, and funds for enriching college library programs.

I am particularly glad that the Senate added provisions for a 6,000-member National Teacher Corps and for fellowship grants to elementary and secondary schoolteachers. These programs will mean much to schools in areas of poverty whose students have been the victims not only of impoverished homes but of impoverished schools.

This act has many provisions, but it has only one purpose: to nourish human potential today, so that our Nation can realize its rich promise tomorrow.

Johnson chose to go to Southwest Texas State on November 5, 1965, to sign this legislation into law. His words and promises are worth remembering in a time when politicians of conservative persuasions are blaming him for bankrupting America, encouraging slothful dependency, and of cluttering up college campuses with "the riff-raff" of America. Johnson said:

In the next school year alone, 140,000 young men and women will be enrolled in college who, but for the provisions of this bill, would have never gone past high school. We will reap the rewards of their wiser citizenship and their greater productivity for decades to come.

It ensures that college and university libraries will no longer be the anemic stepchildren of Federal assistance.

I consider the Higher Education Act — with its companion, the Elementary and Secondary Education Act of 1965, which we signed back in the spring of this year — to be the keystones of the great, fabulous 89th Congress.

This Congress . . . was the Congress that was more true than any other Congress to Thomas Jefferson's belief that: "The care of human life and happiness is the first and only legitimate objective of good Government."

This is a proud moment in my life . . . because here a great deal began for me some 38 years ago on this campus.

Here the seeds were planted from which grew my firm conviction that for the individual, education is the path to achievement and fulfillment; for the Nation, it is a path to a society that is not only free but civilized; and for the world, it is the path to peace — for it is education that places reason over force.

Was Johnson merely engaging in hyperbole, self-puffery, fantasizing about the ultimate fruits of his vision? The Bob Doles and Newt Gingriches of this generation will credit LBJ with very little, but the record shows that the Higher Education Act did produce the results that Johnson expected. It has tripled the number of Americans who attend college, thus enriching their lives and adding to the productivity that makes ours the richest society on earth. When Johnson spoke at Southwest Texas State, the nation's total college enrollment was 5,675,000. By the fall of 1994 it had risen to 14,279,000, just less than triple the number when Johnson spoke so proudly in San Marcos.

Minorities have benefited magnificently from that piece of legislation. There were only 274,000 African Americans in college in 1965. By 1994 the number had increased almost fivefold to 1,448,000. No one even bothered to count the number of Hispanics in college in 1965. But by 1976 there were 384,000 Hispanics in institutions of higher education, and 1,057,000 in 1994.

But the Higher Education Act was no "doles for minorities" program. It gave opportunities to more than 5 million white youngsters, raising the total of Caucasians in college to 10,416,000 in 1994.

And the benefits were a blessing in every state and region. College enrollment doubled in Michigan between 1965 and 1994. It more than doubled in Mississippi, rising from 55,790 to 121,000 in that period.

This nation came to value learning to the point that, in 1979 during Jimmy Carter's tenure, Congress created a cabinet-level Department of Education.

Americans took pride in their Fulbright fellowships abroad and their Pell Grants, tuition loans, and work-study programs at home. I still saw the pride emanating from these programs when I made four commencement speeches in 1995. Many of the graduates in the audiences were the first in their families to attain college educations.

But support for America's public schools may wane, and contempt for teachers — especially unionized ones in the National Education Association and the American Federation of Teachers — may grow. Racial conflicts on college campuses may become more commonplace. Those arguing that none of this is the business of Congress may be heading powerful committees. We are likely to find, incredibly, that education has become hostage to the most ignorant people in the land.

I cannot describe the major developments in education, at every level, during the last decade as anything other than a social tragedy. If we wanted deliberately to make our public schools and our colleges snake pits of violence, cesspools of venom, breeding grounds of racism, camps of ugly little armies known as "gangs," we could not have done a more despicably "successful" job.

If we wanted to cloud America's future by refusing to see what we have done, except when blaming someone else for it, we could not find more myopia in higher places than in the current American reality about education.

Two years ago, on the fortieth anniversary of *Brown v. Board of Education*, just about every daily newspaper in this country carried stories saying that racial resegregation was taking place with growing speed.

SEGREGATION IN SCHOOLS INCREASES; U.S. STUDY SAYS 70% OF BLACKS, HISPANICS ARE RACIALLY ISOLATED, said a headline in the *Washington Post.*"

PUBLIC SCHOOLS BECOMING AS SEGREGATED AS IN THE 1960s, blared a *USA Today* headline.

A headline about Boston, once wracked with violence over court desegregation orders, said, MANY HAVE GIVEN UP ON CITY SCHOOLS. A Dallas headline read, HISPANICS FACE A NEW AGE OF ISOLATION.

JUDGE ORDERS DESEGREGATION OF SCHOOLS IN PHILADELPHIA was, incredibly, a 1994 headline, four decades after the *Brown* case out of Topeka, Kansas. More incredible was the headline saying that the American Civil Liberties Union was suing Topeka because its schools were still segregated. Some readers were even more incredulous when the Harvard Project on School Desegregation listed the most segregated states insofar as blacks were concerned. More than 59 percent of Illinois public schools had enrollments that were from 90 to 100 percent minority, and 80.2 percent of its schools were at least 50 percent black, Hispanic, Indian, or Asian. Four more northern states — Michigan, New York, New Jersey, and Pennsylvania — had more segregation than all southern states, with the "most Jim Crow" list then citing Tennessee, Alabama, Maryland, Mississippi, and Connecticut.

A lot of change had occurred in schools since the day Richard Nixon expressed his sorrow for the people of the South, whom he considered unfairly hounded, but the record sure indicated that the change was not progress. In Dade County, Florida, the typical black student in 1994 attended a school that was 12 percent white; in the northeast, half of all black and Hispanic students went to schools where whites made up just 10 percent of the student bodies.

Professor Gary Orfield, who did the Harvard studies, told *USA Today:* "We're building escalating segregation and inequality into our school districts. It's a recipe for disaster."

Signs of that disaster were everywhere in 1995. Along with an escalation of segregation came a stark increase in racial tensions and violence. More suspicions and fears provoked more students to bring knives and guns to school, or to join gangs of their race that they thought would protect them. More cases were reported of students physically attacking teachers or vice versa. A principal in Prince George's County, Maryland, was fired after he was accused of banging students' heads on the wall, and of hanging some students upside down. When the school superintendent in one Alabama district forbade interracial couples to attend the prom dance, someone burned the school down.

The Harvard study attributed increasing racial segregation to the poverty and housing patterns that have concentrated blacks and Hispanics in central cities. Higher birth rates among Hispanics and blacks and immigration, legal and illegal, also were cited as reasons for the sharp increase in minority-majority schools. Professor Orfield saw what he called "a historic reversal." "The civil rights impulse from the 1960s is dead in the water and the ship is floating backward toward the shoals of racial segregation," he added.

The *New York Times* saw an economic as well as general threat to the nation's well-being. It said editorially, "The nation long ago recognized that integration was a moral and political imperative. These statistics . . . make clear that to remain economically viable and competitive, the United States cannot keep pushing large numbers of black and Latino children further and further to the margins of society. Fully one-third of those entering the work force in the next decade will be minorities. It makes no sense to keep so many of these future workers isolated in schools that are educationally inferior." The editorial noted also that during twelve years of the Reagan and Bush administrations, federal policies virtually wiped out funding for voluntary desegregation efforts, even as the Republican leaders "encouraged legal efforts to terminate successful desegregation orders."

Those 1994 reports of onrushing disaster failed to provoke even a ripple of efforts to allocate funds to encourage voluntary desegregation, the consolidation of school districts, or even the creation of more magnet schools.

Many influential whites believed that (1) segregation wasn't all that bad; why punish intelligent white kids by forcing them to go to school with intellectually inferior African Americans? And (2) no addition of funds would make a difference, because they would be swallowed up or wasted by teachers' unions, especially the National Education Association.

Blacks were not exactly clamoring for more funds, or magnet schools, or other ways to halt resegregation. In fact, many black leaders and parents were becoming more and more disillusioned with promises about the fruits of school integration. Farrakhan and others pushed the argument that "it is an insult to black people to tell them that they can't learn except in the presence of whites." The separatists were believable when they told black audiences that "Whitey" would never let black people, however brilliant, be a real part of "their society."

So, in their disillusionment and anger, millions of blacks had grown lukewarm about enduring the threats to their children and the sacrifices they had to make for the "fantasy benefits" that hadn't shown up for forty years. Black parents were especially gullible in the face of a greater fantasy — that they could get vouchers from the state to pull their children out of public schools and enroll them in private schools. They had not yet learned that this was a snare and a delusion fostered by people who want to abolish public schools and want state funds for their private schools, but ultimately will admit to their private schools only the scrubbed-cheek minority children who "know how to behave," to repeat Nixon's formula for determining which blacks should be "allowed in the body politic."

Gingrich, Dole, Armey, Kasich, and other congressmen saw as a first step to wiping out public schools the abandonment of a Department of Education. So this, the voucher program, deep cuts in federal scholarship programs, cuts in the school lunch and breakfast programs all became part of the Republican plan to end "the welfare state."

It was clear by mid-1995 that education was still the answer, but this time the education of millions of white Americans as to what education could mean if it were distributed fairly. Three educational researchers, Greg Duncan at Northwestern University and Jeanne Brooks-Gunn and Pamela Klebanov at Columbia University were imploring white Americans to accept their findings about IQ, which were diametrically opposite those of *The Bell Curve*. While Murray and Herrnstein had argued that low IQs were the cause of black poverty, their study of the development of 483 black and white children from birth to age five showed that "poverty causes lower IQs."

Noting that three times as many black children as whites live below the poverty line, these three researchers found that the IQs of children are affected by poor nutrition, more stress, and fewer educational choices. When they factored in poverty, they found that the IQ gap between black and white youngsters was about three points, which is statistically meaningless.

Evidence abounds, however, that the mentality of the Freemen, the skinheads, and the Aryan Nation is so forceful in all of white America that the majority would rather fight over education than accept the Northwestern-Columbia findings.

If that is true, the fight is coming.

# Chapter 11

# How
# to Prevent
# "Armageddon"

*When . . . you have succeeded in dehu-
manizing the Negro; when you have put
him down and made it forever impossible
for him to be but as the beasts of the field;
when you have extinguished his soul and
placed him where the ray of hope is blown
out in darkness like that which broods
over the spirits of the damned, are you
quite sure that the demon you have roused
will not turn and rend you?*

Abraham Lincoln,
in Edwardsville, Illinois
September 11, 1858

I must say honestly that I doubt there is any way to prevent
bloody racial strife in America. So many hate groups are at
large that a few of them are bound to try to make good on
their threats to make parts of America, or all of it, the exclusive
home of superior Aryan whites. Too much rage has built up in
the minds of young blacks who are trapped in the corridors of
resentment and hopelessness for me to assume that they will not
strike out with firepower, especially if provoked.

But it is possible to formulate a prayerful program to prevent
a race war that would be based on the open boasts and predictions of those who say they want one — that is, the new "patriots" who say they are arming to take back America for the white
race.

I can see some of these militias and hate groups not only
blowing up federal and state buildings in a lot of cities, but also

raiding armories and other weapons warehouses. They are already using automatic weapons to rob banks, so I have no doubt that they will try to make good their threats to attack police stations in Washington, D.C., and other cities. Most likely to draw black retaliation of the wildest, fieriest sort would be a rash of white-supremacist assassinations of prominent black leaders, a choice part of the formula of conquest spelled out in *The Turner Diaries* and other manifestos of the white supremacists.

It is clear to me that an essential step toward preventing "Armageddon" would be to disarm to the extent the law allows the eight hundred or so militias that have sprung up across America. To allow these groups to continue to pile up caches of war-level weapons and bomb-making compounds would be suicidal lunacy.

What magnitude of weapons am I talking about having authorities seize? No one can be sure. When twelve members of the Viper Militia in Arizona can stockpile materials capable of making a bomb half the size of the one used in the Oklahoma City explosion, plus scores of rifles that were lawful and unlawful, and other death-dealing devices, we have to assume hidden in the woods of America, or perhaps in your neighbors' homes, are enough guns, grenades, rockets, and bombs to blow up half of America. It just makes no sense to leave such instruments of destruction in the hands of nuts and kooks who declare openly that their goal is to destroy the government of the United States and of the individual states and replace them with people who will wipe out the threats imposed by "niggers" and Jews.

I know the dangers of even talking about disarming the "patriots." They say that they have taken to the woods precisely because they know that "the System" is bent on destroying their right to bear arms. Any official talk of disarming them would be taken as proof of their fears, as well as justification for having hidden away their arms. An official disarmament decree would provoke threats of standoffs more dangerous than those with the Branch Davidians in Waco, Texas, and with the Freemen in Montana. I doubt that the BATF or the FBI, or state and local law enforcement agencies, have the stomach for trying to disarm the militias.

But there can be no tranquillity without a mandatory disarmament program of colossal magnitude. It would be folly to assume that law enforcement people can infiltrate every violent, underground militia group the way they burrowed inside the Vipers in Phoenix.

Still, there is no widespread public clamor to disarm militia and militia-type groups except perhaps in the northwest areas where some weirdos are robbing banks with machine guns and are claiming that God exempts them from prosecution for these and other crimes. It will take perhaps two more terrorist acts akin to the Oklahoma City bombings to make the great mass of Americans see just how dangerous these bands of renegades are.

Even after the best of disarmament efforts, authorities will have to monitor these groups with an array of tactics that would break a civil libertarian's heart. Infiltrations, buggings, wiretaps, inspections of bank accounts, and more will become routine if we are to have a genuine sense that we have a serious threat under control.

Obviously, it is now too easy for anyone to purchase ammonium nitrate fertilizer and other compounds that can be used to build bombs of awesome power. If a bank has to report to Uncle Sam any cash transaction of $10,000 or more, surely it is not unreasonable to demand that manufacturers put tracers in bags of fertilizer, or that hardware and farm stores and others keep records of and report to a federal office all sales of even moderate amounts of explosive compounds.

We will need to enforce laws banning "practice" explosions, even in the countryside.

In short, our law enforcement people need to read *The Turner Diaries*, which spelled out in such detail how to blow up an FBI headquarters that someone decided to do it to the Murrah building. Legitimate government people need to read the detailed instructions on how to commit acts of terror that can be gotten by mail from Pierce's friends in West Virginia and elsewhere. Can we, or do we want to, halt the dissemination of such materials?

I probably would be in the front row of those protesting efforts to censor or ban the publication of materials that can be found on the Internet or other public places. I doubt that I would oppose prosecuting publishers on grounds that they aided and abetted terrible crimes.

A civil suit is now in the federal courts in which Paladin Press of Boulder, Colorado, is accused of aiding and abetting a Detroit man, James Perry, in carrying out a triple murder in 1993.

A Washington, D.C., lawyer contended that Perry used a Paladin publication, *Hit Man: A Technical Manual for Independent Contractors*, as a twenty-seven-step guide when he went to a Wheaton, Maryland, home on March 3, 1993, and killed Mildred Horn, her eight-year-old quadriplegic son, Trevor, and the boy's nurse, Janice Saunders.

Police said Perry might have committed "the perfect crime" if he had just stuck with the book, but he was caught because he used his own name to rent a car in Detroit for the trip to Maryland, and when he used his own name to rent a motel room in Gaithersburg, Maryland. Perry has been convicted and sentenced to death. He had been hired as a hit man by Lawrence T. Horn, a former Motown Records sound engineer who was Trevor's father and who hoped to inherit $1.7 million in the boy's medical malpractice trust fund. Horn was convicted and sentenced to life in prison without possibility of parole.

Paladin argues that it is in no way responsible for the three deaths just because it published the *Hit Man* book. Its president, Peder C. Lund, has told the court that the book was not meant to be taken seriously but was designed to "tease the reader with ambiguity."

In August a federal judge expressed personal disgust for the book, but ruled that Paladin Press is totally protected by the First Amendment. The plaintiffs said they will appeal.

No disarmament program would be effective, of course, if it did not take millions of guns out of the hands of the urban youth gangs that are likely to tangle with the militia in the first stages of any race war. Fortunately, the Clinton administration now has a computer system ready to help seventeen cities track the illegal sale of guns to young people and thus cut off the supply of firearms with which so many young people are killing each other.

The Bureau of Alcohol, Tobacco and Firearms now runs a computer data base called Project LEAD that can trace a gun seized in a crime and check the serial number and computerized records to determine where it entered the market. The BATF has discovered that of the 160,000 federally licensed gun dealers in the country, fewer than 1 percent are responsible for more than half the guns used in crimes. This small number of licensed dealers is especially big in the trafficking of guns directly to juveniles, or through "straw" buyers who then sell them to adolescents.

With BATF help, the Boston police found that all the handguns being used by gangs in one part of the city originated in Mississippi. They found that a Boston man, Jose Andrade, a student at Mississippi State University, was bringing the guns home on weekends and peddling them. Police say that in the five months before Andrade's discovery and arrest there were ninety-one shootings in the affected neighborhood, but there were only twenty shootings in the five months after his arrest. Andrade was convicted on federal gun trafficking charges.

In another case, federal agents traced four thousand guns seized in New York City to one store in Alabama.

Project LEAD is a remarkable crime-fighting tool in a nation where the number of homicides committed by juveniles toting guns has risen 418 percent since 1984.

The point should not be lost that the same corrupt people who supply juvenile gangs with guns are probably providing firearms to members of the alienated "patriot" militias.

Some Americans will despair at my suggestion that a domestic arms control program would help us avert a race war, because they do not believe the National Rifle Association and similar groups would ever let the politicians vote for such a program. But when Bob Dole walks away from a promise to the NRA to lead a fight to repeal the federal ban on certain assault weapons, anything seems politically possible. Dole's reason for reneging was not especially brave. He said no repeal is necessary because eleven of the seventeen banned guns are "back on the market in some other form." The NRA backed Dole's call for a national instant background check of gun buyers.

[I know from my mail that many readers may now be thinking, "This author Rowan is the same hypocrite who used his handgun to shoot a white kid who was just taking a dip in his swimming pool." That is a lie that got around the world before the truth got its boots on. Just after 2 A.M. on June 14, 1988, a drugged-up, six-foot four-inch man tried to break through my patio door and enter my house. He was 175 feet from, and out of sight of, my pool and Jacuzzi. I stopped the intruder by using a gun owned by my former-FBI-agent son to shoot him in the wrist. A corrupt District of Columbia mayor, Marion Barry, seeking revenge for my written criticisms of him, tried me on "illegal gun" charges, but a jury refused to convict. I have never owned a handgun personally, and have always supported gun control.]

## Restore the Public's Trust in Law Enforcement People

We cannot carry out an effective gun control or domestic disarmament program without restoring the people's faith in those who enforce the nation's laws. Note that the would-be domestic terrorists speak first of bombing the FBI building, or other facilities that house the BATF, the IRS, and other law enforcement authorities. How astonishing that these same federal authorities are viewed with distrust and contempt by the very African Americans whom the white supremacists want to kill.

I say categorically that there is not a law enforcement agency in America that does not reek with racism and sexism. I have written earlier about the good ol' boys roundup where assorted state, federal, and local lawmen met in Tennessee for an orgy of racism. Note that BATF, the agency in which this bigotry celebration was conceived, last July agreed to pay $5.8 million to black agents who had charged in federal court that the bureau discriminated against them in hiring, promotion, and evaluation. John W. Magaw, head of the BATF, went on television to concede that a pattern of discrimination had existed, and to talk of the "progress" now being made.

Mark Jones, one of two black agents who filed the class action suit, said the BATF "still has today the mind-set of southern plantation culture. This [settlement] puts a check on their behavior. You may never change their attitudes, but you can damn sure change their behavior."

The settlement came to about $19,500 for each black agent claiming discrimination.

The FBI, the Secret Service, and most other federal law enforcement agencies also have been sued for racist practices. All of them are hotbeds of bigotry that is covered up and perpetuated by old boy networks.

President Clinton has said repeatedly what the most authoritative fighters of crime emphasize: community involvement and cooperation with the police are essential to any successful crime-reduction program. There was a time, in cities such as Detroit and Memphis, when it was assumed that community cooperation would arise naturally as blacks were given a chance for promotions, even to the level of police chief. But the community goodwill created in most cities has evaporated in the anger over courts reversing consent decrees agreed to many years earlier.

When officials of a city concede that for generations they have had a pattern of racial discrimination, or even exclusion of blacks, in their fire and police departments, and the city and complainants agree with a judge as to how to make amends, that consent decree ought to be settled law. But as we have seen in the Memphis case cited in this book, one white claiming "reverse discrimination" can come along and roil a whole city by asking an appeals court to undo an established settlement.

In order to give established law enforcement officials primacy over private race warriors, we citizens must insist upon proper and speedy prosecution of policemen believed guilty of breaking the law. Neither blacks in corporate boardrooms nor those living in ghetto filth will trust our criminal justice system when O. J. Simpson, a man found not guilty, is punished outside the law in every way his detractors can punish him, but the city of Los Angeles shows no sign of ever prosecuting detective Mark Fuhrman, who in his own taped voice has admitted to egregious violations of law.

## Acknowledge the Validity of Black Rage

I am sure that upon seeing the title of this book, you thought immediately that I was warning that "the fire next time" is upon us, because hordes of disillusioned black youth will soon roam a thousand American cities, torching and looting everything in sight. You're surprised that the war I foresee will most likely be provoked by white men afflicted with incredible hatreds.

Well, don't let anything I've written diminish your fear of an uprising by young blacks. If you will read for a second time Abraham Lincoln's 1858 remarks in Edwardsville, Illinois, I will concede that there are black people in the hellholes of America who live like animals and behave like savages — African Americans who would kill a skinhead, a total stranger, or me with a sardonic smile. White readers will say, "your people," but remembering Lincoln I will say, "your creation." But none of us can afford just to call names to assign blame. Those whites with the most to lose are absolutely irresponsible in not trying to take sane steps to ensure that black rage does not destroy almost everything worth keeping in America.

Many whites find solace, or escape, in the fact that black "liberals" and "conservatives" seem in such disagreement. The truth is that we see the same America but propose different solutions to a bewildering array of injustices. What I have written in Chapter 10 of this book is the same, though less eloquent, as what professor Glenn C. Loury of Boston University wrote in the July/August issue of the *New Democrat* magazine:

> The civil rights movement broadened the scope of this moral revolution to the private sphere in the years following *Brown.* Segregated restaurants, housing developments, workplaces, and hotels were declared unlawful by Congress. The power of the federal prosecutor, and the weighty threat to withhold federal funds, were employed to achieve equality of opportunity for blacks. Again, although many conservatives objected at the time, the moral principle embodied in this legislation is now broadly accepted. Racial discrimination, whether the result of public policy or private business practice, will not be tolerated.
>
> The Conflict Between Ideals and Practice
>
> These reforms succeeded, but they also failed. *De jure* segregation is dead. But, due to the continuing desires of whites and blacks to associate with persons of their own choosing, *de facto* segregation is very much alive. The assault on racial discrimina-

tion has made it possible, for the first time in American history, for millions of college-educated black professionals to live the American Dream. Yet it is a measure of the gravity of our racial problems that, as Princeton political scientist Jennifer Hochschild has recently reported, they seem to be enjoying it less. Meanwhile, an equally unprecedented black underclass, also numbering in the millions, lives beyond the reach of conventional social remedy, casting a pall over the idea that genuine equality of opportunity for black Americans can ever be achieved.

Sad to say, only white Americans can answer that question whether genuine equality of opportunity for black Americans can ever be achieved. I would have to say, on the basis of seventy-one years of life in America, that the answer is no. But that does not mean that I personally will ever accept anything less.

But neither Loury nor anyone else ought to think me naive enough to believe that what Loury calls an "unprecedented black underclass" is interested in a debate over the merits of integration and separatism. Neither genuine integration nor a "separatism" under terms set forth by people like Farrakhan is remotely within their grasp.

The reason there is danger of this black underclass engaging in a race war is that they have no meaningful stake in the America that most whites and privileged minorities know. People with a real stake in something of value are loath to piss on it, let alone destroy it. But the mass of blacks can't get close enough to the American dream just to piss on it.

Are American power brokers willing to do anything to make "integration" meaningful to the millions of blacks who did not get college degrees and well-paying jobs out of the Federal Aid to Higher Education Act of 1965? We damned well had better find ways to make the hewers of wood and haulers of water believe that they, too, can find out what social mobility and economic justice are all about.

The challenge could not be set forth more succinctly or frighteningly than in the woes of Hartford, Connecticut, where the public schools attended almost exclusively by blacks and Hispanics in 1996 were so wretched that the Connecticut Supreme Court has declared them unconstitutional. In a 5–4 verdict, chief justice Ellen Ash Peters wrote:

We conclude that the existence of extreme racial and ethnic isolation in the public school system deprives schoolchildren of a substantially equal educational opportunity and requires the state to take further remedial measures.

The decision raised the specters that the legislature would have to mandate the busing of white children back into Hartford; wipe out the district lines between the suburbs and the city and let Hartford's blacks and Hispanics attend suburban schools; or amend the Connecticut constitution to state specifically that de facto racial segregation (94 percent minority in Hartford schools) is not unconstitutional.

Republican governor John G. Rowland quickly vowed that there would be no "forced busing" as long as he is governor. James Connelly, school superintendent in Bridgeport, where the public school enrollment is 88 percent minority, asked: "How do we remedy the problems without ripping apart town lines and boundary lines, which I don't think anyone wants to do?"

Supreme Court justice David M. Borden, who wrote the dissent, said, "The necessary implication of the majority's reasoning is that virtually every school district in the state is now unconstitutional or constitutionally suspect ... the majority has effectively struck down, not just for the greater Hartford area but for the entire state, the municipality-based school system that has been in effect in this state since 1909."

In a Detroit case way back during the heart of the civil rights movement, the federal courts said no to busing across city and suburban lines. The old black spiritual just had to be wrong when it said to white people, "There's no hidin' place down here."

All the proposed solutions to Hartford's dilemma probably sound worse to the average white citizen there than any talk of a race war. There is little or no respect for the children who are the victims of de facto Jim Crow, and there is not enough fear of them. The assumption is that there will always be enough jails and concentration camps to contain them. And therein lies part of the American dilemma.

If we Americans are ever to escape the threat of "Armageddon" and the "rivers of blood" that *The Turner Diaries* predicts, we are going to have to make early and massive interventions in the lives of the millions of children who constitute a hopeless underclass. I mean interventions at home, in schools, and in teenage life choices. The education and lifestyle initiatives must be financed in part by government, in part by private institutions, and otherwise carried out by volunteers.

But such interventions can never come about if Americans persist in basing public and private policies on *The Bell Curve* notions of weak races and superraces, and on the assumption that whole groups of people are incapable of absorbing the education and civilized traits that benevolent intervention would offer.

We must adopt instead the findings I cited earlier by Jeanne Brooks-Gunn and Pamela Klebanov of Columbia University and Greg J. Duncan of Northwestern University. They followed 483 low-birthweight children for the first five years of their lives and concluded that "age-5 IQ differences between black and white children are almost completely eliminated by adjusting for differences in neighborhood economic conditions, family poverty, maternal education, and learning experiences." They found, in layman's terms, that a child's IQ is stunted when he or she lives in deep poverty in a poor neighborhood with an uneducated mother, and when that child gets relatively few learning experiences. And their study showed that black children are far more likely than whites to suffer all those disabilities.

Of the kids studied, 40 percent of the black tots were in "persistent poverty" — families below the poverty line for at least five years of a six-year period. Only 5 percent of the white children faced this level of poverty.

Fifty-seven percent of the black children lived in neighborhoods where at least 20 percent of their neighbors were in poverty, compared with 7.5 percent of the white youngsters living in such neighborhoods.

More than one-half of the black children who were not poor still lived in poor neighborhoods, compared with fewer than 10 percent of the comparable white children.

The researchers emphasize that they are not arguing that there is no genetic component whatever in the IQ gap between blacks and whites. But they are arguing that poverty and disadvantage cause low IQs.

The authors say their study suggests "that a focus on poor black families is critical to altering the life chances of black children." They suggest such possible IQ-boosting steps as wider application of the earned income tax credit, increased efforts to enforce laws requiring support payments from absent fathers, and changes in housing policies and practices to prevent so many black youngsters from growing up in impoverished neighborhoods. That would mean more public housing in scattered sites, and possibly more vouchers to support rentals in the private housing market.

Taking steps to liberate the IQs of black kids would mean more blacks in good jobs and fewer on welfare. One of the attendant benefits would surely be a reduction in the racial jealousies and hatreds that are making America a more violent place every day.

I am convinced by the history of my own family, and that of others I know in which no one graduated from high school until my generation, that well-run, believed-in programs of assistance to deprived families would produce remarkable changes in just one generation.

On the governmental side we must retain programs such as Head Start, which has been under attack by the white supremacists. In fact, we would save the nation a lot of money a decade from now if we had a huge expansion of programs designed to nurture and inspire disadvantaged preschoolers and those in the first few years of elementary school. Such programs must be supplemented by private forces, particularly the churches of the black and Hispanic communities.

School officials in the most deprived districts need to be aware that at every age their pupils need a lot more than classroom instruction. Every feasible opportunity must be seized to provide poor youngsters with life-altering experiences outside their neighborhoods. Affluent Americans, black and white, are rarely cognizant of the fact that our worst communities include millions of youngsters who have never been to a concert, a ball game, or much of anything outside their squalid neighborhoods.

Last November, more than five hundred black high school seniors, each with a grade point average in excess of 3.5 on a 4.0 scale, attended the Project Excellence–Freedom Forum Scholarship Day. One student from the poorest ward in the District of Columbia wrote to say that she was "amazed and inspired to see so many brilliant black students showing so much confidence about their futures. That sure opened my eyes!" It opened everyone's eyes when forty-five colleges offered these five hundred youngsters $9.4 million in scholarships.

With just a pittance of money we can help open the eyes of youngsters who otherwise would expect little good from America or themselves.

The Columbia-Northwestern findings make it clear to me that it would help the poorest of children immensely if we stopped herding them into housing — persistent pockets of poverty, misery, and fear — where they rarely see anyone who does not share their plight, their hopelessness.

Public housing has been turned into high-rise clusters of violent racial ghettos because bigoted, or timid, politicians have insisted that jobless welfare people could never be housed with the working poor, and surely not with middle-class families. Sociologists and politicians have talked of scatter-site housing for the poor and of giving needy families vouchers with which to purchase housing in the private market, but such ideas have met a lot of resistance.

This may soon change because, incredibly, Republican senator Christopher Bond of Missouri has joined HUD secretary Henry Cisneros in producing reforms that will soon make it possible for children living in public housing to see people of proud achievements in their communities every day.


With proper intervention in the earliest teen years, we could discover our best chances to reduce crime, sexual promiscuity, illegitimate births, and the proliferation of sexually transmitted diseases.

We need a revival of the Civilian Conservation Corps (CCC camps) that Franklin D. Roosevelt used to maintain hope within youngsters during the Great Depression of the 1930s. In 1934, 52 percent of blacks in northern and border states were on relief, and the situation was worse in the South. That's when the federal government first became interested in black education. The Works Progress Administration (WPA) sponsored an artists' project that produced Langston Hughes, Ralph Ellison, Richard Wright, and other notable black writers. Some two hundred thousand young blacks got training in the Civilian Conservation Corps for employment in forestry and related fields.

My recollection is that CCC camps were like a poor man's military academy, a boot camp, and a summer camp for the needy all rolled into one. These were not places of punishment, and there was no stigma in going to one. Many black youngsters came home to report with pride that their camps in New England and the Pacific states were integrated. Unlike today's Job Corps, the youngsters in the CCC camps had not been in difficulty with the law.

How marvelous it would be to give millions of idle city youngsters a chance to know the discipline and high standards of such camps. How helpful for ghetto youngsters to get work experiences that are not available in their neighborhoods, and to make daily human contacts that involve human beings from remarkably different backgrounds.

I hear someone asking how these CCC camps would be paid for. I say, with the money we're spending for new prisons — or that Gingrich proposes to spend on stockades or orphanages.

The first requirement is to convince the nation's leaders that they want to do something for young minority men and women other than locking them up where presumably they can't hurt anyone. Well, not until they are released back into society, as all but a few of them must be. A youngster graduating from a Job Corps center, or a CCC camp, will not have been dehumanized, stripped of all pride and self-respect. But those leaving our new jails and prisons, believing in their hearts that they never should have been incarcerated, will have been turned into human killing machines. They will be more than eager to rumble — strike out at any and all groups that issue the threats of the white supremacists who are the heroes of *The Turner Diaries* and the bombastic leaders of the "patriots" movement.

Can we reverse the current suicidal trend? Only if the government programs suggested above are supported by thousands of initiatives by foundations, corporations, and individual citizens.

In May 1996 the W. K. Kellogg Foundation announced a twenty-year program to improve the lives of disadvantaged black men. After a five-year, $11.6 million grant program, a forty-eight-member board convened by Kellogg announced, it will seek to raise $50 million from corporations and other foundations to make profound changes in the lives of black males. The committee noted particularly that "although black men account for just 6 percent of the U.S. population, they make up 45 percent of prison inmates." The Kellogg program is designed to help black people themselves shatter the links between black males and crime.

"We are trying to save urban America, not for black people, but for everybody," said former UN ambassador Andrew Young, the former mayor of Atlanta and chairman of the Kellogg committee. "We're focusing on African American men and boys because that's where the biggest breach is in our society."

The great danger is that the nation as a whole will do little or nothing of the sort that the Kellogg Foundation proposes.

With these innovations, we should begin to see signs that we can actually do something to reduce crime. We should have enough confidence to see that we should change the mandatory minimum sentencing policy for minor drug offenders and clear our prisons of most of those small fry who are now overflowing the cells. Without mandatory sentences, judges could target the real threats and the money saved could be used to hire more police or expand drug education and social programs that would help prevent crime. Miami has set up a model drug court, which since the late 1980s has diverted first-time drug offenders to treatment instead of jail.

Harvard professor Philip Heymann notes that reducing the sentences of low-level, nonviolent first-time drug offenders to around three years — about the median sentence of someone who commits extortion — would save $80 million a year, which could hire a lot of police or FBI agents. By one reckoning, electronically monitored home confinement costs about $7 a day, compared with $55 a day for a state prison inmate.

A second step is to explore alternatives to prison. Among the possibilities are halfway houses, home confinement, community service, financial restitution, and drug/alcohol management. By some estimates, as many as four out of every five inmates are likely candidates for these programs.

I'm aware that letting people out can backfire, that a man on house arrest can rape or rob or murder. Better systems and more parole officers will be needed to keep track of released prisoners. But we must not forget that incarceration also produces failures.

To cut down on those failures, let's make drug treatment, job training, and education available for men and women in prison. Let's reinstate Pell Grants to enable inmates to take college courses. Experience has shown that the proportion of parolees who return to criminal behavior drops from about 65 percent to 10 percent for those who have been educated through Pell grants while in prison. In North Carolina, experimental programs have put seventeen thousand of the state's twenty-seven thousand inmates to work or in job training.

These are not wild-eyed radical-liberal schemes. Prison wardens, correctional officials, some crime victims, and even conservatives are advocating new ways of handling criminals.

Wisconsin governor Tommy G. Thompson, who won headlines and conservatives' plaudits for overhauling his state's welfare program, has vowed not to build any more prisons and has hired a former state commissioner of corrections to study alternatives to confinement.

We cannot rescue America from wanton violence simply by imprisoning and executing more people. To avoid calamitous conflict this society must develop social and economic policies that are saner than the lock-'em-up approach that is so popular these days in Washington.

What we must say "yes" to are expanded summer, weekend, and after-school programs — even much-maligned "midnight basketball" — that offer children alternatives to mean streets. Also to drug treatment and education efforts. We have a Job Corps that does magnificent work with disadvantaged youngsters who have had minor confrontations with the law, without making them think of themselves as criminals or enemies of society. Why not expand this program instead of pumping millions of dollars into boot camps and juvenile detention centers?

If with anger and tunnel vision we abandon programs like these — and shred our basic antipoverty, health, and education safety net — all we will do is create larger armies of hopeless American outcasts who will turn to crime to express their rage.

Time is short. The large cohort of children born in the mid- and late 1980s will start reaching their dangerous teen years

around the turn of the century. Then watch out. Three-fourths
of the young teens who set records for criminal violence in the
early 1980s were born to married mothers and fathers. Three-
fifths of the black children in the upcoming group of teens were
born to single mothers.

They have grown up with the scars of "illegitimacy," abandonment, and abuse. They have been shortchanged by a perverse
set of government and private sector priorities that allocates billions to the Pentagon to fight a two-front war while spending
just pennies to combat the war on children in America. Add to
all that a burning sense of rage and entitlement, and you have a
devastatingly explosive mix.

It will be infinitely easier to take the steps needed to avert a race
war if we can mute the cries of the hatemongers. It is hard,
though, to ask Bob Grant and G. Gordon Liddy to show restraint
when Washington politicians are behaving in ugly irresponsibility. What foul-mouthed broadcaster cares what Congress thinks
when he sees House majority leader Dick Armey of Texas take
the House floor and refer to the openly homosexual Representative Barney Frank as "Barney Fag." Or sees Representative
Robert Dornan call President Clinton a "traitor."

We need politicians who will exhort the people of the United
States to be better than they think they can be.

I know that the seeds of violence lie in some of these proposals
for preventing violence. But we must be bold, because the haters
have a head start on us. We have for too long been afraid to talk
openly to each other about the threat of widespread racial conflict in America. We have been like a cruise ship and a trawler,
carefully parting the fog as we go our separate ways, with no one
listening to the voices of the people closest to the sea.

The voices are now saying that there can be no separate ways,
because destiny has lumped us together in a crisis that involves
our national and personal well-being.

Are we equal to this challenge?

# *Acknowledgments*

A few friends have told me that writing this book could become the most futile effort of my long career in journalism. They say, correctly I'm sure, that nothing can be more frustrating than trying to awaken a person who is drunk on power or stultified by ignorance. They say that jarring wake-up calls are rarely greeted with thankful smiles.

Still, there are friends who know that I had to write this book, hoping that even those Americans who sleep are not yet dead or beyond caring about what is happening to this country. I value beyond words their care and support.

Foremost among the supporters is my wife, Vivien, who pretended to forget my 1994 promise not to write another book. She indulged me in two more years of having her dining room table, living room sofas, guest room bed, and dozens of chairs covered with documents about the curse of racism in America. She understood that my sea of paper represented the refuse of a bloody social storm.

Vivien's sense of duty was matched by the enthusiasm of my incredibly perceptive—and persistent—editor at Little, Brown, Fredrica Friedman, who helped immensely to make national bestsellers of my autobiography, *Breaking Barriers*, and my biography of Justice Thurgood Marshall, *Dream Makers, Dream Breakers*. Fredi demanded a clarity of message in this last and probably most controversial of my importunings of those white Americans who seem increasingly inclined to defy all the lessons of history.

I have struggled to be sure that the force of my feelings never got ahead of the facts. I have been blessed by the eye and mind of Betty Power, a copy-editor whose commitment to accuracy saved me from a barrage of letters saying, "On page so-and-so you really goofed." Her caring editing here, as with *Dream Makers, Dream Breakers,* was infinitely valuable. I also appreci-ate the work of assistant editor Amanda Murray.

I cannot overstate the importance of the contribution of my special assis-tant, Pam Paroline, on this book. She drove two computers crazy shifting paragaraphs and passages and reorganizing chapters. She, David Mazie, Mar-ian Rowan, and others did marvelous research. When the computers got viruses, my former assistant, Kristine McDevitt, and her expert husband, Pat McDevitt, delivered healing hands.

Regarding research, I offer a special thanks to Phyllis Lyons and Nancy Stewart of the Freedom Forum, who in times of urgency reached into cyber-space or someplace and provided me with the oldest and newest information about many people and things.

I am especially grateful to my "home newspaper," the *Chicago Sun-Times,* for publishing and making available my columns that are quoted frequently in this book.

I make special mention here of Professor William H. Tucker's marvelous book *The Science and Politics of Racial Research,* published by the University of Illinois Press. No one has written more incisively about the political pur-poses of those who espouse theories about IQ tests revealing the superiority or inferiority of races. I found his book extraordinarily helpful.

I thank the whole crew at Little, Brown for their efforts to make this wake-up call heard across this and other lands.

# Index